T0302044

ON THE ORIGIN OF PRODUCTS

THE EVOLUTION OF PRODUCT INNOVATION AND DESIGN

In this new work, Arthur Eger and Huub Ehlhardt present a "Theory of Product Evolution." They challenge the popular notion that we owe the availability of products solely to genius inventors. Instead, they present arguments that show that a process of variation, selection, and accumulation of "know-how" (to make) and "know-what" (function to realize) provide an explanation for the emergence of new types of products and their subsequent development into families of advanced versions. This theory employs a product evolution diagram as an analytical framework to reconstruct the development history of a product family and picture it as a graphical narrative. The authors describe the relevant literature and case studies to place their theory in context. The "Product Phases Theory" is used to create predictions on the most likely next step in the evolution of a product, offering practical tools for those involved in new product development.

Arthur O. Eger is a Professor of Product Design. He has a broad experience in industrial design engineering, wrote and edited more than fifteen books, and published more than 100 articles and papers. He is a member and Chairman of the Board of the Department of Industrial Design Engineering of KIVI, the Royal Institution of Engineers in the Netherlands.

Huub Ehlhardt has studied Industrial Design Engineering at Delft University of Technology and worked on a PhD project at University of Twente. He has worked more than 20 years in different roles in the manufacturing industry.

On the Origin of Products

THE EVOLUTION OF PRODUCT INNOVATION AND DESIGN

Arthur O. Eger

Huub Ehlhardt

CAMBRIDGE
UNIVERSITY PRESS

CAMBRIDGE
UNIVERSITY PRESS

University Printing House, Cambridge CB2 8BS, United Kingdom

One Liberty Plaza, 20th Floor, New York, NY 10006, USA

477 Williamstown Road, Port Melbourne, VIC 3207, Australia

314–321, 3rd Floor, Plot 3, Splendor Forum, Jasola District Centre,
New Delhi – 110025, India

79 Anson Road, #06–04/06, Singapore 079906

Cambridge University Press is part of the University of Cambridge.

It furthers the University's mission by disseminating knowledge in the pursuit of
education, learning, and research at the highest international levels of excellence.

www.cambridge.org
Information on this title: www.cambridge.org/9781316638187
DOI: 10.1017/9781316941539

First published 2018

A catalogue record for this publication is available from the British Library.

Library of Congress Cataloging-in-Publication Data
Names: Eger, Arthur O., author. | Ehlhardt, Huub, author.
Title: On the origin of products : the evolution of product innovation and design / Arthur O.
Eger, Huub Ehlhardt.
Description: New York, NY, USA ; Cambridge, United Kingdom : University Printing
House, [2017] | Includes bibliographical references.
Identifiers: LCCN 2017030640| ISBN 9781107187658 | ISBN 9781316638187 (paperback)
Subjects: LCSH: New products. | Technological innovations.
Classification: LCC TS170 .E39 2017 | DDC 658.5/75–dc23
LC record available at https://lccn.loc.gov/2017030640

ISBN 978-1-107-18765-8 Hardback
ISBN 978-1-316-63818-7 Paperback

Contents

Figures

Preface

This book addresses the question of how new (types of) products come about and develop through time into a family of more advanced versions. The content of this book is organized around three topics. First, theoretical perspectives from different schools of thought deemed relevant are collected in order to provide an inclusive background. Second, the question of the origin of new types of products is explored based on the observation that products do not appear as a *generatio spontanea*,[1] but build on previously developed versions and/or accumulated learning. Case studies of various kinds are included to provide context. Third, using the perspective of accumulated learning, this book provides a low-risk new product development strategy that builds on recurring patterns in products introduced through time. For editorial reasons, these topics do not appear in a strict numerical order. Finally, using the maxim that products "are both the means and the ends of technology" (Basalla, 1988, p. 30, and Section 10.5 of this volume), a product-centric perspective is presented.

Since the dawn of mankind, we have been making things, tools, products. Today we live in a world that depends on technology and is characterized by abundant products: the consumer society. The twentieth century saw an explosion of ever more advanced products. During the past few decades, the process of developing new products was refined and became an engineering discipline. Until the late 1980s, product development was generally considered a linear process. Successful new (versions of) products were considered the next logical step in the continuous improvement of the product with regard to price and performance. The basic thought behind this idea was the – in practice nonexistent – principle of perfect competition, a term derived from neoclassical economic theory. According to this theory, a product can only survive in a market if it has an improved performance/price ratio, relative to its predecessors.

---

[1] Aristotle used this term to explain that new generations spontaneously arose as he observed eels and flies coming from cadavers.

In the last quarter of the previous century, this principle received a great deal of critique. Development processes (e.g., product development) seemed to be much less predictable and unambiguous than the linear model suggested. In different fields of interest in which innovation processes are studied, such as economics and technology studies, research was initiated to find new explanatory models that focus on the complicated way that innovation progresses. It is striking that this research, which is based on very different points of view due to the many research backgrounds, ended with the same type of explanations, namely evolutionary models. Nelson and Winter (1982) defined a new nonlinear view on the economy referred to as "evolutionary economy." Several authors – such as Steadman (1979), Petroski (1992), and Norman (1988, 1992) – engaged in the field of product development and suggested an evolutionary process, although the practical consequences of this point of view remained unnoticed for many years. The linear model remained the generally accepted theory in studies of product development and innovation management, as can be seen, for instance, in the approach followed in almost all introductory texts on design methodology. Despite this, those practical implications are far-reaching. A number of economic phenomena, such as partial path dependence, embeddedness, and technological lock-in, cannot be explained by the linear model and are therefore traditionally considered anomalies. However, they can be explained when technological innovation is regarded as an evolutionary process. This conception has been used to devise a low-risk strategy in new product development based on the observation that products commonly develop through phases.

Evolutionary Product Development is a framework that can be used for developing products that is based on the observation that new products are always based on previous versions and/or accumulated learning. This is an important reason for continuing to investigate the possibilities of an evolutionary vision of product development and innovation.

The theory of Evolutionary Product Development originates from the design practice of Van Dijk/Eger/Associates (nowadays referred to as WeLL Design), a leading Dutch design company founded in 1979. From the very beginning, Arthur Eger – one of the founders of the company – tried to describe the experience of the bureau in terms of a model. The first publication was realized in 1987 in *Dutch Design* (Eger, 1987) on the occasion of a large exhibition that five museums in the Netherlands had organized on the subject of design in the Netherlands. This publication identified five product phases. The sixth product phase, namely awareness, was first described in an article in *NieuwsTribune* (Eger, 1993), and afterward in the book *Succesvolle Productontwikkeling* (*Successful Product Development*) (Eger, 1996).

In the theory of Evolutionary Product Development, all matters that play a role in the evolution of products are the starting point. The model states that each of six product phases displays a typical pattern of product characteristics.

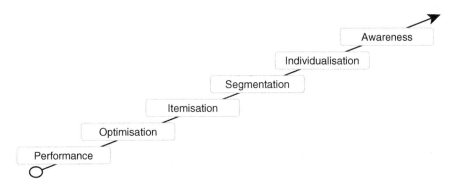

Figure F.1 The six product phases first version (1993) (Source: authors)

Any company making money through the development, production, or marketing of products will have to deal with this phenomenon. Managing it requires skills with respect to management of product development and design methodology, as well as a sound awareness of design history. In practice, products in each phase can be found on the market and specific knowledge is required for every phase.

Generally speaking, the emphasis in the first phase – performance – is on new technologies. New product functions are developed for which the functional performance of the products is the main challenge at this point. In the second phase – optimization – other knowledge is required. The market no longer accepts imperfections and other disciplines become important. Manufacturing technology and quality control become increasingly relevant. Product development is aimed at improving performance, reliability, ergonomics, and safety. In this phase, and in the following one, involving clients in the product development process is beneficial for both the product performance and the financial results of the company (Candi et al., 2010). In the third phase – itemization – high quality and safety no longer suffice. Here, ergonomics and styling are important success factors. Research in the field of man-machine interfaces also starts playing a role. The aim of product development is to develop extra features and accessories, including special editions of the product for different trade channels and target groups (segmentation).

According to the research presented in earlier publications (summarized in Eger, 2013) and in this book, the last three phases coexist (Figure F.2). Product development is either aimed at target groups that become increasingly smaller and differentiated according to specific needs (segmentation), or at mass customization or cocreation by which the customer is able to influence the final result (individualization). The ethical behavior of the company or organization behind the product is also becoming more and more important for customers (awareness).

When applying Evolutionary Product Development it is crucial to understand the history of the product in focus. Designers do not usually investigate

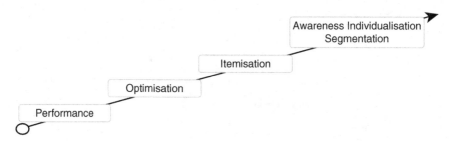

Figure F.2 The six product phases with the last three occurring simultaneously (Source: authors)

the development history of products, as this is a time-consuming activity normally reserved for economic historians or the like. In addition, traditional engineering and design courses lack embedding in the theoretical background of innovation studies required to recognize and interpret mechanisms and phenomena that shape the development history.

Given the aim to provide a method for mapping and extrapolating the development of products, a PhD research project was carried out entitled "Technological Innovation as an Evolutionary Process." This produced a thesis entitled "Product Evolution" (Ehlhardt, 2016) that presents the Theory of Product Evolution and the Product Evolution Diagram. The Theory of Product Evolution describes how the process of variation, selection, and retention drives the accumulation of "know-how" (to make) and "know-what" (function to realize) to provide an explanation for the emergence of new (types of) products and their subsequent development over time into a family of more advanced versions.

Using analytical concepts from innovation studies, the product evolution diagram (PED) is proposed as a systematic approach for analyzing the development history of products. This method uses two elements. First, a tree diagram similar to the family tree known from biology is used to map a product's development path. Second, a so-called PEST diagram is used to map the influences from the environment or ecosystem that affected the evolving product. A timeline reference connects the evolving product with the ecosystem. The Product Evolution Diagram is an analytical concept complementary to the product phases theory that is used as a guideline in new product development.

This book is intended for an audience of academics, students, design engineers, and others interested in new product development. It is an attempt to combine practical experiences from the field of new product development with theoretical insights from various academic schools of thought. The aim of this book is to provide a comprehensive answer to the question, "How do new products come about?" Besides this, it provides clues to the design direction of an evolutionary next version of products.

Acknowledgements

Conversations and discussions with colleagues and students of industrial design engineering at the University of Twente were of great help while we were writing this book. Special thanks go to Laura Schäffer for her contribution to the understanding of the awareness product phase, Noor Reigersman for her contribution to the chapter about the child restraint systems, and Maarten Michel for his research and design of the basketball shoes.

The *Consumentengids*, a publication of the Consumentenbond, has been used as a source of information for both case studies and education. We would like to thank Ronald Vroman and his colleagues from the Consumentenbond for their support in providing background information. We would like to thank Erik Tempelman for his contribution to the discussion on the Product Evolution Diagram and the case study of the CFL. And finally, Howard Turner, translator and native English speaker, contributed with his support in reflection on the use of the English language.

1 On the Origin of Products

1.1 Introduction

According to Grove (1997), human history has evolved through four stages. The oldest stage was that of the hunter-gatherer. About 7000 BC, the second stage, that of agriculture, began. New stages are usually enabled by new tools and/or knowledge, in this case, the tools and knowledge to cultivate the land. The third stage began with the Industrial Revolution around 1770 in England with the first textile mills. The fourth and last stage is the Information Age that began with the first computer in 1946. Perez (2002), however, sees the Industrial Revolution as the beginning of five periods of technological revolutions of about 50 years that correspond with the "long waves" of Kondratiev (1922, 2004). The five technological revolutions are the following:

- The Industrial Revolution (ca. 1770)
- The Age of Steam and Railways (1829)
- The Age of Steel, Electricity, and Heavy Engineering (1875)
- The Age of Oil, the Automobile, and Mass Production (1908)
- The Age of Information and Telecommunication (1971)

Within each "long wave," both Kondratiev and Perez distinguish four stages. Kondratiev distinguishes Recession, Depression, Improvement, and Prosperity; Perez distinguishes Irruption, Frenzy, Synergy, and Maturity.

The first phase – Irruption/Recession – begins with the results of the key technologies of the new "long wave." These results are improved; they attract new investors and companies. Existing companies that ignore the emerging technologies, or that manufacture products that become redundant because of the new technologies, get into trouble. This may result in increasing unemployment and will lead to a recession.

The Frenzy phase – or Depression – marks the time when some people make and some people lose a lot of money. Many individuals and companies invest in the new technologies and the supply of new products is very diverse; some of them succeed, a lot of them fail.

The turning point begins when dominant designs manifest. Perez calls this stage Synergy; Kondratiev called it Improvement.

In the final stage – Maturity/Prosperity – product development shifts from product improvement to production improvement. This stage will last until a new technology emerges and starts to threaten the existing products.

1.2 How Revolutionary Is Revolutionary Really?

In many publications (among others Schumpeter, 1939; Dosi, 1982, and Section 10.13 of this volume; Anderson and Tushman, 1990, and Section 10.3 of this volume; Christensen, 1997, and Section 10.10 of this volume), it is suggested that technology proceeds in two different ways: incremental development of existing products or processes, or discontinuous leaps caused by the invention of new (technological) possibilities. Rosenbloom (2010) and Rosenberg (1996) however argue that the immediate impact of these "discontinuous leaps" is shortly after their introduction rather small.

> Indeed few if any of the innovations we would characterize today as revolutionary appeared so momentous at the time they were first introduced.
>
> (Rosenberg, 1996 as cited by Rosenbloom, 2010, p. 11)

The explanations they give are that new technologies are often rather primitive at the moment of their introduction. They mostly perform quite poorly and in many cases, it takes a long time before their performance is good enough to become a threat to existing products. Another limiting factor of the success of new technologies is the interdependence of different technologies. The substitution of black-and-white by color TVs was only worthwhile after enough of the broadcasted programs were also in color. Rosenbloom and Rosenberg conclude that determining whether a development was revolutionary is most of the time only possible afterward.

Hybs and Gero state that the process that a designer goes through when developing a product is nothing more than:

> Selection, refinement, modification and combination of existing designs or objects considering the current performance requirements and constraints ... It assumes an intrinsic evolutionary process in design, where any novelty, even a so-called innovative or creative design, is a result of recursive steps of generation and evaluation, and where each new solution is based on pre-existing solutions.
>
> (1992, p. 274)

In an afterword in his revised edition of *The Evolution of Designs*, Steadman (1979, revised edition 2008) writes – paraphrasing Basalla (1988) – with regard to the opinion of the general public that many innovations are revolutionary:

> There are always precedents according to Basalla for these apparent radical novelties. The general public only believes otherwise because the crucial antecedents have been lost or hidden, because technological change is confused with socioeconomic change, and because nineteenth century biographies of inventors depicted them as lonely heroic figures conjuring new machines entirely out of the air.   (2008, p. 264)

1.3 Innovation

Innovation is generally defined as a process of introducing new products, processes, or technologies to better meet existing, new, or unarticulated needs. Innovation is regarded as the key to advancement and economic prosperity. As such it receives much attention.

This book addresses the following questions:

– How do new products come about?
– How do new products typically develop through time?
– How does the development of technologies and products relate to the context?
– How can designers apply evolutionary strategies?

1.4 Patterns and Mechanisms of Innovation

Many authors have discussed patterns and mechanisms of innovation and provided analytical tools to investigate them (Schumpeter, 1939; Rogers, 1962, 1995, and Section 10.25 of this volume; Abernathy and Utterback, 1975, and Section 10.1 of this volume; Dosi, 1982; David, 1985, and Section 10.12 of this volume; Anderson and Tushman, 1990; Von Hippel, 2005). Evolutionary metaphors have been used by several authors in this context (Nelson and Winter, 1982; Mokyr, 1996; Geels, 2002, and Section 10.16 of this volume). This book expands on this work, originating from a wide range of disciplines such as economics, sociology, science policy, innovation studies, evolutionary models, industrial design engineering, and design methodology, with the aim being to extend the descriptive and predictive power of the evolutionary paradigm as applied to technological innovation in general and the emergence of new (types of) products in particular. The next section summarizes major perspectives and conceptual models used to describe patterns and mechanisms of innovation that fit the chosen perspective.

1.4.1 Economics

Creative Destruction

Being key to economic advancement, innovation is the subject of the study of economics. The observation by Schumpeter (1942) that innovation is associated with creative destruction is a well-known comment. When new products, processes, or technologies are introduced that outperform earlier versions, the incumbent is ousted. The creative force of innovation destroys that which it improves upon.

Neoclassical economic theory assumes that the behavior of actors is based on relations between supply-and-demand and so sets prices for goods. It assumes stable prices once supply-and-demand are in equilibrium. However, it went not unnoticed that the economic process is a dynamic process and that innovations disturb equilibriums.

Nelson and Winter (1982) developed an evolutionary theory of economic change, which they based on continuous change to overcome limitations in conventional neoclassical economics that do not well explain the economic process of change or renewal. Instead, evolutionary economics describes the process of change along trajectories, based on the argument that economies grow because they are fueled by technical advancement. Nelson and Winter refer to all regular and predictable behavioral patterns within firms as "routines." Put simply, the term "routines" encompasses all "know-how" and "know-what" those firms apply in their processes, and these can range from hiring personnel to research and development. Firms compete on the basis of the fitness of their routines that evolve over time, based on the premise of continuous change.

The economic historian Mokyr (1996, 1998, 1999, 2000a, 2000b) proposed an evolutionary theory of technological change, according to which it is more useful to analyze the change in techniques rather than the change in the artefacts based on those techniques. The argument provided is that a lot of techniques do not involve artefacts and that a lot of artefacts only acquire meaning once "how-to" instructions are included.

Path Dependence and Lock-In

Path dependence is a concept used to explain how a certain state, for example the design of a product, is explained by the preceding course of events. A broad and generic interpretation of path dependence is that "history matters." However, this is regarded as trivial. A narrower interpretation of the concept holds that small events are a disproportionate cause of later events.

By its theoretical definition, path dependence has implications for the evolution of products. It is used to argue how a historical course of events can explain the outcome of a particular development. This course of events leads to a certain outcome, which is not a predefined equilibrium. A different course of events leads to a different outcome. It also suggests that a design that becomes dominant is not necessarily superior to other possible designs. Instead, small events in the course of history can make certain designs more viable in a market, which leads to self-reinforcing mechanisms that provide it with a continuing dominance, or lock-in. Based on this reasoning, the potentially superior design cannot develop sufficient momentum, or is locked out from the market, and therefore becomes unviable. The evolutionary race continues along the "lock-in" path until a next dominant design is set. In retrospect, the moments at which these paths are defined become important nodes in the evolution of products.

The concept of path dependence was developed by economists to explain how technology adoption and evolution of industries take place. Since then, the concept has also been applied to other fields. David (1985, and Section 10.12 of this volume) described path dependence in his iconic paper on QWERTY. Since then, QWERTY has been adopted as the paradigm case of path dependence. David argues in his paper how this particular keyboard layout became dominant in the course of time. Although the case and the arguments used are criticized by authors who distinguish different types of path dependence (Liebowitz and Margolis, 1990), the idea that development processes are path dependent is commonly accepted. The QWERTY case became one of the most influential articles in social sciences and developed into a polemic. Kay argues that if one would rerun the tape of history, QWERTY would always win. Basic probability theory is used to showcase that "the probability that the seven letters that make up 'typewriter' could finish up on the top row by chance is one in 5000" (Kay, 2013, p. 1177). In plain English, it is highly probable that these letters were arranged this way on purpose in order to allow salesmen to impress potential customers with rapidly typing the word "typewriter." Further, probability arguments are provided that the Dvorak Simplified Keyboard (DSK) layout has letter pairs prone to jamming that appear 16 times more frequently than in QWERTY. Hence, this layout would not have outcompeted QWERTY if it would have been around in the beginning of the typewriter evolution. Kay argues that DSK did not win the competition over QWERTY because it is inferior. Besides, DSK was patented 69 years after Christopher Latam Soles patented QWERTY in 1867 in the United States. And Soles was not the only one working on typewriters. In 1864, carpenter Peter Mitterhofer from Austria made the first typewriter from wood. In 1865, Rasmus Malling-Hansen from Denmark invented the writing ball, a typewriter with the keys placed on a sphere. The apparatus used a battery-activated escapement (Robert and Weil, 2016).

Another reflection on the topic of path dependence by Vergne (2013) argues that the theoretical concept itself is not to be disputed, but empirical evidence for path dependence cannot be provided by *ex post* case studies like that of David. For the record, Vergne notes that David did not claim evidence of path dependence, but described QWERTY as a rather intriguing case, believing many more similar cases to be around, which we do not fully perceive or understand. Vergne argues that as with most case study research, path dependence theory is not falsifiable. To illustrate his point, Vergne provides an overview of different research methods including simulation and laboratory experiments, and evaluates their strengths and weaknesses. He closes with a remark that scholars have done a poor job in empirically exploring path dependence. Better research is required, or else the concept remains as a trendy catchall phrase to explain virtually every sequence of events where history seems to matter.

Although QWERTY has become the dominant design for Latin alphabet typewriters and computer keyboards, some countries use variants adapted better to language specifics. In Germany and much of Central Europe, the QWERTZ variant is used. In the German language, the Z is more commonly used than the Y, hence their positions are switched. In France and Belgium, the AZERTY layout is the dominant design for typewriters and keyboards. In addition to a slightly modified sequence of letters, the localized layouts include language-specific characters like ä, ö, and ü (QWERTZ) and ç, à, é, and è (AZERTY). Anyone in doubt of the strength of the "lock-in" is advised to try a variant other than the one he or she uses daily. It is a frustrating experience.

A well-known, more recent example of path dependence is the triumph of VHS over other videotape formats. The VHS format was not superior to Betamax. On the contrary. The greater availability of VHS tapes compelled consumers to buy matching equipment. This network effect reinforced itself and eventually led to a win for VHS. Standards or standardization are often associated with path dependence. Standards can be coordinated through agreements set by industry bodies, as was the case with JPEG, which was defined as the file format for compressed digital pictures by the Joint Photographic Experts Group. In other cases, standards are set as the outcome of development processes, as was argued to be the case for the QWERTY keyboard layout.

Standardization defines compatibility between various products and users who use the particular standard. It shifts the locus of the evolutionary battle from the interface design defined by the standard toward application of the particular standard. It is not so much the technical superiority of a particular standard at a certain point in time that defines its evolutionary fitness. Rather, the versatility of use of the standard greatly influences the extent to which it is used, and so its economic success and with it, its evolutionary faith. An example of such a battle of standards can be witnessed at time of writing between standards for interfaces used for data communication and connectors.

FireWire, also known as the IEEE1394 standard, was developed by Apple in the late 1980s and early 1990s and first used in products in 1999. USB (Universal Serial Bus), developed in the mid-1990s by a partnership of companies, became quickly more used than FireWire. Both standards evolved through various versions that competed on the bandwidth of data possible to communicate with them as well as their versatility of use. USB replaced a variety of earlier interfaces such as serial and parallel ports, as well as power chargers. USB acquired a greater market share, and a larger diversity of types of use. FireWire declined in use, and Apple replaced it with the Thunderbolt interface in 2013. The evolutionary race continues with new versions of standards being released every few years. USB released a power delivery (PD) specification in 2012 that enables up to 100 Watts to be provided, where as few as 10 Watts was previously possible, with the intention of bringing about uniform charging of electronic devices. Based on this new specification, an interface named USB Type-C was developed, which prompted Apple to remove the connector used only for power delivery in its laptops released in 2015. Chances are these new standards will open evolutionary paths to many new types of use and new types of products not viable before.

1.4.2 'Sociology

Diffusion of Innovation

One of the best-known models on innovation was developed by Rogers (1995, and Section 10.25 of this volume) and describes how new products, methods, or technologies diffuse through a population. In his book, of which the first edition was published in 1962, Rogers characterizes users according to their degree of willingness to adopt innovations. Those users most eager to adopt particular innovations are named innovators. They are followed by the early adopters, the early majority, and the late majority. Those users most skeptical and waiting to adopt innovations are called laggards. The definitions coined by Rogers are commonly used in popular culture and became a staple in marketing literature.

Rogers attributes five key characteristics that influence why potential adopters will consider using the innovation:

- Relative advantage, the advantage the innovation has over existing products.
- Compatibility, the compatibility with existing values, experiences, and needs of potential users. This is reminiscent of the Most Advanced Yet Acceptable (MAYA) principle of Raymond Loewy from the early 1950s (Loewy, 2011).

- Complexity, perceived ease of understanding and use.
- Trial ability, the degree to which the innovation can be tried (first-hand experience).
- Observability, the easier it is for potential users to see the result of the innovation, the better the chances are that it will be adopted.

The characteristics are all rather rational; however, aspects such as emotional benefits, habits, or status are not taken into consideration.

Over time, several theories of why consumers adapt an innovation have been developed. Ajzen and Fishbein (1980) introduced the Theory of Reasoned Action (TRA). Key in the TRA model is the postulation that behavior is driven by behavioral intention, which is a function of the person's attitude toward the behavior and a subjective norm, which is defined by the perception of whether people in the social network will approve the behavior. A limitation of the model is the assumption that an individual is free to act without any constraints. In reality, the intention to act can be restrained in many ways. Time, contextual limitations, existing habits, and abilities can and will limit a user in his or her feasibility to act. For instance, age-related functional loss will limit elderly users in their ability to act freely, as it limits their possibilities. The same limitations apply to the Technology Acceptance Model (TAM) proposed by Davis (1989) and Bagozzi, Davis, and Warshaw (1992). TAM tries to describe an individual's intention to accept and use a technology. In this theory, perceived usefulness and perceived ease of use determine the user's intention to actually use the technology (or the innovation using the technology).

Venkatesh and colleagues (2003) have tried to improve the Technology Acceptance Model. In their Unified Theory of Acceptance and Use of Technology (UTAUT), they describe four determinants for the use intention of the new technology and four influencers that describe the impact of the new technology. The determinants are performance expectancy, effort expectancy, social influence, and facilitating conditions. The influencers are gender, age, experience, and voluntariness of use. In contrast to TRA, TAM and UTAUT, the Lazy User Model (LUM) of Collan and Tétard (2007) aims to explain how a consumer selects a product from a set of possible, available solutions. LUM states that users will select the solution that fulfills their needs with the least effort.

All the mentioned models help to explain how decision making may be influenced, but lack explanations on how "effort" is to be understood, or how the different factors influencing the user's decision have to be weighed against one another, and therefore they do not answer the question how to use the models in a design process.

Social Construction of Technology

Another influential sociological perspective on innovation, referred to as the Social Construct of Technology (SCOT), argues *that technology does not determine human action, but that rather, human action shapes technology*. SCOT (Pinch and Bijker, 1984; Bijker, Hughes, and Pinch, 1987) takes us away from the common technology-centric view and underlines the forming pressures different social groups exert on innovating products and technologies. Bijker (1997) uses the SCOT perspective to describe among others how fluorescent lamp technology emerged and competed with incandescent bulbs. Fluorescent lamps were from the outset superior in efficacy terms. However, this appeared not to be sufficient to oust the incumbent incandescent lamps. According to Bijker, the struggle was not so much over pure technical benefits for the end user. Rather, Bijker argues, it was literally the power struggle between social groups that shaped the evolution of fluorescent lighting. Utilities that produced electricity wanted to further grow their revenue stream and rejected energy-saving technologies. Lamp manufacturers who competed among each other for market dominance feared losing market share and needed to cooperate with fixture manufacturers. Consumers were not a strong voice in this game. Hence, according to Bijker, we need to understand how social groups such as producers of electricity, manufacturers of lamps, and users interact to comprehend how in this case fluorescent light came about (see also Chapter 7).

From "Commodity" to "Experience"

In their book *The Experience Economy*, Pine and Gilmore (1999, and Section 10.23 of this volume) distinguish between the following four phases for products and services: Commodity, Good, Service, Experience. According to them, "Commodities" are taken from raw and basic materials. They are very similar, and that makes price the main means of competition. As an example they refer to coffee beans. If a company burns, grinds, and packages coffee beans, it makes what Pine and Gilmore call a "good." Although the company can demand a better price than if it only sold burned coffee beans, the level of competition means its price cannot be set very high. "Services" are aimed at individuals. Service products use goods to create services for their clients. According to Pine and Gilmore, people are more interested in services than in goods and are therefore willing to pay more for them. They call the fourth level "experience." Companies that offer an "experience" use their products and services to commit the customer. They explain: it is the memory that makes an experience stand out.

Designing Pleasurable Products

A model that is comparable to that of Pine and Gilmour is described by Jordan (2000, and Section 10.18 of this volume). According to Jordan, features such as the usability of a product start as – what in marketing terminology is referred to as – satisfiers. Later, however, they come to be expected, and this transforms them into dissatisfiers, in the meaning that they become dissatisfiers of the product if they are not a feature of it. He identifies three hierarchical levels of human factors: Functionality, Usability, Pleasure. Each level is a satisfier until most of the products have reached a certain quality. From that moment on, the lack of enough functionality or usability causes them to become dissatisfiers.

1.4.3 Innovation Studies

Sources of Innovation

Drucker (1985) argues that there are seven "sources of innovation": unexpected occurrences, incongruities, process needs, industry and market changes, demographic shifts, changes in perception, and new knowledge.

1 UNEXPECTED OCCURRENCES Companies should always consider that political, economic, social or technical occurrences can influence the requirements with regard to their products or services and can offer opportunities for innovations. An example, described in further detail in Chapter 8, is a car accident in 1994, when three-year-old Dana Hutchinson was killed after being struck by an airbag deployed while in a rearward-facing child seat in the passenger seat. This resulted in legislation changes that made warning labels on child seats and airbag cut-off switches for cars obligatory.

2 INCONGRUITIES An example of incongruity is when a company is trying to solve the wrong problem. Drucker describes the incongruity in development of new ships in the ship-building industry. For many years, the involved parties tried to reduce fuel consumption and improve the speed of the ships to save on costs without much result, until they discovered that most costs were made when the ships were in the harbor for loading and unloading. Once they understood where the costs lay, the solution was obvious: the roll-on and roll-off ship and the container ship – solutions that had been in use on trains and trucks for many years.

3 PROCESS NEEDS This concerns products that are needed to make a process go (more) smoothly. The world is full of them: a mobile phone frees you from a wire, a car navigation system makes it possible to find your way in unknown areas even when driving alone, which used to be quite dangerous in the times when you needed to read a map while trying to drive safely.

4 INDUSTRY AND MARKET CHANGES This comes close to what Christensen (1997, and Section 10.10 of this volume) describes as "disruptive innovations."

> Established companies, concentrating on defending what they already have, tend not to counterattack when a newcomer challenges them. Indeed, when market or industry structures change, traditional industry leaders again and again neglect the fastest growing market segments. New opportunities rarely fit the way the industry has always approached the market, defined it, or organized to serve it. Innovators therefore have a good chance of being left alone for a long time.
>
> (Drucker, 1985, p. 69)

A recent example of a company missing an innovation and losing its market leadership is Nokia, which missed the market of smartphones with touch screens because it waited too long to enter this market.

5 DEMOGRAPHIC SHIFTS According to Foot (1996, and Section 10.14 of this volume), two-thirds of "everything" that will happen in the near future can be predicted based on demographic shifts. A well-known example is the aging of the population of Western countries. A more recent development is the designing of products for what is called the "Bottom of the Pyramid": people with very small budgets.

6 CHANGES IN PERCEPTION Probably the most famous quote on changes in perception is "I think there is a world market for maybe five computers." This statement was attributed to Thomas J. Watson, but no real evidence of him saying this has been found. However, there is a documented version of a similar quote in 1946 by Sir Charles Darwin, head of Britain's National Physical Laboratory, who wrote: "it is very possible that one machine would suffice to solve all the problems that are demanded of it from the whole country."

7 NEW KNOWLEDGE That new knowledge offers opportunities for innovation seems so obvious that there is no need to further explain this.

Product Life Cycle

In the mid-1970s, Abernathy and Utterback (1975, and Section 10.1 of this volume) proposed a model of innovation process characteristics that is currently known as the technology life cycle. Their model describes the relationship between innovation patterns for two distinct but complementary aspects, competitive strategy (what) and production process characteristics (how).

According to Abernathy and Utterback, the locus of innovation is first found in new insights on "needs." During this stage, new products are conceptualized and new product specifications emerge. The technology life cycle model describes how the rate of "product innovation" decreases after

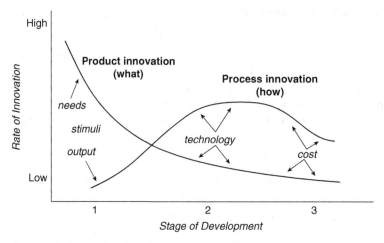

Figure 1.1 The technology life cycle (Free after Abernathy and Utterback, 1975)

introduction of the innovation (Figure 1.1). Product innovation refers to the "what" that is innovated rather than to a physical product. Improvements in the "how" of a product or technology are called "process innovation." The rate of innovation starts low in process innovation and then increases to a certain point and subsequently decreases. Process innovation includes both technology to fabricate a product and details in the design (of a product) aimed to improve manufacturability of the product. In the first stage, product innovation (design or specification changes/improvements) is focused on maximizing performance. In this stage, process innovation is at a low rate.

In the second stage, "technology" serves as the main stimulus for innovation. Innovation in the product is targeted at sales maximization. Here the locus of innovation is found in better ways of (re)producing. Production systems are increasingly designed for efficiency. Some sub-processes become highly automated while others are essentially manual or based on general-purpose equipment.

The third stage finds its main stimulus for innovation in "cost" (reduction). Cost minimization is a dominant strategy (for changes in the product design or specification) and process innovations become systemic. According to Abernathy and Utterback, one can expect "a greater degree of competition based on product differentiation with some product designs beginning to dominate" when firms start to focus on maximizing sales (pp. 643–644). This notion is the first use of the "dominant design" concept in literature.

Technological Discontinuities and Dominant Designs
Anderson and Tushman (1990, and Section 10.3 of this volume) propose an evolutionary model of technological change. Their model (Figure 1.2)

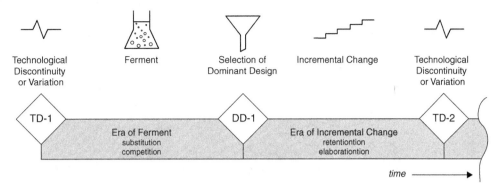

Figure 1.2 Technological discontinuities and dominant designs (Source: authors)

recognizes that technology develops in cycles. Periods of fermentation and periods of incremental change alternate and are demarcated by technical discontinuities and dominant designs. The eras of fermentation are essentially "trial-and-error phases" characterized by intense technological variation and selection that culminate in one, sometimes a few, dominant design(s). Subsequently an era of incremental change starts in which a dominant design is further elaborated until a new technological discontinuity punctuates the equilibrium. The model is called evolutionary as it recognizes that the process of (technological) "variation" provides designs that compete, a "selection" produces a dominant design as an outcome, and subsequent reproduction of this variant leads to "retention" of product characteristics. In Chapter 4 of this book, these dominant designs will be pictured as the successful branch in an evolutionary process that is visually displayed in a product family tree. The designs that are substituted or outcompeted are the evolutionary dead-end twigs.

Technology Cycles and Dominant Designs as Nested Hierarchies
Tushman and Murmann (1998) recognize that products are composed of a nested hierarchy of subsystems and linking mechanisms and note the following:

> Not all subsystems are equivalent. Rather, products are composed of hierarchically ordered subsystems that are coupled together by linking mechanisms that are crucial to the product's performance as are the subsystems themselves. Those more core subsystems are either tightly connected to other subsystems or represent a strategic performance bottleneck. In contrast, a peripheral subsystem is one that is only weakly connected to other subsystems.   (p. 249)

One can also depict these constructs as a nested hierarchy with the "system" as the highest level on top, cascading down via "subsystems" of various orders toward "components" (Figure 1.3). For example, a car can be considered a unit of analysis at the system level. Cars contain a power

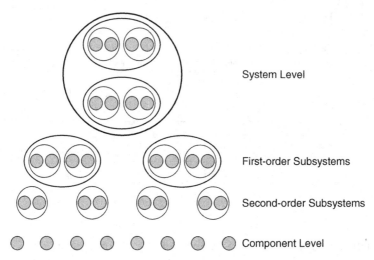

Figure 1.3 Illustration of a four-level nested hierarchy (After Murmann and Frenken, 2006)

train, which is a first-order subsystem that consists of the second-order subsystems engine, transmission, driveshaft, differentials, etc. The engine can be implemented technically in different ways (e.g., as internal combustion engine, hybrid, or electric). A car with an internal combustion engine contains third-order subsystems like the cylinder block, crankshaft, and pistons. The piston is built up of the components piston-head, piston ring, gudgeon pin, piston-rod, bolts, and nuts.

According to Tushman and Murmann, each of these systems and subsystems goes through technology cycles (Figure 1.4) that can be regarded as evolutionary sequences of variation, selection, and retention. A first "technical discontinuity" (TD1) disturbs equilibrium and a series of competing design variations is produced during an "era of ferment" (EoF). Selection results in a first "dominant design" (DD1), which is subsequently refined during an era of incremental change (EoIC). These cycles succeed each other over time and so represent technological trajectories.

As complex systems constitute different subsystems – each of which is subject to its own technology cycles – the evolution of complex systems can again be described as a nested hierarchy of technology cycles (Figure 1.5). An example of a nested hierarchy is provided for the telephone network system in Figure 2.2. The case studies described in Chapters 7 and 8 elaborate how technology cycles contribute to the evolution of products investigated. To illustrate the cases, system diagrams have been included that show the products (systems) are made up of subsystems and components.

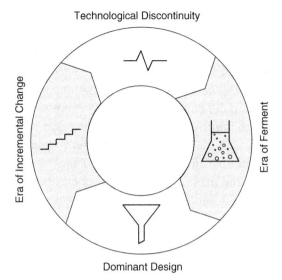

Figure 1.4 Technology cycles over time (Source: authors)

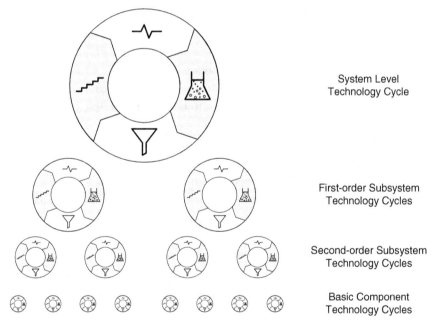

Figure 1.5 Nested hierarchy of technology cycles over time (Free after Murmann and Frenken, 2006)

Disruptive and Sustaining Innovations

In his book *The Innovator's Dilemma*, Christensen (1997, and Section 10.10 of this volume) makes a comparable distinction as Anderson and Tushman do; he differentiates between disruptive and sustaining innovations.

According to Christensen, innovations are sustaining most of the time. A sustaining innovation is an innovation that fulfills a desire held by existing clients. Often this means improving the performance of the product. Sustaining innovations hardly ever lead to the failure of an organization. A sustaining innovation leads to an improved product with an immediate, positive result for the company. In the event of a disruptive innovation there is, according to Christensen, no improvement of the product that the existing relations are interested in. On the contrary, the present clients will not want the innovation. Disruptive innovations have to find their own, new market. The problem for the present organization comes later, after the product has been developed in more detail, and sometimes only after several years, when the disruptive innovation has been improved in such a way that it has become interesting to their clients. In many cases, it is then too late. The new organization will have acquired such a strong position in the market that the existing organizations are unable to catch up.

Administrative and Architectural Innovations

In her article "Types of Innovation," Garcia (2010) differentiates – among others – between technological, administrative, and architectural innovations. Administrative innovations change an organization's structure or its administrative processes. As examples, she mentions: management by objectives, six-sigma processes, job rotation, staff incentive systems, and telecommuting. Architectural innovations refer to how shifts in subsystems or new ways of combining existing technologies can create new solutions. A well-known example of an architectural innovation is the Apple iPhone. The combination of a smartphone with a touch screen was new; however, the used technology was not the latest available and the performance was less than that of existing smartphones.

Technological Paradigms and Trajectories

Dosi (1982, and Section 10.13 of this volume) introduced the term "technological paradigm" in an analogy with the scientific paradigm as posed by Kuhn (1962). Dosi defined technological paradigm as follows:

> A "model" and a "pattern" of solution of selected technological problems based on selected principles derived from natural sciences and on selected material technologies.

Subsequently, a technological trajectory is defined as follows:

> The pattern of "normal" problem solving activity (i.e. of "progress") on the ground of a technological paradigm.

The technological trajectory is the direction of advance within a techno-logical paradigm. The technological paradigm strongly narrows the directions of technological change (solutions) pursued (investigated). It provides a framework that guides technological development. At the same time, such a framework also prevents investigation of alternative types of solutions. Thus, a technology paradigm has an exclusion effect, blinding technologists and engineers to other technological possibilities. According to Dosi:

> Paradigms are an "outlook" that focus the eye and the efforts of technologists and engineers in defined directions.   (1982, p. 158)

Dosi describes two different states of technological development, "normal progress" and "extraordinary innovative effort" or breakthroughs. During "normal progress," technology develops along a path or trajectory that is framed or limited by the boundaries of the technological paradigm. This is also called "continuous technological change." Trajectories are disrupted by changes in the technological paradigm. When a technological paradigm changes, the problem-solving activity starts almost again from the begin-ning. This type of technological change is referred to as "discontinuous." Often, the emergence of new technologies is characterized by new emerging firms.

Dosi describes two phases of technological change. First, in a "trial-and-error" phase, institutions produce and direct the accumulation of knowledge, experience, etc. A multiplicity of risk-taking actors tries different technical and commercial solutions. Then, a second phase starts, the oligopolistic maturity. In this phase, the production, exploitation, and commercial diffusion of inno-vations are commonly executed by a less diverse group of actors. Therefore, this phase is referred to as an oligopolistic competition. Actors in this phase derive their oligopolistic power from the asymmetric capability to innovate successfully. Static entry barriers (such as economies of scale) protect the oligopolist from competition entering the market. This possibility for firms to enjoy oligopolistic positions is a strong economic incentive to innovate as it provides market and technological leadership.

Technological Transitions

Geels (2002, and Section 10.16 of this volume) developed an analytical model to describe technological transitions, which are long-term and large--scale technological developments. Examples of technological transitions are the replacement of horse-based transportation by automobiles and the replacement of the current hydrocarbon-based energy systems by renew-able energy. The model Geels developed employs a so-called multilevel perspective (MLP) because it uses three analytical levels in its description of technological transitions: the micro-level or the niche, the meso-level or socio-technical regime, and the macro-level or landscape. The micro-level describes how radical innovations occur in small networks or niches. The meso-level describes a web of interlinking actors that together define so-called socio-technical regimes. The regime level slowly aligns with radical innovations that stabilize over time into dominant designs. A macro-level or landscape describes a broad range of factors such as social trends, economic pressure, or cultural values that together change even more slowly than the regimes. The three levels influence and interact together, describing different actors and dynamics that collectively effectuate long-term technological change or technological transitions. The multilevel perspective model recognizes that technological transitions are multidimensional in nature with technological change being only one aspect of change next to, e.g., culture or industrial networks.

1.4.4 Universal Darwinism and Evolutionary Perspectives

Adaptation and Selection

One and a half century after Darwin published his book, we are still further exploring concepts rooted in his theories on evolution. The evolutionary ideas are now applied to other fields like economics, languages, psychology, physics, and computer sciences. Collectively this is referred to as Universal Darwinism. Some of them have been mentioned in previous paragraphs.

When biological evolution (Darwin, 2008; originally published in 1859) is compared with cultural evolution (Dawkins, 1976), it can be concluded that the basic principles are the same, but that there are some important differences. Darwin published his book *On the Origin of Species* to explain how species evolve by adaptation and selection. This process became known as biological evolution. Since Darwin, the biochemical process of evolution has been unraveled. The current prevailing thought is that life started very simply with some kind of replicating molecular structure, although the form of the first replicating units and their origin remain a mystery. Over billions of years, more complex and advanced forms of life evolved, generally referred to as organisms. These organisms use a large, helical molecule named deoxyribonucleic acid, commonly referred to as DNA, as storage medium for biological information. We call the smallest unit of heredity information genes. The complex life-forms appeared later in time as they could not have evolved without their less complex predecessors. The genetic information found in the genomes of current living organisms is the result of a process of accumulation of biological information that started with the origin of life on earth. This allows us to trace back how long ago and along which paths organisms evolved into different species (see also Chapter 3).

Dawkins (1976) discussed the evolution of ideas and introduced the term "meme," by analogy with "gene." A meme is postulated as a contagious information pattern that replicates by parasitically infecting human minds and altering their behavior, causing them to propagate the pattern.

Biological Evolution: Genetics

Based on, among others, his study of finches from the Galapagos Islands, Darwin concluded that different populations of species would develop in different ways when living in different environments. He observed that the species would develop in other directions and that certain, favorable adaptations to the local circumstances would become dominant. Biological evolution, according to Darwinism, is commonly described by the following three steps:

1: Variation (random mutation) > changes to a species trait (laid down in genes)
2: Selection > survival of the "fittest,"[1] or maybe better of the "best adapted"
3: Retention (reproduction with heredity) > traits of the fittest are passed on to offspring and so retained

Changes in traits (mutations) can be harmful to species; they can be beneficial or neutral. If they are harmful, they will give organisms a disadvantage and most likely a shorter life expectancy and or reduced reproductive capability. If they are beneficial, they will provide an advantage and a higher life expectancy, which will make organisms more prolific as they have a higher chance to reproduce these advantages and pass them on by means of their carriers: the genes. Finally, if the changes in traits are neutral, they will have no effect. As will be shown, the fact that changes in traits (caused by mutation or recombination of genes) are random and genes are the "carrier" is the most important aspect that differentiate biological evolution from the evolution of ideas and products.

Cultural Evolution: Memetics

In his book *The Selfish Gene*, Dawkins (1976) introduces a new conception, the meme, a unit for carrying cultural information that can be compared to the gene as a unit for carrying biological information. Memes are postulated to play an elementary role in communication and sharing of ideas. Ideas – or memes – can be reproduced by word of mouth, by printing, by broadcasting, etc. Memes have one important difference from genes. They can mutate or recombine without intention, randomly, or they can be mutated or recombined with intention in a certain purpose and direction,

---

[1] The phrase "survival of the fittest" was introduced by Spencer in his book *The Principles of Biology* (1864).

by transforming them or by adding new or existing thoughts or ideas, or by changing the original idea. In the first case, there may be a misunderstanding: the person sharing the idea did not quite get the point. Anyone who has ever participated in an experiment where people are sitting in a circle and a short sentence is passed on by whispering the sentence in one's neighbor's ear knows that the chances are good that the sentence that returns to the person who started the experiment is not the same (or even completely different). Cultural evolution by memes can be described by the following three steps:

1: Variation > changes to an idea (or, e.g., product)
2: Selection > survival of the fittest or best-adapted ideas
3: Retention > passing on of fittest of best-adapted ideas by reproduction

Two decades after Dawkins coined the meme, several authors further elaborated his idea (Brodie, 1996; Blackmore, 1999; Aunger, 2000, 2002). They introduced conceptions like memetics (the study of memes and their social effects), memeplexe (a group of memes), and meme pool (a set of memes accessible to a culture or an individual). Concepts like something "going viral" have also been derived from the meme.

Steadman (2008) brings up several issues of discussion and doubts regarding memes. The first question is how and where memes are "stored." According to Dawkins, they are stored in the brain. Other authors suggest that they can be found in speech, acts, books, tools, and buildings as well. Steadman suggests that to transfer the memes from one person to another, most of the latter are necessary. He concludes that without writing, the ability to store information is quite limited.

Other questions are whether it is possible or useful to break down information into smaller units such as memes, and how selection of memes takes place:

> The difficulty, it seems to me, is that if all thoughts, ideas and beliefs are memes, does this not mean that memes are being selected by other memes?
>
> (Steadman, 2008, p. 244)

Langrish (2004) tries to solve this problem by introducing recipemes, selectemes, and explanemes.

> Recipemes are transmittable ideas about how to do things – recipe ideas.
>   Selectemes are ideas about what sort of thing you want to do. They are involved in making decisions between alternatives. ...
>   The third type of meme, the explaneme, must be added because of the human propensity to ask: "why?"   (p. 17)

This division, however, does not solve the issues under discussion. It seems to have many parallels with the efforts of Bense (1954, Section 10.6 of this volume) to find a formula to measure aesthetics: the unmeasurable concept of aesthetics is split in several new concepts that are just as unmeasurable. Steadman speaks of an "infinite regress" (2008, 244).

According to Edmonds (2005), memetics has not been very successful in providing "explanatory leverage upon observed phenomena." The huge number of publications in the first few years of this century quickly diminished and became almost nonexistent after 2005.

Similarities and Differences

What do genetics and memetics have in common? For one thing, they both allow for variation, selection, and retention. But there are also a number of differences. Take for example the different ways in which organisms reproduce and evolve. Sexual reproduction is the primary method of retention (of genetic information) for the vast majority of macroscopic organisms, including almost all animals and plants. Sexual reproduction also plays a crucial role in providing large amounts of variation as it recombines genetic information from both parents. Besides, there is asexual reproduction, arguably at least as important being an older type and used by the majority of organisms (see also Chapter 3). Cloning of an organism is an example of asexual reproduction where a genetically identical copy is created. In organisms like bacteria (Prokaryotes; see also Chapter 3) that reproduce asexually, variation can occur by mutation. Also bacteria are known to exchange their genetic information laterally (instead of from parent to offspring), allowing for recombination. Many species can reproduce sexually as well as asexually (many plants and some type of starfish).

Biological variation whether by mutation or recombination is always random. Biological evolution is unintentional as a result. Species do not originate because of a master plan that foresaw their appearance (intelligent design). Instead, species originate by means of adaption and natural selection. Different selective environments would have produced different species.

Genetic manipulation, like, for example, selective breeding or genetic engineering, is intentional, on purpose. Likewise is innovation and/or product development. Products are developed with an intention, for a specific group of users, for a certain type of use. Nevertheless, long-term evolution of products is not intentional, as we do not direct product development over many human generations. If a time scale of centuries is used, product evolution starts to resemble biological evolution in the sense that it then clearly becomes unintentional. The selective environment influences the origin of products as well as their evolutionary future in a similar fashion as it does for species.

Genes in asexual reproduction can exchange laterally. Also, asexual reproduction allows for very fast growth of a population (e.g., for bacteria). On the other hand, genes in sexual reproduction are transferred much more slowly and in one direction only, from parent to offspring. Each step is toward the next generation. And the length of a generation is commonly a substantial part of the length of the lifespan of species. The speed of replication of genes in sexual reproduction is constrained by time (to sexual maturity and pregnancy cycles) and the number of females with which a male can practically mate.

Memes replicate and evolve particularly well within a group of like minds such as colleagues, peers, or people with similar interests. While memes replicate from sender to receiver the roles of sender and receiver can vary. This type of lateral memetic exchange and replication is therefore often compared with lateral genetic exchange and replication as observed in asexual reproduction of bacteria.

Memes can replicate rather swiftly and toward a theoretically unlimited number of receivers. Twitter provides us an example of how fast memes can replicate, or perhaps more strikingly, propagate. Bad news (on popular topics) travels fast and "goes viral" on Twitter. And finally: unsuccessful genes will disappear once unviable (once died out they do not reappear), but unsuccessful memes can become viable again swiftly if their carriers (e.g., books) have not been destroyed.

For the purpose of this book, we will park memes and memetics in this chapter and leave them as a philosophical concept. Studies into its unit of reproduction have not led to commonly accepted ideas on how to better organize the process of product development.

1.4.5 Architecture and Design

For centuries, design solutions provided by biological evolution have served as a source of inspiration to architects and engineers. Steadman (1979) explores the many analogies that have been made between the evolution of organisms and human-designed objects. With a background in architecture, Steadman describes many interesting examples, not only of architects and designers, but also of philosophers and other theorists, who have looked to biology for inspiration. Although this work is extensive in the examples and references listed, it does not provide a clear explanation of how designers can benefit from the evolutionary analogy. There does not appear to be a method for design analogous to the process of growth and evolution in nature, or at least not one that is easy to grasp.

Many authors, inventors, and engineers have suggested words to describe how nature is used as source of inspiration for the world of made. Otto Schmitt coined the term "biomimetics" in the 1950s as the imitation of elements from the biological world for the purpose of solving human problems. Benyus (1997) describes "biomimicry" as a new discipline using nature's best ideas as inspiration for design solutions. And finally Jack E. Steele coined the term "bionics" in 1958, describing a comparable principle as biomimetics or biomimicry. Among other things, the nature-inspired design perspective has received attention in the context of sustainable design (Tempelman et al., 2015). Next to inspiration for designs, biological evolution has been used as an explanation for certain evolutionary mechanisms in the world of made. Gould and Vrba (1982) introduced the term "exaptation" for the process by which features acquire functions for which they were not originally adapted or selected. For example, feathers that most likely originally evolved for thermal insulation are now an indispensable trait for flying birds. An often-quoted example of functional shift in the world of made is the radar, whose technology also proved useful in microwave ovens. Adriani and Cattani (2016) brought together several papers in a special section of a journal in an effort to introduce the concept of exaptation to a broader audience and exposing it as a (possible) solution to questions about the emergence of manmade novelty, particularly radical innovation.

1.4.6 Industrial Design Engineering

Most Advanced Yet Acceptable

One of the first principles from an industrial design perspective was formulated in the 1950s by Raymond Loewy: "MAYA, Most Advanced Yet Acceptable."

> The adult public's taste is not necessarily ready to accept the logical solution to their requirements if the solution implies too vast a departure from what they have been conditioned into accepting as the norm. (2011)

Product Phases

In the last decades of the twentieth century, the process of developing new products was mastered and taught in various engineering courses. Eger (1987, 1993, 2007b) recognized that products develop through phases and proposed a step-by-step product development or innovation strategy named Evolutionary Product Development (EPD). Recognizing that radical, new innovations imply both a promise of potential high returns and a substantial risk of failure and loss of money, Eger introduced Evolutionary Product Development as a strategy, reducing risk in new product development. EPD recognizes phases in the development of products. Each phase is defined by 10 product characteristics, of which five apply to the product itself (newness, functionality, ergonomics, product development, styling) and the others to its market, its production technology, the services that accompany it, and the ethical aspects of the product. The six product phases are performance, optimization, itemization, segmentation, individualization, and awareness. In the first phase, the product is new to the market, the performance is often poor, and few competitors offer the product for a high price. Over time, the product starts improving in reliability, ergonomics, and safety. Competition increases and prices decrease. The product receives more features and achieves a high market penetration.

Initially the phases postulated were assumed to appear sequentially. In a later study, Eger (2013) defined three sequential phases plus another three that appear to coexist as a fourth phase.

1.5 Patterns and Mechanisms of Innovation Framed

The models discussed earlier describe different perspectives (social, economic, technological, and evolutionary) on the process of innovation. Time is a common dimension and used to route from earlier to later versions because innovation processes are path dependent. Over time, periods with specific innovation dynamics are recognized.

Kuhn (1962) and Dosi (1982, and Section 10.13 of this volume) describe how a specific regime or "paradigm" defines a period characterized by one and the same frame of reference. Geels (2002, and Section 10.16 of this volume) describes how the process of technology transitions is driven by interactions within and between different levels (micro/meso/macro). Typically, longer time frames are assigned to the technological trajectories and technological transitions.

Abernathy and Utterback (1975, and Section 10.1 of this volume) as also Anderson and Tushman (1990, and Section 10.3 of this volume) describe how technology cycles are defined by periods of rapid change alternated by periods of slower change. These periods of alternating rapid and slower change are associated with shorter time frames and nested in a technology trajectory.

Altshuller (1999, and Section 10.2 of this volume) formed the theory of inventive problem solving (in Russian, the acronym is TRIZ). Altshuller studied thousands of predominantly Russian patents on features of innovative solutions, and then looked for similarities between the innovative steps. The result is TRIZ, and the accompanying algorithm of inventive problem solving (ARIZ). As the name suggests, TRIZ is a method for technical problem solving during product development, rather than a method for finding novel product ideas. Technical systems develop during their existence. Each generation of a technical system will be the result of ongoing development toward "the ideal result." There are seven paths along which a product or part of a product can develop:

1. Dynamics: from a fixed to a flexible connection, then to several flexible connections, finally to fully flexible;

2. Number: one object, two objects, many objects (the same principle applies to part objects);
3. Big to small: macro to micro (and finally to nano);
4. Synchronization: from continuous to periodical to resonating;
5. Dimensionality: from 1D to 2D to 3D;
6. Disparate development of components;
7. Automation: from manual to supported to fully automated to autonomous.

A Few Examples of the Development Paths

Dynamics (1): A mobile phone in one piece, a phone with one hinge (clamshell models), a fully flexible phone that can be rolled or folded up and will adjust to the shape of clothing.

Big to small (3): Storage of computer data. First on punched tape (macro structure: one hole punched in paper tape for each bit of data); then, magnetic storage on tape and disk (microscopically small magnetic fields for each bit of data); and one atom per data bit.

Dimensionality (5): From a display of one line at a typewriter (showing one line of text), to an entire field at a time (computer monitor) to a holographic 3D projection.

These development patterns can be used in forecasting the direction in which an existing product may develop. That is why this is a very suitable method for solving design constraints in product development.

Eger (1987, 1993, 2007b) describes how products evolve from a poor performance toward more advanced and refined versions.

Most of these models have in common that they assume a sequence as well as a gradient (from course to finer) in a process that delivers new products referred to as innovation. However, an integrative perspective on how products come about, develop into families of related products over time as also the causal link between new products and their predecessors, is generally absent in literature. An exception is formed by the evolutionary theories. This book addresses the gap between sequential models and evolutionary models. In Figure 1.6, an overview is given of a number of the described models.

1.6 The Evolution of Products

Based on the two described evolutionary models (Darwin and Dawkins), a third model is developed that describes the evolution of products (see also Chapter 4). Every product mankind develops today builds on earlier products, on earlier knowledge. Newly developed knowledge builds on previously developed knowledge. Knowledge accumulates and so does the specific knowledge we use to design and build products. New products that do not

Eger and Ehlhardt (2017)	Performance		Optimization	Itemization	Segmentation / Individualization / Awareness		
Geels (2002)	Niche Innovations		Socio-Technical Regime		Socio-Technical Landscape		
Jordan (2000)	Functionality		Usability		Pleasure		
Pine and Gilmore (1999)	Commodity		Good		Service		Experience
Christensen (1997)	Disruptive Innovation				Sustaining Innovation		
Eger (1993)	Performance		Optimization	Itemization	Segmentation	Individualization	Awareness
Anderson and Tushman (1990)	Era of Ferment / Radical Innovation (starts with a Technological Discontinuity)				Era of Incremental Change / Incremental Innovation (starts with a Dominant Design)		
Bijker (1990)	Outside the Technological Frame				Inside the Technological Frame		
Eger (1987)	Performance		Optimization	Itemization	Segmentation		Individualization
Dosi (1982)	Trial and Error Phase		Oligopolistic Maturity		Continuous Technological Phase		
Abernathy and Utterback (1975)	Fluid Pattern		Transitional Phase		Specific Phase		
Rogers (1962)	Innovators	Early Adopters	Early Majority		Late Majority		Laggards
Loewy (~1950)	Most Advanced Yet Acceptable (MAYA)						

Figure 1.6 Conceptions that are used in different disciplines but that come close to each other with regard to their meaning; left to right: new products often start with "more revolutionary strategies" and are more attractive to innovators, but in the course of time the strategies become more "evolutionary" to make the products attractive for a bigger audience. The concepts are vertically organized by time of appearance and horizontally by sequence or gradient (Source: authors)

function well do not survive. We continue the design of next-generation products with the learning experience of the previous ones. Introducing as much newness in a product as possible (radical innovation) in general is not a viable strategy. It is known that if one introduces a new product to the market, the more newness it contains, the higher the risk of failure. Only very few "really new products" that are introduced survive long enough to become the start of a new type of product. And in the beginning of their life as a new type of product, they commonly function poorly. By far the majority of products introduced on the market are in fact facelifts, possibly a next generation or a new version targeting a new segment in the market (segmentation phase). They are not what is referred to in this book as "new types of products." Hence, for the majority of all (new) product development work, it makes sense to grow new designs carefully. Such an "evolutionary" approach greatly reduces the risk of failure. This book provides a methodological framework called "Evolutionary Product Development" as a low-risk strategy for New Product Development.

In the next section, the question will be discussed if it is possible to translate the evolutionary concepts into a model of the evolution of products and what the building blocks of this model would look like.

Evolution of Products: Itemetics

The most prominent marker in the evolution of products and organisms is the variation-selection-retention mechanism. However, in product development, variation is not unintentional. A similarity between products and ideas is the possibility of purposely transforming them (intelligent design). Or, one could say, products (or artefacts) are a specific appearance or materialization of ideas. When it comes to reproduction, there is a major difference between (immaterial) ideas and (material) products. Ideas that do not require matter reproduce easily. Products that consist of matter require raw material, machineries, and lots of energy to reproduce. A known example is the comparison between hardware (which consists of matter) and software (which is by its nature immaterial, an idea laid down in a series of 1s and 0s). It is more expensive to reproduce hardware than software. The reproduction of software (or services) is nearly as easy as the reproduction of ideas. Products will not be improved through random variation (mutation). Rather, many product variants are developed, manufactured, and marketed that are developed with the intention to provide an improved version. A variety in items that provides a functional, social, or environmental benefit to a product can be compared to a variety in traits found in species. Some will be more successful than others. Hence, selection will take place beyond the influence of the designer. The transformation applied to the product is assumed intentional (and called the process of new product development). With regard to selection, products have more in common with organisms. Disadvantageous characteristics of products will disappear, just like bad genes do most of the time. Note that selection does not operate on possible products, but on existing products that are available in the market. This brings us to the following three steps of the evolution of products:

1: Variation > changes to a product resulting from product development or modification
2: Selection > survival of the fittest or best-adapted products under selective pressures resulting from influences from the context such as buying behavior, legislation, etc.
3: Retention > fittest or best-adapted products are reproduced and items passed on to next-generation products

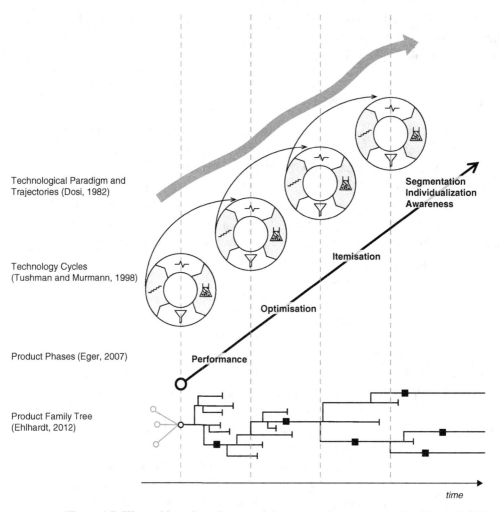

Figure 1.7 Hierarchic order of some of the conceptions presented in Figure 1.6. The concepts are vertically organized by time scale and measure of detail and horizontally by sequence of appearance (Source: authors)

Evolution in biology is "embedded" in genes, evolution of ideas is embedded in memes, evolution of products is regulated through what we will here call "items." Items are product characteristics laid down in the product specifications. In Chapters 5 and 6, the items are described that refer directly to the product. They are called "product characteristics." In Chapters 4, 7, and 8, the context (the ecosystem) in which the product has to survive is described in different elements. The ecosystem plays a major role in the selection of items (through selection processes in the context where the product evolves). The elements of the ecosystem are referred to as political, economic, social, and technical aspects also referred to by the acronym PEST (Chapman, 2006). Contrary to memes, we expect items to be explanatory with regard to the

"Building Block"	"Building Instructions"	Elements	End Result
Gene	DNA, RNA, ...	Organs, Muscles, Bones, ...	Living Creature
Item	(Construction and Detail) Drawings, Bill of Materials (BOM), RAL numbers, ...	Components, Subassemblies, ...	Product

Figure 1.8 A comparison of the building blocks in the biological- and the "product-world" (Source: authors)

Product:	1939, the Cigar	1946: Steel Beard	1947: the 'Egg'
Item:			
Form of the enclosure	Shaving head in line with shaver	Shaving head in line with shaver	Shaving head on the side (90°)
Material of the enclosure	Bakelite	Bakelite	Urea formaldehyde
Colour of the enclosure	Black	Black	Ivory
Number of shaving heads	1	1	1
Size of shaving head	17mm	22mm	22mm
Material of knives	Bronze	Steel	Steel
Number of knives	3	6	6
Material of head	Chromed steel	Chromed steel	Chromed steel

Figure 1.9 An example of the first electric shavers by Philips/Norelco shows how items "variate" ("mutate") separately (Source: authors)

evolution of products. With regard to variation, genes and items even seem to come closer to each other, since genetic manipulation starts to look like goal-oriented product development. While with memes selection does not necessarily lead to the disappearance of a poor idea, in biology a disadvantageous feature will disappear, often even a complete species may vanish. The same is the case with products. Product characteristics (items) that are not successful will not survive, and unsuccessful products will – under the influence of their ecosystem – vanish as well. In Figure 1.8, genes and items are compared. In Figure 1.9, it is shown how items "variate" separately: some items remain the same and others change, in a way that is comparable to genes.

1.7 Definitions

The terms "product development," "innovation," "design," "styling," "industrial design engineering," and "functionality" are used with different meanings. Some use product development only in relation to the development of a new or improved product. For others, the search that precedes the design of the new product, the development of production methods, and the development of the market introduction are also elements of what they call product development. The term "design" is even used in a wider context. While an optician may have a "designer collection" of glasses in his shop, someone who develops software may also call his concept a "design." To avoid misunderstandings about the definitions of these terms, the definitions used in this book are presented first. Most of the time, the term "product" refers to a physical object that performs a function. However, in this book, a "product" can also be software, a service, or a combination of a product and a service, meaning that products are not only bicycles, shavers, or mobiles, but also holidays, traveling, or bank services. This results in the following definitions of an artefact and a product.

Artefact: An artefact (from Latin phrase *arte factum*, from *ars* = skill + *facere* = to make) is something made or given shape by man, such as a tool or a work of art.

Product: A construct designed to realize a specific basic function, resulting from accumulated know-how (to make) and know-what (function to realize). Products can be tangible (e.g., lamp, car, chair) as well as intangible (e.g., word-processor, package holiday). Some products realize their function independently (e.g., a chair), while other products typically are used nested in other products (e.g., a navigation system in a car). And some products (e.g., a telephone) are elements of larger technological systems (telephone networks).

Also: A (physical) result of the creative or artistic mind, intentionally designed or developed. In this book, we refer to products that are "produced" in series, or mass-produced, and offered for sale.

This book excludes from the scope of products those artefacts that are not intended to realize a specific basic function and/or are considered works of art such as a painting or a piece of music. The reason for this exclusion lies in the importance attributed here to "function" and "production," which leads to a clear distinction in technology cycles (see also Section 3.3) between "application-based products intended to be used for a basic function and need to be efficiently produced" and those regarded as "art." Without dismissing art, this book inclines toward engineering because of the utilitarian character of products (function), and the way they are reproduced makes them stand out.

New type of product: A construct that provides a new basic function, or a basic function in a fundamentally different way that commands a decisive performance, cost, or quality advantage over previous products.

New types of products commonly originate from technological discontinuities and become well established and recognizable once a dominant design is achieved. New types of products typically fulfill their basic function initially poorly against relatively high cost. Over time, products mature through the product phases, improving in basic function performance, against lower cost, differentiating into embodiments that serve different segments of the market.

One example is the incandescent lamp, which was a new type of product that originated at the end of the nineteenth century and provided a basic function (providing light) such that it held decisive performance, cost, and quality advantages over previous products providing the same basic function (e.g., candle, paraffin lamp, gas lamp, arc lamp).

Product class: A group or range of products that may serve as substitutes for another, depending on how wide or narrow the definition used for product class. A product class is a functional classification designating products with the same basic function. Products within a class compete with each other in the marketplace, but need not belong to the same product family, i.e., share a common root or ancestral product and use the same or similar architecture and technology.

For example, the product class General Lighting Service (GLS) originated as a designation for an incandescent lamp standard also known as the standard "incandescent light bulb." Currently GLS bulbs might use incandescence, gas discharge, or LED technology. They all belong to the same product class, but different product families descending from different ancestral products based on different technologies. A narrow product class for "lighting" would include incandescent lamps, halogen incandescent lamps, tube lamps, and LED bulbs, while a broad product class would include candles and paraffin lamps. An adjective can be used to narrow a product class (e.g., electric lighting or GLS lamps).

Function: The natural or characteristic action performed by a product (SAVE, 2015).

Basic function: The primary purpose or most important action performed by a product. The basic function must always exist, although methods to achieve it may vary (SAVE, 2015).

Product development: The activity of dealing with the design, creation, production, and marketing of new products. Also referred to as new product development (NPD).

Innovation: 1. The act of innovating; introduction of a new idea into the marketplace in the form of a new product or service, or an improvement in organization or (production) process. 2. A change effected by innovating.

Evolution: 1 (biology). The process by which life forms change over time. 2 (general). The process of gradual change and development.

Niche: 1 (biology/ecology). The specific area an organism inhabits in an ecosystem (affecting its survival as a species). 2 (general) A special segment of the market.

Path dependence: A concept used to elucidate how a certain state (e.g., the design of a product or a standard) is explained by the course of events that took place before. Path dependence is most likely to arise in "network" industries, where the benefits of adopting a particular design, standard, or technology, depend on choices made by others. At a certain point, a *lock-in* is achieved, making the choice for the particular design, standard, or technology quasi irreversible. Path dependence and lock-in are commonly associated.

Lock-in: A situation where a particular design, standard, or technology becomes dominant, despite other potentially more economic alternatives being around. Lock-in may occur either because of sunk cost or because of external economies and a lack of coordination mechanisms that prevent individuals from switching to another (potentially superior) design, standard, or technology. Path dependence and lock-in are commonly associated.

Design (verb): The process of purposely developing ideas into, e.g., a construction, engineering drawings, etc.

Design (noun): The arrangement or scheme to which an product is made, intended to accomplish a goal by satisfying a set of requirements.

Design (adjective): The appearance of the whole or part of a product, including any pattern or texture applied to its surface.

Dominant design: 1. A design that is widely adopted and that changed the nature of competition in the corresponding industry (Murmann and Frenken, 2006). 2. A single configuration or narrow range of configurations that accounted for more than 50% of new product sales or new process installations and maintained a 50% market share for at least four years (Anderson and Tushman, 1990, p. 620).

Dominant designs are associated with change in industry dynamics. However, scholars differ on whether a dominant design is the cause or the consequence of these changing competitive dynamics. Dominant designs remain in their position until a disruption causes new designs to evolve, which then compete with the incumbent until a new dominant design is established.

The term "dominant design" is used in different levels of analysis. Most commonly it is used to define a configuration on the product level. The term "dominant design" is also used for subsystems like landing gear in airplanes (Tushman and Murmann, 1998). In this book, the term "dominant design" is used for products and in analysis on the level of products unless stated otherwise. Further, we will distinguish between dominant designs in a subsystem (e.g., the Edison screw base as an interface), in a product family (e.g., CFL lamps), and in a product class (e.g., GLS lamps).

Styling: A distinctive manner or way of form giving, e.g., a unique decoration or an expressive shape.

Industrial design engineering: The design and engineering of functional objects that can be produced in a series, or that can be mass-produced.

Function analysis system technique (FAST): A method developed to systematically analyze the functionality of products (Bytheway, 1965). Functions are described using a verb and a noun. FAST distinguishes between basic and secondary functions and their subsets. The FAST method uses a diagram to map functions from the WHY on the left (highest-order function or output) to the HOW on the right (lowest-order function or input). FAST is a tool used in Value Engineering, a systematic method to improve the "value" of goods or products and services by using an examination of function (SAVE, 2015).

Functionality: In this book, the word "functionality" relates to the technical performance of a product. Does the product function – in a technological way – as the user expects? According to this definition, the functionality can be good while, for instance, the comfort, safety, and user friendliness of the product are insufficient. Consequently, this functionality is sometimes referred to as technological functionality. Wherever this study refers to another kind of performance, this will be stated, for example, in the case of ergonomic or economic functionality.

This book introduces some new concepts.

Item: A unit of information describing or defining a characteristic of a product.

Product phase: A phase in the marketing product life cycle (M-PLC) of a product that has distinguishing features defined by product characteristics.

Product (phase) characteristic: A feature of a product phase that is characteristic for this phase. Product characteristics may concern the functionality, emotional benefits, price, market, product development, production, ethics, etc.

Product family: A series of (the same) type of products designed to realize the same basic function, that share a common root or ancestral product, and that commonly use the same or similar architecture and technology. The branches in a family are separated by differences in user segments to which their designs and architectures are optimized. A young product family typically consists of product variants in the performance or optimization phase. Once a product family matures to the segmentation phase, it consists of variants that evolved to serve specific segments of the market and commonly apply architectures optimized to the type of use or users that define the segment.

For example, an incandescent lamp bulb type-A and a halogen incandescent lamp of the PAR type (including a parabolic reflector) belong to the same product family derived from the same ancestral product (carbon filament lamps) using the same technology (tungsten filaments). However, the GLS incandescent and GLS LED bulb are not in the same product family originating from different technology families, but do belong to the same product class. Having the same producer, being made from the same material, or providing the same function also does not define a product family.

Product family tree (PFT): A mapping technique to visualize the evolution of a product family through time by relating inventions, dominant designs (standards) that designate the most prolific variants and discontinued products. A PFT emerges from a single node, a first-of-a-kind product, and then branches out into different designs that exist in parallel and cater to different segments or types of use. Some branches have dead-ends as certain technologies, designs, or product architectures become outdated and are discontinued.

Ecosystem: Context in which a product evolves. Used to map influences on the development of a product family in a product evolution diagram.

Product evolution diagram (PED): An analytical framework that graphically relates evolving products to a context of factors influencing that particular evolution. Using a timeline, it combines a PFT with an ecosystem. The graphical narrative provided by the PED visualizes the complex relationship between technological developments and their context.

2 Technological Innovation as an Evolutionary Process

2.1 Introduction

Stone tools in general are regarded as the oldest and most primitive tools and as such are associated with the dawn of mankind. Evidence of direct stone tool manufacturing dates back more than 2.5 million years (Semaw et al., 1997), and stone tool–assisted consumption of animal tissues even 0.8 million years earlier (McPherron et al., 2010). It is possible that other tools of softer materials prone to decay, like wood, were made even before then. With the oldest discovered remains of our own species, *Homo sapiens*, being an estimated 0.2 million years old, it is clear that toolmaking goes back a long way among our ancestors. As the first stone tools date 2.5 million years back, the rate of development in these products was rather slow, at least by today's standards. For more than 2 million years, the most prominent tools of which remains have been found were based on stone technology. The technological era in which these tools were produced is therefore referred to as the Stone Age.

The oldest stone tools were flakes chipped off from larger stones. Over time, stone technology advanced and produced complex, meticulously shaped products like the hand axe (Figure 2.1), which requires deliberate planning in manufacturing and dexterous craftsmen. Stone technology further advanced, e.g., by improving functionality with heat treatment to harden sharp edges (Schmidt et al., 2013), or adding wood or bone extensions to sharpened stones. This led to the creation of improved axes, as well as new tools like spears, daggers, or arrows. People then started to write and live in cities, and various specializations of labor arose. People discovered how they could use metal to make tools such as axes and arrow points. This marked the transition from the Stone Age to the Bronze Age.

Ever since our technological history has been characterized by the increasingly rapid development of new and more advanced types of tools. This book builds on the observation that tool manufacturing started with simple tools and that the complex types we use today were only recently produced.

Figure 2.1 A stone hand axe (left) and a bronze axe (right). Note: not the same scale (Source: authors)

2.2 Knowledge Accumulation and Innovation

As described in Chapter 1, various authors have explained the process of innovation in evolutionary terms. Basalla (1988) described how a process of invention accumulation eventually led to the current diversity as well as complexity in tools. He writes that:

> Continuity implies that novel artefacts can only arise from antecedent artefacts – that new kinds of made things are never pure creations of theory, ingenuity, or fancy. If technology is to evolve, then novelty must appear in the midst of the continuous.   (pp. vii–viii)

In other words, Basalla postulates that inventions like the bicycle or smartphone build on previous inventions and he states that the evolution of technology implies a continuum in which one artefact can be invented by building on knowledge associated with previous artefacts. Consequently, there is no "inventive leap" that explains the sudden appearance of inventions like the bicycle or smartphone. Instead, the emergence of these products can be explained by a continuum, in which step-by-step product-technology combinations evolve.

This reasoning implies that next-generation products evolve that, over time, lead to more advanced products whose existence was not intended by the initial developments, nor could initially have been conceived. The process of know-how and know-what accumulation over time therefore explains how new products emerge and give rise to new types that could not have been envisaged initially. The introduction of new products, let alone new types of products, is therefore not an example of *generatio spontanea*. Rather it is enabled by a long process of accumulation of know-how to make elements of the first elementary version of the product, which enables the exploration of the know-what with a view to providing new functionality.

The notion that our current knowledge builds on previous discoveries was first used in the twelfth century by Bernard of Chartres (McGarry, 1955), who introduced the metaphor of "dwarfs standing on the shoulders of giants." The metaphor compares our current generation with dwarfs who can look beyond previous generations not because of better vision, but because we are lifted up by the knowledge accumulated. The knowledge accumulation referred to in this metaphor also holds for know-how (to make products) and know-what (products to make) used in today's products or technologies.

Technological innovations accumulate over time and cannot skip a generation. Each step from one generation to the next, although technically challenging, has to be feasible based on new combinations of know-how and know-what available at that time. After all, skipping a generation would require an inventive leap or a knowledge fundament that is unavailable. The philosopher Dennett (1995) uses the metaphor of skyhooks (which use no fundament) and cranes (which rest on a fundament) to explain the difference between the emergence of a new design by a divine intervention (for which a skyhook suffices), and Darwinian evolution in which adaption and selection elucidates how accumulated changes (that build the fundament) over time explain how new designs in biology come about. This metaphor also supports the accumulation of know-how and know-what as a more plausible argument for the emergence of new types of products by technological evolution[1] rather than divine intervention (also referred to as intelligent design).

Arthur (2009, and Section 10.4 of this volume) adds to this the observation that evolution in technology in particular is a matter of recombining knowledge and techniques used before for solving other problems. Hence Arthur describes this as combinatorial evolution.

As argued earlier, any innovation is an "inventive step," which builds on prior art. Before new types of products can be invented, a fundament of know-what (functions to fulfill) and know-how (to make these products) has to be accumulated. It is this knowledge and skills accumulation process that can explain the appearance of highly complex tools, such as the smartphone.

---

[1] Dawkins (1986, 43–74) developed a computer program to explore how accumulating small changes explain diversity and complexity in organisms. The biomorph program takes evolution into virtual reality and shows how a succession of small changes can produce evolving fictitious two-dimensional animals and so visualizes the power of evolution.

Today's smartphones would not exist without preceding mobile phones, which were, in turn, developed to overcome limitations of telephones using landlines. Every new type of telephone was not only introduced to improve upon earlier models, but could not have been invented or developed if these prior models and a rich source of adjacent knowledge were not available. The next section illustrates how products (telephones) evolve, nested in a large technological system (telephone networks) that is inextricably linked to evolution in components (e.g., transistors).

2.3 System Evolution: The Case of the Telephone

This section will show that to understand how a nested product evolved, it does not suffice to regard it as a stand-alone product. Instead, one has to look at the evolution at different levels (system and component) to understand how they influence each other.

To understand how telephones evolved, it is required to understand their position as an element of a large technological system (Figure 2.2), consisting of a network of landlines, telephone exchange facilities, and telephones to allow users to talk to each other over a large distance. In other words, the product (telephone) is nested in a larger system (telephone networks). This large technological system can be analyzed at different levels. Although the

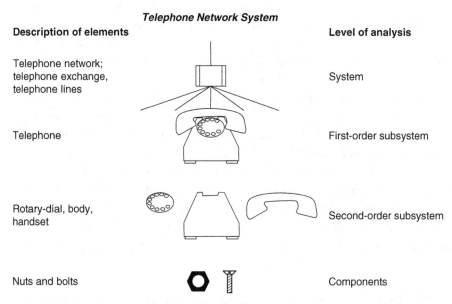

Figure 2.2 The telephone network system as a nested hierarchy consisting of a system, subsystem, and components. In this perspective, the telephone is a first-order subsystem. (Source: authors)

breakdown in levels is ambiguous, in the case shown in Figure 2.2 we assume four levels when analyzing the telephone system. The reason is that it requires four levels here to show how changes in a network technology (system) affect design details in the telephone (subsystem/product). In addition, changes in, for example, electric circuits (components) explain the changes in network technology (systems). Apparently, the process of evolution in technology acts across all system hierarchy levels.

The telephone was commercially introduced in 1876. It consisted of a speaker and a mouthpiece next to a wood panel body with various electrical parts. There is disagreement about who should be given credit for the invention of the telephone, although the Bell and Edison patents dominated early telephone technology and are regarded as commercially decisive (Wikipedia, 2015a). However, the invention of the telephone and its network technology was clearly not the work of a single inventor. Instead it was the accumulated inventive work of many individuals over several decades.

Over the years, telephone usage grew and had an enormous impact on our society. The telephone allowed more efficient communication and was instrumental in societal modernization. For example, it enabled women to participate in jobs like switchboard operator, outside the confines of the house. Women turned out to be avid users of this new technology and were first discouraged from using the telephone for "mere idle gossip" as the telephone was emphasized as a device for practical use in business. After a while, the industry wholeheartedly encouraged women to use telephones (Fischer, 1994). As is the case with many products, the way we use and perceive them evolves over time. The aversion of inventors and businessmen to unforeseen uses of the telephone proved only temporary. In the end, increased use stimulated business.

The growth in the number of users also led to raised expectations of telephone systems. Initially, telephone exchange facilities were filled with operators using switchboards to manually establish connections. Operator-established connections turned out to be expensive and not always available, as operators did not work 24/7. To overcome limitations associated with human operators, the pulse network technology was developed, which automated the process of establishing connections.

In order to allow the system to work with pulse network technology, the first-order subsystem (telephone) needed a second-order subsystem to generate pulses. For this purpose, a second-order subsystem (the rotary dial) was developed. In the case of the first pulse network telephones, the rotary dial was simply added as a "Fremdkörper" to the body of the telephone model that existed at that moment (Jacobs et al., 1987) in the 1920s. Then, over time, a more advanced telephone model was introduced, integrating the second-order subsystems rotary dial and base. The second-order subsystems speaker and mouthpiece

Figure 2.3 Evolution in early telephones: at the system level, operator networks were replaced by the pulse network, the second-order subsystem rotary dial was introduced, and then the second-order designs like the dial and the handset were further integrated. (Source: authors)

became integrated into an assembly named the handset (Figure 2.3). With the adoption of pulse network technology, the operator-switchboard networks slowly disappeared. The dial pulse network technology is also referred to as Plain Ordinary Telephone Service (POTS) and was the standard until about 1960.

Increased use placed higher demands on the networks; the volume of calls increased, not only for local calls, but also for long-distance calls. The dial pulse network technology had a technical limitation as regards the physical distance over which it could automatically make connections using dial pulses. To overcome this problem, operators were still used to connect long-distance calls, using special equipment based on multi-frequency signaling and a 16-digit keypad. Operators used this equipment at the system level to contact the next downstream operators to establish connections. This semi-automated signaling and switching equipment proved successful from the point of view of both speed and cost-effectiveness. Based on this success, new equipment using dual-tone, multi-frequency (DTMF) signaling was developed that could be operated without intermediate operators. The DTMF system uses 16 signals established by combining two frequencies from a matrix of four by four (Figure 2.4).

Engineers who developed the DTMF system envisioned phones being used to access computers. To facilitate this, they used two symbols (asterisk or * and hash or #) and four letters in addition to the 10 digits. The letter keys were used for menu selection and were dropped from most phones (Wikipedia, 2015b). The keypad required a new telephone design (Figure 2.5) using a second-order subsystem with push buttons replacing the rotary dial. Again, the new design of the product telephone, a first-order subsystem, was due to changes in the network technology at the system level.

According to Jacobs and colleagues (1987), the product telephone design evolved toward an archetype with an integrated handset similar to the one

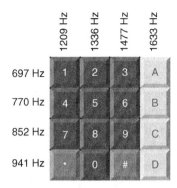

Figure 2.4 The dual-tone, multi-frequency matrix, and the push-button keypad (Source: authors)

Figure 2.5 Evolution in telephones from pulse toward tone networks (Source: authors)

pictured in the middle of Figure 2.5 in the 1930s. The beginning of the telephone archetype referred to by Jacobs is a Siemens & Halske telephone produced in the early 1920s (not pictured here). It is described as a cube with a dial on a chamfered front side, a handset with an integrated speaker, and a mouthpiece placed transversely to the body. Initially, plenty of both small and large firms brought a wide variety of telephone models to the market. Once the generally applied design solution for speaker and mouthpiece had converged toward an integrated handset, a new design standard appeared (i.e., dominant design). Smaller firms purchased this subsystem from the larger manufacturers and assembled it on a variety of body subsystems, targeting different types of use. Then, over time, the number of manufacturers decreased and with that the diversity in models. The (wired) handset appears to have become the core element in the design of telephones. The importance of this subsystem for the product telephone became evident in the manner in which Jacobs summarizes the results of the research with the following statement: the device is a telephone once it contains a handset.

The telephone evolved in a wider context that influenced its development. New ways to match supply-and-demand were introduced by using the telephone. This increased market transparency, which had economic effects as markets changed for both producers and consumers. Increased participation of women in the labor market was another effect. In general, widespread use of telephone technologies had an enormous impact on society. Reciprocally, how people used telephones and what telephone types they preferred affected selection from available variants and therefore had an effect on telephone evolution. This illustrates that social and economic forces are an example of context affecting evolution in a product.

Another example of influences on the evolution of the telephone comes from the technological domain. Innovations in electronics delivered new components like the transistor. Researchers at Bell Labs, a research laboratory of a large telephone company, produced a first working transistor in 1947. Ironically, this resulted from wartime efforts to improve radar technology, not telephony. The transistor heralded a new era of technological opportunities, enabling a dramatic reduction in the size of electrical components, which, in turn, led to microelectronics and microprocessors, which became key components of the computer technology that developed in the following half century. This new technology, by no means specifically developed for telephony, contributed as an enabling technology to further innovation in telephone network systems. The transistor was key to the development of computer and associated digital technology, which allowed voice to be converted into digital data, which, in turn, could be carried over networks more efficiently than analog voice signals. At the system level, the increased capacity of networks contributed to a further reduction of cost, which again increased use. With the advance of computing technology and the introduction of the Internet, the networks that initially carried only voice now changed into digital data networks. Currently telephone conversations are carried over networks using a so-called voice over Internet protocol (VOIP), often using glass fiber instead of copper lines.

Each time a new telephone network technology was introduced that allowed more technical functionality and capacity, this translated into lower cost and led to the ousting of incumbent telephone network technologies. Over time, the appearance of telephones evolved together with network technologies. The first-order subsystem telephone evolved in conjunction with the network technology applied at the system level. The evolution of the product telephone therefore appears to be nested in the evolution of a larger-order telephone network system and the evolution of system, subsystems, and components appears to be influenced by a context of diverse factors ranging from enabling technologies and business interests to social factors. Figure 2.6 shows successive telephone network technologies.

2.4 When the Time Is Ripe, New Types of Products Emerge from a Fundament of Know-How and Know-What

The previous text shows how a succession of network technologies and associated telephone models led to today's models. The example of the telephone

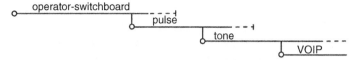

Figure 2.6 Evolution in telephone network technologies (Source: authors)

shows how technology is a means to an end, in this case allowing people to speak to each other over a long distance. The telephone network system was developed to make this basic function possible. The product telephone is an element nested in the larger system and has no function without it. The technology used in modern telephones is by no means the exclusive result of developments targeting this product. Instead, it builds on the wider know-how and know-what developed in many adjacent fields. The technological knowledge accumulates over time, enabling a first version of the system. Over time, change occurred in many elements of the system and changes in the dominant design on the system level led to changes in first- and second-order subsystems. In addition, changes in components (e.g., transistor, glass fiber cables, VOIP) led to changes at the system level. Evolution in elements of the system affect each other across system levels and the evolution of the product cannot be explained without interaction with its context.

As observed before (e.g., Eger, 2007a), the first products of a new type perform their function in a simple way, at rather high costs, and are developed using knowledge available at that point in time. These products first appear in a niche (Geels, 2002) catering to a small group of users. The first users to adopt such new, expensive products, which do not yet function that well, are referred to as "innovators" (Rogers, 1995). Note that not only professional inventors, engineers, or designers (the "producer side") contribute to new products. A share of the renewal comes from what is referred to as "lead users" (Von Hippel, 1986), who are known to experiment with products and tweak their designs to fit their needs more effectively. Known examples of users modifying products for their own use range from professional software to extreme sporting equipment (Von Hippel, 2005). Ideas for improving the product and/or the technology used to perform the functionality resulting in new designs are therefore generated by a wide community from both the producer and user sides. Over time, newer, more advanced versions appear on the market that could not have been made if the first product of this family had not been developed because the required know-how and know-what would simply not have been available. When the first telephone was introduced, there was no intention for it to pave the way for the smartphone. Nevertheless, it is very unlikely that smartphones would exist today unless these primitive telephones had first existed. Although this is exactly the point to be made here, other theoretically possible development paths that could have led to the smartphone will not be further explored. This would simply take too much time. Besides, it is debatable if we should consider the smartphone an advanced telephone or a successor of what was once referred to as a personal digital assistant (PDA), including a telephone function (see also Chapter 6, the case of the mobile phone). Recent publications on the use of smartphones indicate that making calls is now the fifth most used function on smartphones (O2, 2012). Apparently, making phone calls has lost its position as the basic function. It is a mere case of "one damn thing follows another" (David, 1985, 332).

Today's products, such as smartphones, are intentionally designed. This determination probably holds for most products. However, when one considers long-term accumulation of innovations, for example, from early telephone to smartphone, one has to conclude that, although it can be argued that the small steps result from intentional actions, the long-term outcome (i.e., the direction of evolution in products over many decades) is not the result of a deliberate, continuously aligned set of actions designed to achieve a predefined goal. Rather, technologies and products evolve autonomously by building on prior art in and under the influence of a context, without a preset goal many decades ahead. And the telephone is by no means a unique example, as will be shown in the case studies of compact fluorescent lamps and child car seats later in this book. New types of products do not appear out of the blue. Instead of standalone, serendipitous inventions or intelligent design, they can better be described as the result of the accumulated, inventive work of many individuals fueled by many knowledge domains and shaped by selective pressure from various contextual forces. Evolving products are therefore the result of a long selection process in which many designs are ousted and discontinued. Competing manufacturers (their development teams), lead users, and the like provide *variation* by developing many competing designs each to a greater or lesser extent having different characteristics. After that *selection* takes place as an interactive process by different forces (buying behavior of consumers, competing manufacturers, legislation, etc.), leading to the survival of the best-adapted product variants, of which the most prolific are also referred to as dominant designs. Then *retention* of know-what (product characteristics, items) and know-how (manufacturing technology) is achieved as best-adapted variants are reproduced.

Several sources mention cases of similar inventions having been described and patents filed prior to an invention that is regarded as the start of a new type of product. As regards the incandescent lamp patented in 1879 by Swan in the UK, and in parallel by Edison in the USA, 19 prior inventors of incandescent lamps are described (Friedel and Israel, 1985, 91). In the case of the telephone, four inventors preceding Gray, Bell, and Edison are mentioned as being associated with the invention of the telephone (Wikipedia, 2015a). According to

David (1985), Christopher Latham Sholes, known for the QWERTY keyboard, was preceded by 51 inventors of typewriters. Apparently, at a certain moment, the time is ripe for a particular type of invention. No skyhooks are required. Once the fundament is laid, we can wait for new (types of) product to emerge on it. The know-how and know-what required for the invention (the fundament) is available, and creative individuals, whether cooperating or not, envision new functionality and find novel combinations of available technology that produce the invention. People experiment with functionality and therefore cause further know-what development. Knowledge developed for one particular domain influences other domains. Product evolution is a complex process that shapes know-what and know-how that evolves in a context. Prior art or the fundament explains the emergence of new and ever more complex and advanced inventions.

2.5 Subsystem Evolution: The Case of the Electric Bicycle

Bicycles evolved over time from a first primitive type into designs that dramatically improved in functionality and price (Eger, 2007a). The first man-driven vehicles with wheels appeared at the end of the eighteenth century and were used as a sort of running machine. Many different configurations for cycling without feet on the ground using two, three, or four wheels were proposed in the second half of the nineteenth century. See also Section 6.3 for an extensive description of the manner in which the bicycle evolved over the course of time.

The evolution of bicycles and the introduction of dominant designs for different subsystems are pictured in Figure 6.25. It shows how, according to Bakker (2013), different design configurations for a bicycle evolved over time and led to the Rover Safety Bicycle as the first type using the configuration still used by contemporary variants. Based on this design, contemporary variants evolved, such as the city, racing, and folding bicycle. All variants are designed for specific types of use, also referred to as niches.

Although patents for electric bicycles like Figure 2.7 date back to the end of the nineteenth century, these variants did not thrive. In the 1990s, enabling technologies became available with torque sensors, power controls, and improved batteries (nickel-cadmium (NiCad), nickel-metal hydride (NiMH), and thereafter lithium-ion polymer (Li-ion)). This led to a new design variant for the electric bicycle. Compared to the conventional bicycle, it features two new subsystems, namely an electric motor to support propulsion and a battery to provide energy. Initially, the new electric bicycle was met with skepticism and frowned upon as a product for the elderly.

However, this changed over time with improving technology, more design variants, and decreasing cost. The electric propulsion was used as a booster and enabled the range comfortably covered by bicycle to be increased and led to its

O. BOLTON, Jr.
ELECTRICAL BICYCLE.

No. 552,271.   Patented Dec. 31, 1895.

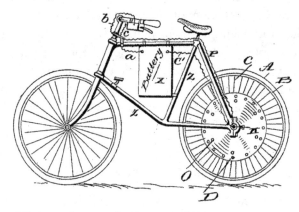

Figure 2.7 An early example of an electric bicycle patented in 1895. Figure reconstructed from patent document (Source: US Patent Office)

frequent use for commuting. This resulted in competition across a transportation product class (mopeds, cars, etc.). The sales of electric bicycles increased rapidly, making up 21% of new bicycles sold in the Netherlands in 2014, up from 10% in 2008 (CBS, 2015).

At the time of writing, the electric bicycle is a typical example of a product design in the ferment phase with different competing subsystem designs. The technology cycle had not yet reached closure in terms of the selection of a dominant design for its motor and battery subsystems (Figure 2.8). The electric motor is currently offered in three positions: A-front wheel, B-rear wheel, and C-crank axle. All solutions have their pros and cons. Having the motor in the front wheel (A) is technically the simplest and cheapest solution. However, this position has a negative effect on the controllability of steering as the e-motor kick is a bit abrupt and pulls the front wheel through corners. It is known that this causes an increased level of fall incidents, especially among elderly people, who sometimes have a reduced level of responsiveness. Placing the motor in the rear wheel (B) is more expensive as the construction of the rear wheel is more complicated. This position does not have the same drawbacks of the motor positioned in the front wheel. However, it requires a sophisticated mechanism to control the tension on the chain which, in turn, controls the e-motor. A third, more recently offered solution is to place the motor in the crank axle (C). This solution is the most radical in technology and design terms, as it requires the construction of the frame around the crank axle to be changed. This implies

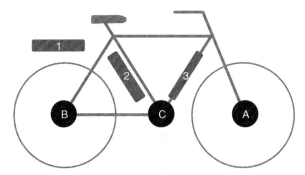

Figure 2.8 The electric bicycle for which designs compete for dominance in subsystems motor (A, B, C) and battery (1, 2, 3) (Source: authors)

the use of a nonstandard and therefore more expensive frame. However, the advantages of this solution are a more direct drive, robustness, positioning close to the center of gravity, and the use of conventional wheels.

As far as the battery is concerned, three design solutions are offered: beneath the rear carrier, between the seat tube and the rear wheel, and in the down tube. The position beneath the rear carrier is often used. It has the advantage that the battery can easily be exchanged and it enables a simple construction. However, it is the highest position used for batteries and significantly raises the center of gravity, which makes the bicycle less stable. The advantage of the position between the seat tube and the rear wheel is that it lowers the center of gravity, which increases stability. The battery can also be exchanged, although not as easily as in the first position. Besides that, the frame needs to be adjusted in order to position a battery, as normally there is insufficient space available to place a battery here. The position in the down tube also has the advantage that it lowers the center of gravity and thus enhances stability. A disadvantage is that the down tube needs to be designed to house the battery, which implies a frame that is not standard and therefore more expensive.

The different design solutions for subsystems of electric bicycles compete in an evolutionary race. Time will tell whether dominant designs for the electric bicycle will emerge. This example makes clear that subsystem evolution allows for major changes in a product family and that this evolutionary race is not confined to technological changes. How people use technologies and products, shapes evolution in these technologies and products. Types of use for bicycles stretch and/or change, made possible, for example, by the increased range of electric bicycles. Consequently, the influence might extend beyond the product family and affect the use of other types of products. It is also illustrative that many countries still struggle with the legal status of electric bicycles. Some variants with strong motors easily exceed 40 km/h, which often means they are classified in the same legal class as mopeds.

2.6 Evolving Products

As described in Chapter 1, evolutionary metaphors have been used before to describe the process of innovation in domains such as economics, sociology, science policy, innovation studies, industrial design engineering, and design methodology.

The variety of schools of thought listed indicates the number of angles from which one can view the process of innovation. It cannot rightfully be described from a single perspective. However, the many perspectives on technological innovation that have been described form a fragmented landscape when it comes to exploring origins of products that contribute to the ever-increasing diversity of man-made goods. So far they have been explored from technology-centric and behavioral perspectives. A product-centric perspective appears to be barely used. What is more, a "theory of product evolution" that explains how new (types of) products emerge appears to be absent. It may therefore come as no surprise that there is a yawning gap between journal-based academic literature on the topic of innovation targeting scholars, and practical tools and methods for those involved in the development of new products.

This book aims to bridge that gap and combine perspectives by proposing a "theory of product evolution" that employs the product evolution diagram (PED) in Chapter 4 as an analytical framework to study how new types of products come about and develop over time into a family of more advanced versions. The PED provides a graphical template for capturing the development history of products, revealing relationships in complex technological developments and their context that would be otherwise difficult to see. By doing so, the PED contributes to a comprehensive view on the question of how new products emerge, develop through time, and relate to the context in which they develop. As such it provides a tool to both those who study innovation and those who develop new products. Where most studies of innovation are technology-centric, this book takes a product-centric perspective. Instead of describing innovation as a technological process, it investigates how new (types of) products come about and develop into families of more advanced versions. To that end, the focus is on products as unit of analysis instead of technologies.

The usefulness of a product-centric perspective is exemplified by the way we describe these artefacts. In our daily language, the noun used to designate a specific product also assigns meaning and function to the construct. This is well illustrated by the case of the "bicycle" product. We do not ride a system consisting of subsystems and components like tubes, spokes, chain, metal parts, and rubber profile. Instead, we ride a bicycle because this product has a meaning to us and fulfills a well-recognized function. Note that this book does not explore the concept of "meaning" in relation to "products." Scholars who do explore this topic include Desmet and Hekkert (2007) and Verbeek (2000).

2.7 Conclusion

Authors from many schools of thought have already illustrated that technological innovation can be described as an evolutionary process. However, a product-centric perspective is not commonly used. This makes it hard to comprehend how new types of products emerge. Given the aim of describing this process, a product is defined as a construct designed to realize a specific function.

Various authors have explained technological innovation as an evolutionary process. It has been argued that accumulation of know-how and know-what can explain continuity, diversity, and complexity in man-made goods.

In literature, the term "dominant design" is used to designate a specific design that becomes a common denominator and is also associated with change in the nature of competition in an industry. Dominant designs can be designated at different levels: system, subsystem, and component. It has been shown that products can be regarded as (parts of) systems. Change at the top system level can cause changes in subsystems. Similarly, change at the component level can invoke change at the system level. This appears to be a consequence of the fact that technological evolution happens across different levels, and across different technological domains. The mechanism driving technological evolution can therefore be described as indifferent to system levels or technological domains. Besides that, technological innovation is influenced by many factors that make up a context. This context appears to be part and parcel of the evolution of products. Describing evolution in products from a single perspective does not, therefore, reflect the complexity of the process.

Availability of *enabling technologies* (know-how) provided by one domain is a known cause for technological change in other domains. The know-how is exchanged laterally. Technologies developed for one technology or product family are transferred to others and invoke further product evolution there. New types of products first start to offer a basic function in a simple way, at rather high cost. The availability of a *basic function* (know-what) provides a point of departure to continue exploring and refining that functionality. Experimentation with new ways of using products leads to further evolution of the basic function of products. Different ways of providing a basic function compete within a product class. Evolution in one product family influences another. Altogether, evolution in products can be described as a function of developing know-how, know-what, and context.

Evolution in products is a complex process that takes place at different levels and has, up to now, been commonly described from different perspectives. It is assumed that describing technological innovation in general, and evolution in products specifically from isolated perspectives, does not promote a comprehensive understanding of these phenomena. Therefore a new analytical framework is needed that continues to build on existing schools of thought and integrates various perspectives developed. To that end, a "theory of product evolution" is proposed that employs the product evolution diagram proposed in Chapter 4 as a tool to integrate perspectives and supports an understanding of the way new (types of) products emerge.

3 Lineage

3.1 Introduction

This book investigates how new (types of) products come about and develop over time into a family of advanced versions. This implies that we investigate how products *relate* to each other. To that end, the concept of *lineage* is explored.

The concept of lineage is derived from the world of life, where it is used to describe how a sequence of species evolved from a predecessor. This chapter provides an overview of methods used to map lineage and describes how they originated and then became used to explain how the world of life evolved. Lineage is also applied to elements of human culture, as will be shown here. However, due to its different nature, depicting lineage for the world of made requires different rules to be applied than those used to map lineage for the world of life.

3.2 Theoretical Background and Embedding

A first attempt to view technical change as an evolutionary process can be attributed to the archaeologist Pitt-Rivers who, at the end of the nineteenth century, believed that the form of artefacts was based on small modifications of preexisting versions. He collected primitive artefacts and organized them in a sequence of closely related shapes. As an example, he organized Australian aboriginal weapons in a picture (Figure 3.1) in a way that makes them appear as evolutionary sequences radiating from the most simple version in the middle (Basalla, 1988, 19). Pitt-Rivers argued that every made thing could be placed within a sequence that could ultimately be traced back to the earliest human artefacts. Since the 1980s, evolutionary theories have been applied more prominently to technological change.

Basalla (1988) is particularly interesting for his extensive exposition of "the evolution of technology" as an explanation of how the process of technological

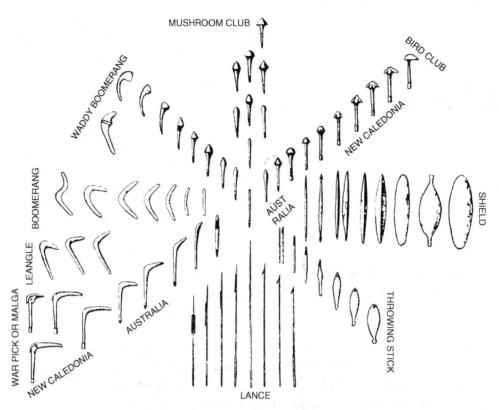

Figure 3.1 The evolution of Australian aboriginal weapons according to Pitt-Rivers (Source: Basalla, 1988, 19)

innovation produces novel artefacts, and how society applies selective pressure to available artefacts. Basalla argues that technological novelty and diversity can only be explained if there is continuity in artefacts, just as there is continuity among species through lines of descent. As an historian of technology, Basalla speaks of artefacts rather than products or technologies.

Besides Pitt-Rivers and Basalla, there is a wide body of literature on innovation that is interesting to review in this context. Most of these authors analyze one particular element, such as the innovation adoption rate (Rogers, 1995), the locus of innovation (Abernathy and Utterback, 1975), periodical change in the speed of innovation (Anderson and Tushman, 1990), or the limiting effects of a development path (David, 1985). Evolution is often described as a process of variation, selection, and retention. Evolutionary economics (Nelson and Winter, 1982) builds on this view to describe how economies continuously change or innovate instead of being frozen in stasis and equilibriums. Another perspective regards evolution as a process of unfolding and creating new combinations that destroy the old ones (Schumpeter, 1942), resulting in paths and trajectories (Dosi, 1982). Geels (2002) notes that technological evolution starts with novel configurations in niches, which become influenced by a patchwork of socio-technical regimes that aggregate finally as technological transitions.

This book does not pretend to provide a complete new perspective on the process of innovation. Rather, it assumes that the process of innovation cannot rightfully be described from a single perspective and therefore builds on many previously published theories. This book presents the product evolution diagram (PED) as a graphical narrative rather than prose to picture the developmental history of products. The objective of the PED is to map how new types of products emerge and develop over time into more advanced versions. The PED makes it easier to comprehend the interdependencies between technological developments, their predecessors, and their context, which are indispensable for understanding how products evolve. As an introduction to the use of the concept of lineage, as well as a visual means to represent it, this chapter explores its use in both biology and human culture and also discusses its limitations.

3.3 Mapping Lineage in Biology

In the eighteenth century, the Swedish biologist Linnaeus (1707–1778) started to systematically organize different types of plants based on their taxonomy, i.e. based on their shared physical characteristics. Subsequent naturalists further organized natural life according to the methodology that has since become known as the Linnaean taxonomy. Linnaeus proposed a formal system of naming referred to as binomial nomenclature, giving all species a name consisting of two parts, using Latin grammatical forms. The first part of the name identifies the genus to which a species belongs. The second part identifies the species within the genus. This naming convention is still in use today and is used to classify biological life in eight major taxonomic ranks.[1]

Linnaeus based his work on similarities he observed in species (Figure 3.2, left side) and did not question the origin of species. According to the prevailing beliefs of the time, divine design explained the diversity of life found on earth. Lamarck (1744–1829) was a French naturalist and the first proponent of the idea that evolution occurred and then shaped life-forms. His idea of transmutation of species, altering one type into another, received a lot of opposition from the scientific community of that day. However, it became an important step in the development of evolutionary thought. Today Lamarck is widely remembered for his theory of inheritance of acquired characteristics.

In the nineteenth century, scientific knowledge continued to accumulate and fueled the debate of the process that is responsible for the diversity of life. Charles Darwin (1809–1882) traveled around the world on HMS *Beagle* from

---

[1] These taxonomic ranks from small to large are; Species, Genus, Family, Order, Class, Phylum, Kingdom, and Domain.

Figure 3.2 On the left a picture from a book by Linnaeus (1738) in which plant leaves are organized according to their physical characteristics. In the middle, the finches as Darwin encountered them in the Galapagos archipelago (1831–1836). On the right, a note by Darwin (1837) on his idea for the evolutionary tree structure (Source: Linnaeus, 1738; Darwin, 1845, 1837)

1831 to 1836. Darwin was puzzled by the geographical distribution of wildlife and fossils that he collected on his trip. He developed ideas to explain, by an evolutionary process, the origin of species and their diversity, which he had observed, as well as their relationship with fossils of extinct types (Figure 3.2, right side). Aware of the controversy his ideas would cause, Darwin waited decades before publishing his ideas until he was forced into action. To his dismay, Darwin was approached by his contemporary Russel Wallace (1823–1913), who had independently conceived a theory of evolution through natural selection as well. Apparently the new theory of evolution was crystallizing in like minds. In order not to lose his claim to a theory of evolution by natural selection, Darwin opted to coauthor a paper with Wallace entitled "On the Tendency of Varieties to Depart Indefinitely from the Original Type," published in 1858. Swiftly Darwin proceeded to publish his book *On the Origin of Species* in 1859, which describes how all species of life have descended over time from common ancestors (Bryson, 2003). Darwin's observation of finches that adapted beaks to types of food available on the different islands in the Galapagos archipelago became the archetypical example of adaptation by natural selection. Ultimately these ideas led to the understanding that biological species relate to each other and their kinship can be graphically portrayed as a sort of family tree. This tree was organized according to the taxonomic ranks proposed by Linnaeus (Figure 3.3 left).

The ideas that accumulated in *On the Origin of Species* remained controversial until the ideas from several fields of biology came together a century later in what is referred to as the modern evolutionary synthesis (Huxley, 1942). Koltsov proposed in 1927 that traits were inherited via a giant molecule

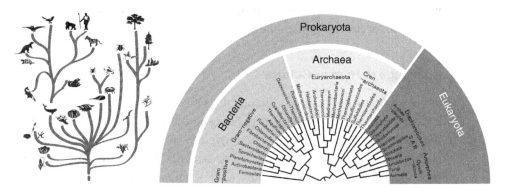

Figure 3.3 Two versions of the tree of life. Left: Linnaean classification (1738) (Source: authors), right: Phylogenetic tree of life by Woese (1977) (Free after Wikipedia (2016a))

made up of two mirror strands that replicate, using each strand as a template. Finally, the shape of this molecule, with a double-helix known as deoxyribonucleic acid, commonly abbreviated as DNA, was first claimed in 1953 by Watson and Crick. The discovery of DNA marks the beginning of modern biology. The technique of analyzing DNA coding allowed the genetic characteristics of species to be read and organized according to their degree of genetic kinship or genetic distance (Figure 3.3 right). This in turn allowed the construction of a so-called phylogenetic tree with a single root, which represents the first life on earth. This technique was pioneered by Woese (1928–2012) and led to the discovery that the Linnaean classification was incorrect. Woese and Fox discovered a new type of microbial life, which they called the archaebacteria or Archaea. Archaea did not fit in the traditional tree of life and Woese redrew the taxonomic tree to create a three-domain system. The new phylogenetic tree of life shows an overwhelming diversity of microbial life (Bacteria and Archaea) whereas the more complex multicellular life-forms (part of Eukaryota) are less diverse. It became evident that the vast majority of diversity is not found in large complex organisms, but rather in single-celled organisms. Many scientists have contributed to modern biology, our current view on the origin of species and the diversity found in biological life. Several individuals have been rewarded with eternal fame for their landmark scientific discoveries. However, it is clear that they could never have achieved these landmark discoveries if they had been unable to continue building on the work of others.

The way in which scientific insights regarding "the evolution of organisms and the role played by genes" have developed over the past three centuries is an excellent example of the way in which knowledge accumulates. Each new generation builds on the knowledge fundaments laid by previous generations, and from time to time overthrows knowledge structures that block the view to new horizons.[2] It is this accumulated knowledge that allows us to look beyond what was possible for previous generations.

3.4 Lineage in Human Culture

Our current view of lineage in biology does not hold for the world of made. Whereas in biology a common code defining heredity has been identified, there is no such thing for artefacts. Although the meme has been postulated (Dawkins, 1976), memetics has not led to scientific breakthroughs as known in genetics. According to Edmonds (2005), memetics has not been very successful in providing "explanatory leverage upon observed phenomena." Nevertheless, family tree structures have been successfully proposed to describe how human culture evolves. A prime example of human culture is found in languages. According to Pagel:

> languages are no more than 160,000 to 200,000 years old although some anthropologists think languages arose even later than this, pointing to the sharp increase around 70,000 to 100,000 years ago in evidence of our symbolic thinking and the complexity of our societies   (2012, 278)

Linguistics, that is the study of human languages, has been using family tree diagrams for decades to show the historical relations between languages (see also Figure 3.4) in a single picture (Southworth, 1964). Such language trees show, for example, how German and English descended from common Germanic protolanguages that together with other pictured languages form the family of Indo-European languages. According to Renfrew (1987), these languages emerged from a common ancestor that some 9,000 years ago was present at times of the origin of agriculture in the Fertile Crescent (roughly the area from the Nile delta with a stretch of Mediterranean coast together with the Tigris and Euphrates). Subsequently the agriculture innovation diffused and in its wake these language(s) spread and formed what we now refer to as the family of Indo-European languages. Millennia of descent with modification subsequently shaped different languages listed at the right side of Figure 3.4.

Stemmatics is a branch of study concerned with analyzing the relationship of surviving variant versions of a text to each other. Based on the analysis of transcription errors, it traces back original versions, for example in religious texts. It uses cladograms (i.e., family trees) to depict lineage in text documents. Family trees have also been used in relation to man-made things. Butler (1863, 1872) explored the idea that machines developed in a way similar to the evolution of living creatures by constructing an evolutionary tree that classified mechanical life. Kroeber (1948) used a tree of cultural artefacts with branches that not only

---

[2] This is what Kuhn (1962) describes as a paradigm shift, a watershed moment in the evolution of scientific knowledge. The new paradigm provides a new perspective on a particular matter.

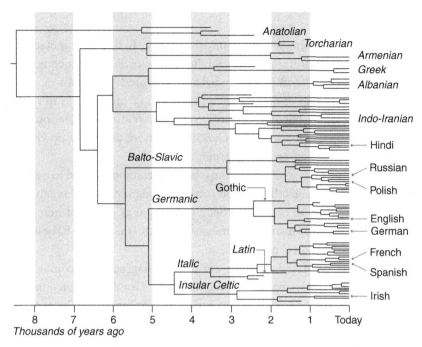

Figure 3.4 Language tree of Indo-European languages. Free after Gray and Atkinson (2003) and Bouckaert et al. (2012)

split from, but also grow through each other, symbolizing the contrast with biological descent.

Steadman (1979, 158) shows a branching diagram that depicts the process of evolution of *standard types* of artefacts (in this case, knives) that was originally published by architect Frederick Kiesler. The diagram departs from a "present standard type" of the artefact via *variations* that evolve to meet the needs for different purposes. Over time, a "new standard type" artefact evolves to meet new needs. A large category of discontinued branches are formed by what Kiesler calls *simulated* artefacts that are characterized by functional inefficiency and designated as insignificant deviations from the standard. Carlson (2000) described the stages in the invention of a telephone by Edison in a tree diagram (Ziman, 2000). A figure attributed to Sanderson has been used to map structural patterns in technological change (Ehrnberg, 1995). Valverde and Solé (2015) analyzed evolution in programming languages and devised a method to map their relationship, claiming their study to be a first full systematic characterization of phylogenetic patterns in a cultural evolving system beyond the human language case. Nevertheless, their paper does not reveal phylogenetic tree-like diagrams, similar to those known in biology, but rather dense webs. The analysis of Valverde and Solé takes account of a high level of horizontal transfer of information (i.e., between different programming languages existing at the same time) and reveals non-uniform rates of change in the evolution of programming languages.

3.5 Conclusion

In biology, life was first classified based on appearance. In the mid-nineteenth century, ideas on how different species might have evolved from a common ancestor were introduced and gradually became accepted. This led to a graphical depiction of biological lineage called the "tree of life." Only after the discovery of genes did it become possible to map evolutionary relations in terms of genetic distance in a so-called phylogenetic tree, which has no visual resemblance to the previous graphical depiction.

In human culture, lineage diagrams have become commonly used to depict how languages relate to each other and descend from common protolanguages.

For human culture, the meme has been postulated as a unit of heredity analogous to the gene. However the meme and its study (memetics) have until now remained a philosophical concept.

It can therefore be stated that the use of tree diagrams is a commonly accepted method for portraying lineage relationships. Graphical depictions of relations have been used to portray human culture, in particular languages (both common human languages and computer programming languages). However, given the lack of an irrefutable unit of cultural heredity, tree diagrams for human culture are not as unambiguous as the phylogenetic tree in biology.

Several authors (Kroeber, 1948; Valverde and Solé, 2015) have mentioned horizontal exchange (i.e., within a generation or between things occurring at the same time instead of from parent to offspring) as an important characteristic of evolution in human culture. So if we were to draw a diagram symbolizing lineage in human culture, then it would need to be possible to depict horizontal exchange. Figure 3.5 symbolizes this contrast between pure parent-offspring lineage as known from sexual reproduction and a more chaotic relationship with a lot of cross-connections.

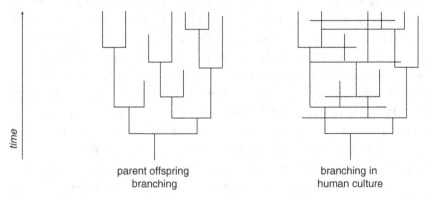

Figure 3.5. Different lineage relationships (Source: authors)

4 Product Evolution

4.1 Introduction

Products are defined in this book (see definitions in Section 1.7) as constructs designed to realize a specific basic function. This is a narrower description than assigned to artefacts, a term archaeologists commonly use for objects made by human beings. Products in this book are therefore a specific type of artefacts designed to realize a specific function and are a distinctive element of human culture. This book proposes a "theory of product evolution" that holds that new (types of) products emerge as a nested hierarchy of system, subsystems, and components on the fundaments laid by previous developments and evolves by means of a process of variation, selection, and retention (first introduced in Ehlhardt (2016)). This theory employs the product evolution diagram to study how new (types of) products emerge. The product evolution diagram makes use of the groundwork described in previous chapters and of the fact that evolutionary patterns are now commonly used to describe innovation processes (Nelson and Winter, 1982; Basalla, 1988; Anderson and Tushman, 1990; Tushman and Murmann, 1998; Murmann and Frenken, 2006; Dosi and Nelson, 2013), as well as the fact that evolutionary relationships in human culture and those between products are now nearly universally accepted.

The product evolution diagram (PED) is introduced in this chapter as an analytical framework for investigating how new (types of) products come about and develop over time into families of more advanced versions. The PED (Figure 4.1) uses a graphical template to relate different versions of a product as they appeared sequentially through time within the context in which its development is interwoven. The PED was introduced in previous publications (Ehlhardt, 2012, 2013) and has since been extended and refined.

The PED is used in evolutionary product development (EPD), which is a design approach based on the observation that products typically go through a series of phases after their initial market introduction. EPD is a low-risk new

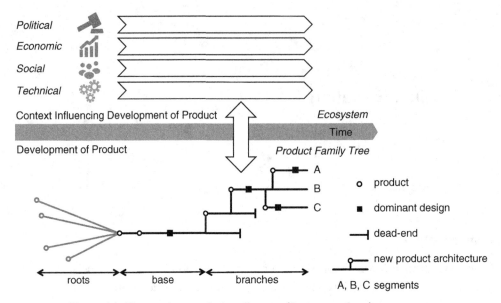

Figure 4.1 The product evolution diagram (Source: authors)

product development (NPD) strategy. The PED comprises two key elements, namely the product family tree and the ecosystem.

4.2 The Product Family Tree

The first element, called the product family tree (PFT), is a tree-like diagram, similar to the family tree based on the Linnaean taxonomy known from biology. However, the PFT has some distinct differences compared to the biological family tree. The biological family tree draws heredity relations from current species toward earlier forms of life according to the Linnaean classification. The more modern phylogenetic tree allows for unambiguous definition of lineage relationships (which the Linnaean family tree could not). This unambiguous lineage description is made possible by genetic analysis of the genome. In the world of made, such unambiguous lineage analysis is, to current understanding, not possible. Memes have not provided an explanatory leverage in the world of made equivalent to that which genes provided for the world of life. Product family trees depict a family of products, starting with a first-of-a-kind, a product that can be regarded as the beginning of a new family of products. Product family trees show how over time product variants have been introduced. Typically, when a product family is in the segmentation phase, the PFT has different parallel branches that each cater to different segments.

The product family tree is intended to be an analytical tool that can be used to reconstruct how new (types of) products emerge. To that end it includes drawing conventions or symbols that designate markers in the evolution of a product, and so helps to read the product family tree, similarly to symbols on a technical drawing or road map (Phaal, Farrukh, and Probert, 2004). Examples of markers these symbols designate are a dominant design, the end of a branch, and forking in a product family. The product family tree as part of the product evolution diagram is intended to support a better understanding of how new types of products emerge and develop into families of more advanced types. For practical reasons, the PFT depicted in Figure 4.1 is oriented horizontally from left to right while biological family trees are traditionally oriented vertically from bottom to top.

The PFT maps the main relations between products through time, connecting a new type of product with later ones as lines of descent. The evolution of products is not bound by strict and unambiguously assignable lineage relationships, as are common in phylogenetic trees used in biology. It is based on progressing know-how and know-what. This accumulation is not restricted to a particular product lineage. Rather, it is a common pool of knowledge from which many product lineages draw. A new type of product constitutes a new "construct fundament" on which a product family evolves. Dominant designs constitute successful incarnations in a lineage of products. New types of products that give rise to new product families are rooted in prior accumulated knowledge, although, as noted, lineage is not strict and unambiguously defined here as in biological heredity as we have no equivalent of the gene for products. Consequently, PFTs cannot unambiguously be combined into a single continuous branching tree, starting at the earliest products (stone stools) through to present-day products. Instead, a PFT is intended to be an analytical instrument to map how products evolve from a new type of product into a product family. It is therefore a simplified representation, limited in scope to a single product family and intended to explain the process of establishment of new types of products and their further evolution into a family of products. Various PFTs connect to other earlier products or technologies via their roots.

4.2.1 Patterns Revealed by the Product Family Tree

The purpose of mapping a PFT is to provide a concise graphical overview of the historical development of products. This reveals patterns in this historical development.

First, it identifies that any developed product builds on previously developed products or accumulated knowledge. At least a share of the elements (know-how and know-what) required to develop a new (type of) product is available at the time of conception. These elements are not all invented at the same time for this particular product. The technology used for the invention, pioneering predecessors, and/or primitive versions of a new type of product are called antecedents or "roots." The new type of product emerges, as it were, on top of the fundaments of preexisting knowledge.

Second, a new type of product commences with a first design somewhere in time that marks the beginning or first node of what is here called the "base" (in Section 6.3 also referred to as the "mother product"). Over time, new variants appear, with their success being defined in commercial terms by the volume produced, the market share achieved, and/or the profit generated. Successful designs that become widely adopted and change the nature of competition in the corresponding industry are referred to as dominant designs (not necessarily the technically superior ones) and, for a period of time, determine dominant branches in the PFT. Dominant designs are marked in the product family tree with a square node (■) to differentiate them from other designs that cannot be regarded as dominant designs. Any other product marked in a PFT that is not defined as a dominant design is designated as an open round node (○).

Third, not all products are continued. The competing and/or incumbent designs that are ousted are marked with "dead ends" in the tree diagram. For example, rooted in earlier professional formats, Betamax and VHS videotape formats were developed and marketed in 1975 for the consumer market. Competition led to the dominance of VHS, although the video quality was known to be inferior to Betamax. Over two decades, VHS was the standard for video recording, only to be ousted by DVD in 2000. The recorders and tapes became obsolete. Tape recording became a dead end in the PFT of video recording.

Fourth, product families often develop into various dominant designs that cater to various segments of the market. In the PFT, this leads to "branches" or variants that together form a family of related products that exist at a certain moment in time, addressing different needs or segments. This branching pattern, revealed by the PFT, is associated with the segmentation phase. The products, catering to different segments in the market, have a level of sophistication in terms of know-what or specification that was not conceivable when the first-of-a-kind of new type of products was designed. An example is provided in Chapter 8, describing the evolution of child restraint systems (Ehlhardt, 2012), which, over time, developed into a family of products addressing different segments, which are distinguished as age, weight, or length groups.

Fifth, last but not least, the combination of PFT and ecosystem reveals how, over time, the context and the evolving product influence each other. The ecosystem is part and parcel of the evolution of products. The case of the evolving child restraint system showed how related legislation developed over the course of the product's historical development and played a prominent role in the evolution of the product family. This legislation was refined after better-performing products appeared, leading to cycles of refinement in both product and legislation. The availability of both product and context was instrumental to the learning cycles and led to knowledge accumulation materialized in advancing products.

4.3 The Ecosystem

The second element in the PED is called the ecosystem and is used to map contextual influences that affect the evolving product. In the biological realm, an ecosystem is defined as "a community of living organisms in conjunction with the non-living components of their environment (things like air, water and mineral soil), interacting as a system" (Wikipedia, 2016b). Speciation, the evolutionary process by which new biological species arise, is driven by isolation or differences in interaction with the environment in which species interact as part of a system. It appears that the environment in which products interact as part of a system also influences the evolution of products. Bijker (1997) uses diagrams to relate artefacts, social groups, and problem to each other to point out how "human action shapes technology." Basalla (1988) frequently refers to environmental, social, economic, and political conditions that influence the evolution of technologies. However, he does not provide a method to systematically map influences on the development of products. For this purpose, use of the PESTmethod (Chapman, 2006) is proposed here. PEST, an acronym for political, economic, social, and technical, describes a framework used in strategic management studies to scan for factors in the macro-environment that *exante* will influence further development of the topic of study.

- Political covers, for example, product safety laws (such as for CRSs) or legislation used to ban the incandescent lamp.
- Economic covers, for example, rising oil prices, high prices for copper, falling purchasing power in times of economic crisis, or increasing purchasing power in rising economies.
- Social covers, for example, demographic shifts such as retiring baby boomers or increasing urbanization.
- Technical, the most obvious perspective in this context, covers inventions such as the transistor and standardization such as USB3.0 or WiFi. Commonly they influence many PFTs other than the one they were originally developed for. They are referred to in this book as *enabling technologies*.

An example of use of the PEST method is found in a strategic study that explored the future of the "End-of-Life Vehicles" supply to scrapyards for Auto Recycling Nederland (PA Consulting Group, 2009). In this case, using the PEST method appeared useful in looking back in time to explain why certain developments based on a context took place, as well as in looking forward in time and identifying those elements in a context that will affect future developments.

Including an ecosystem in a PED allows the juxtaposition of a context to a PFT and lists factors in time that shape the evolution of products and technologies. Chapters 7 and 8 elaborate on two case studies that, for example, show how legislation in completely different products is an important element that shapes the development path of products.

4.4 The Timeline

The timeline in the PED relates the product evolution to the context in which developments took place. By doing so, the PED provides an inclusive overview of the development history of those products. The graphical narrative provided by the PED helps to visualize relationships between complex technological developments and contexts that shape product families. Without that, it would be much harder to grasp those interdependencies that are essential for an understanding of historical developments: this is a clear case of one picture telling more than 1,000 words. As such, the PED promotes a more comprehensive understanding of how products emerge and develop over time into a family of more advanced versions. The PED builds on insights from different schools of thought and aims to integrate them in an analytical framework as an "appreciative theory" (Nelson and Winter, 1982; Geels, 2002). The PED is offered to students of industrial design engineering as analytical framework providing graphical narratives in a product development course. From the work of students, it can be concluded that the PED is easy to understand and apply (see chapter 8 in Ehlhardt (2016) and Section 8.6 and Chapter 9 of this volume).

4.5 Use of the Product Evolution Diagram

In new product development processes, many tools and methods are used to provide structure and direction to designers as well as to reduce risk. Depending on "newness" of the product, the type of product, the reason for developing a new product, and the stage of the development process, different tools and methods are used. Roozenburg and Eekels (1995) provide an overview of product design fundamentals and methods. For example, the ideation stage commonly uses formalized creative processes like brainstorming or TRIZ (see also Section 10.2). In the case of an existing product that requires improvement, value engineering can be used as a method to improve the balance of function, performance, quality, safety, and cost (SAVE, 2015).

New product development (NPD) commonly starts with market research to investigate what features make it likely for a new product to succeed on the market. The findings of such research are embodied in voluminous reports full of text, numbers, and graphs. Designers then have to get to work. According to Sleeswijk Visser (2009), conventional research reports do not meet designers' creative thinking needs. Therefore, a frequently used method for making market research information easier to grasp for designers is the use of "personas" that enable the designer to achieve empathy with the user of the products or services being designed. These are fictional people created for the purpose of representing information on users to whom the design is targeted. The idea of using personas was introduced by Cooper (1999) and then further elaborated toward theory and practice (Pruitt and Grudin, 2003; Pruitt and Adlin, 2010; Miaskiewicz and Kozar, 2011). Currently the use of personas is embedded in the design processes of large and small companies alike (Sleeswijk Visser, 2009).

According to the author's observations during lectures, students following the course "Evolutionary Product Development" at the University of Twente were unfamiliar with concepts of science and technology studies (STS) or other scientific schools of thought that explore the process of innovation. Furthermore, these design students found it difficult to understand the complex relationship between technological developments that lead to new products and the context in which they take place. However, it is known that designers in general are used to working with personas (Sleeswijk Visser, 2009). The product evolution diagram is elaborated as a method that provides a means to represent the complexity of technological developments over time, as well as their interaction with a context, in a single graphical narrative. Similarly to how personas are used to translate the results of market research into concise design briefings, the product evolution diagram can be used as a concise visually oriented means to describe how new types of products come about and develop through time. The product evolution diagram can function as a synopsis of the historical background designers work on and can also offer designers an overview of the present market and developments in the ecosystem that helps them to explore opportunities or new niches for future products.

4.6 Constructing a Product Evolution Diagram

A thorough understanding of the historical development is required to draw a PFT. Sources like patents provide a detailed description of the innovative art of the invention concerned. Patents also contain a clear time stamp and often references to prior art, which means earlier, related inventions. Patents are becoming easily accessible via the Internet, and reviewing them is part of the standard homework of any new product development team. A lot of products are subject to legislation via which the development can be traced and – importantly – upcoming changes identified. Depending on the type of product, books, encyclopedias like Wikipedia, catalogs, or consumer guides provide further historical (or more up-to-date) information. The collected information can be used to construct a PFT. The points at which branches split are markers for changes in addressed user segments, technology, product architecture, and/or dominant designs that have to be identified in the upfront analysis. The level of familiarity cannot be calculated as in phylogenetic trees that are constructed on the basis of genetic distance. Constructing a PFT is a trial-and-error process (like any design), in which various types of diagrams can be used. While collecting information that is used to construct the tree-like diagram, one will come across information about the ecosystem or environment that influenced the development of the product. Tools and methods can be used to make sure different relevant perspectives are included such as PEST (see also Section 4.3).

All these elements can be used to explain past developments, as well as to list factors that are current drivers for change in a product class. The information of the product evolution and ecosystem is combined into one picture separated by a timeline.

4.7 Extrapolating Developments

Any development in products builds on previous developments. For that reason, understanding how a product came about, what influenced the development in the past, and what will influence its future is instrumental when developing a successful next-generation product. Figure 4.2 shows how the PED can be used to explore the solution space for future products. First one maps the product family tree of a product or technology in focus. Second, one needs to investigate which current context factors drive change. Research into historical drivers of change for the product in focus helps assess the extent to which current drivers of change are likely to affect future versions of the product. As a third step, typical innovation patters are projected on the evolving product in order to examine what is a logical continuation in this branch of this product family tree.

A warning should be given here since we must be very careful about predicting the future. Many cases are known of respectable academics who reflect on the future potential of a certain product or technology only to find themselves faced with predictions that turn out to be false.

A first example of a prediction that turned out to be false was made by Basalla (1988, 185), who remarked the following about the home computer.

> Of course it is much easier to identify fads of the past than to recognise those we have so recently foolishly embraced. By the mid-1980s the home computer boom appeared to be nothing more than a short-lived, and for some computer manufacturers, expansive fad. Consumers who were expected to use these machines to maintain their financial records, educate their children, and plan for their family's future ended up playing electronic games on them, an activity that soon lost its novelty, pleasure, and excitement. As a result a device that was originally heralded as the forerunner of a new technological era was a spectacular failure that threatened to bankrupt the firms that had invested billions of dollars in its development.

The line between "home" and "business" computers disappeared once the IBM personal computer compatibles were introduced. These personal computers,

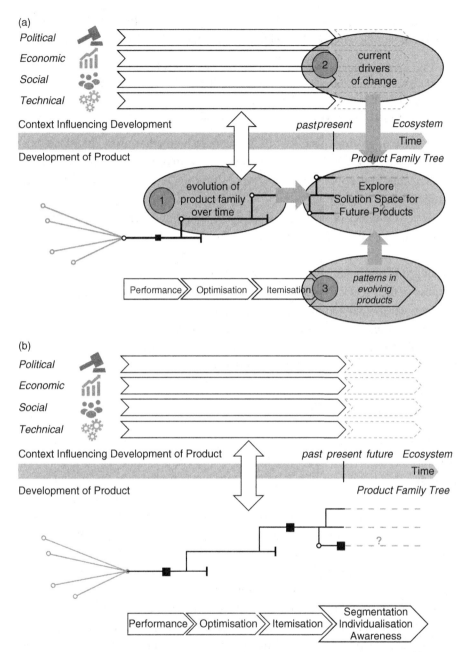

Figure 4.2 Using the PED to explore the solution space for future products (Source: authors)

now commonly referred to as PCs, have become ubiquitous in home environments and (put euphemistically) have drastically changed business environments. Obviously, Basalla would have made a better case if his predictions had been attenuated.

A second example is the prediction made by Van den Hoed (2004, 145), who remarked the following on the development of fuel cell vehicles (FCVs).

> Concerning technological preferences, the case shows how in a period of 10 years the expectations concerning FC technology have shifted from "not considered" to "preferred technological solution" to achieve sustainable mobility. The focus on FCVs was at the expense of BEVs (Battery Electric Vehicles).

At the time of writing this book, FCVs seem to be further away than Van den Hoed predicted. HEVs (hybrid electric vehicles) like the Prius manufactured and marketed by Toyota and BEVs like those by Tesla have taken at least a significant lead over FCVs.

These examples of predictions-not-come-true should serve as an illustration of the caution needed when predicting the future. This especially applies to predictions made with regard to developments further into the future. After all, the future is obstinately difficult to predict. Therefore, it is noted here that the purpose of the PED is to provide a canvas on which the historical development of products can be painted and related to the context in which it evolved. Its first purpose is to support a comprehensive understanding of how particular products came about and only second to provide clues for directions in which the evolutionary next versions of products might develop.

4.8 Conclusion

Building on the groundwork of many scholars who make use of evolutionary patterns to describe innovation processes, a "theory of product evolution" is proposed that holds that new (types of) products emerge as a nested hierarchy of systems, subsystems, and components on the fundaments laid by previous developments through a process of variation, selection, and retention. This theory of product evolution uses the PED as an analytical framework for investigating how new (types of) products come about and develop over time into families of more advanced versions. The PFT has been proposed as a method to map the historical development of a product family over time. The PFT reveals a number of patterns that are characteristic for the way new (types of) products come about and evolve into a family of advanced versions. The ecosystem has been proposed as a means to map the elements from a context that influence the evolution of a product. The ecosystem is part and parcel of the evolution of products. The PFT and ecosystem are linked by a timeline in a PED. The PED is particularly useful to grasp the interdependencies between an evolving product and the context.

Now the PED has been proposed, it will be used in Chapters 7 and 8 to analyze the development history of two products in retrospective case studies.

5 Evolutionary Product Development: Product Phases

5.1 Introduction

The well-known marketing product life cycle (M-PLC) describes the typical pattern of a product's turnover over time. Although it has become a central concept in product development and marketing, it has severe practical limitations, one of the most important of which is its purely quantitative, descriptive nature. It describes the most probable pattern over time in the relative growth and decline of the numbers of a product sold, from its introduction until its extinction, but it does not say anything about the qualitative changes that the product undergoes during the different phases of its own life cycle. In other words, it is impossible to make predictions about the nature of a product's renewal. In 1976, Dhalla and Yuspeh even concluded that the (marketing) product life cycle has little validity: it is "untested" and "without any empirical backing."

5.2 The Marketing Product Life Cycle (M-PLC)

In the first studies where the product life cycle is mentioned, it is divided into four phases: market development (also birth or introduction), growth, maturity, and decline (Levitt, 1965). In later publications, the name of the first phase was changed to introduction or pioneering (see Figure 5.1) (Cao and Folan, 2011). In some publications, the product life cycle starts with a product development phase (before introduction) and the maturity phase is split into a maturity phase and a saturation phase, bringing the number of phases to six: product development, introduction (pioneering, start period), growth, maturity, saturation, and decline. The first phase, development, shows (essentially R&D) costs of the product before its introduction. The second phase, the pioneering phase, starts immediately after the product is launched on the market. If the product is not rejected, a growth phase will set in, leading to an increased turnover. From now on, imitation by other producers will lead to increasing competition. Next

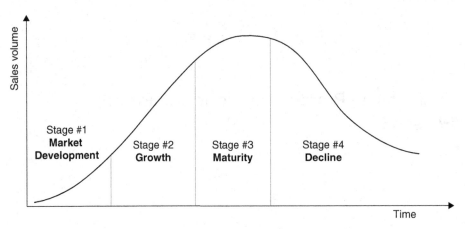

Figure 5.1 The (marketing) product life cycle (M-PLC) according to Levitt (1965) (Source: authors)

comes the maturity phase, characterized by decreasing growth rates in sales and the elimination of weaker competitors. During the next two phases, saturation and decline, turnover will reach its peak, after which sales will decrease in absolute terms, due to, for instance, the emergence of substitute products. During the last phase, the product will gradually disappear. Sometimes a residual market will remain and another phase will follow – ossification. Note that not all products precisely follow this pattern, and that the pattern itself may be influenced by all kinds of external factors. For example, the mandatory wearing of safety belts in the back of cars may result in doubling sales of safety belts during a short period of time, even if the product itself has reached its maturity phase (see Figure 5.2) (Eger et al., 2013).

The marketing product life cycle (M-PLC) lacks predictive validity and empirical meaning, among other reasons, because there are no clear definitions of the turning points between the various stages (Golder and Tellis, 2004). In their paper, they propose four stages and three turning points. The definitions of the stages (or phases) are (see also Figure 5.1):

1. Introduction: the period from a new product's commercialization until take-off.
2. Growth: the period from a new product's take-off until its slowdown in sales.
3. Maturity: the period from a product's slowdown until sales begin a steady decline.
4. Decline: the period of steadily decreasing sales until a product's demise.
   (Golder and Tellis, 2004, 208)

They also define three turning points:

1. Commercialization: the point at which a new product category is first sold to consumers.
2. Take-off: the point of transition from the introduction to the growth stage of the M-PLC. It is the first dramatic and sustained increase in product category sales.

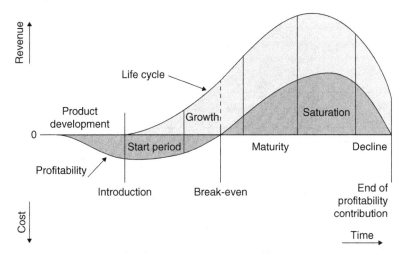

Figure 5.2 A more recent version of the marketing product life cycle (M-PLC) with the profitability curve of a product (Source: authors)

3. Slowdown: the point of transition from the growth stage to the maturity stage of the M-PLC. The slowdown signals the beginning of a period of level, slowly increasing, or temporarily decreasing product category sales. (Golder and Tellis, 2004, 208)

In their results, Golder and Tellis find a difference between time-saving products (washing machines, dishwashers, microwave ovens) and leisure-enhancing products (televisions, games, audio systems). They found that leisure-enhancing products have higher growth rates than time-saving products. They also found that products with large sales increases in the growth phase will also have large sales declines in the maturity phase, and vice versa, slow increase in the growth phase will give slow declines in the maturity phase. Slowdown will occur at a market penetration of 34% on average.

5.3 The Engineering Product Life Cycle (E-PLC)

In the second half of the 1980s, a different type of product life cycle emerged. Cao and Folan (2011) call this the E-PLC, or engineering product life cycle. This life cycle examines the complete cycle of one single product, from raw materials, product development, production, assembly, usage, and support (service) to reuse, recycling, or disposal (Figure 5.3). Research on the E-PLC started with methods such as life cycle assessment (LCA) and life cycle costing (LCC). It was found that operation and support costs of, for instance, military weapon systems sometimes accounted for 75% of the total costs. This knowledge made it very interesting to not only take the product development and

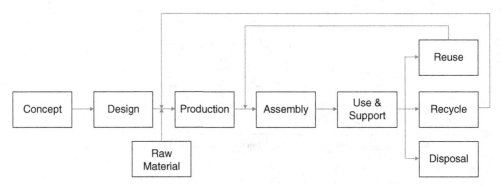

Figure 5.3 The steps of the engineering product life cycle (E-PLC) (Source: authors)

production costs into account. In this research, also known as product life cycle management (PLM), three phases are distinguished: the beginning-of-life phase (or BOL), the middle-of-life phase (MOL), and the end-of-life phase (EOL). According to Cao and Folan (2011), the BOL phase includes product conception, preliminary and detailed design, production, and assembly. They argue that this phase is very important as 70% of the total product costs are determined in this phase. The MOL phase includes distribution, usage, maintenance, service, training, inspections, etc. They mention that after-sales services become more and more important since the profit margins of these activities are often better than the margins on the sale of the product itself. In the EOL phase, the influence of governments by means of rules and regulations is one of the main factors. They further argue that, because of its relatively recent emergence, the E-PLC has not yet undergone any serious questioning of its principles, as the M-PLC has. They conclude that the E-PLC model is now in a phase where it is being tested empirically. One stream of research is the impact of emergent technology on the E-PLC (see, among others, Christensen, 1997; Cao, 2009; Yang, Moore, and Chong, 2009).

5.4 Toward the Product Phases Model

The research and theories described in the previous sections offer industrial designers few starting points for developing or styling new products. In a review of the literature on product development decisions, Krishnan and Ulrich (2001, and Section 10.19 of this volume) conclude that:

> There is essentially no academic research on industrial design, the activity largely concerned with the form and style of products. Yet aesthetic design may be one of the most important factors in explaining consumer preference in some product markets, including automobiles, small appliances, and furniture.   (p. 14)

An exhaustive overview of research in the aspects that explain consumer preference (such as aesthetic, semantic, and symbolic aspects of design) is given by Crilly, Moultrie, and Clarkson (2004, and Section 10.11 of this volume). Some conclusions of this overview match with the theory presented in this study. They mention the appearance after some time of a dominant design (which they call a "stereotype" or "prototype"), and they agree with the conclusion that in mature markets, product performance is taken for granted so that attention on design has to shift to "emotional benefits." They state in their overview that:

> Very few of the scientific studies have led to generalisations which are useful for students or practitioners of design.   (Crilly et al., 2004, 559)

More recent research on new product development in this field was mainly aimed at the effectivity of design. Candi and colleagues (2010) found that giving designers more freedom in their design process leads to commercially more successful products. When product development is aimed at improving the performance or ergonomics of a product, it can be advantageous to involve clients in the development process. However, involving customers in the design of emotional benefits (experience design) does not improve the success of the product.

In 2014, Motiv Strategies (Rae, 2014) showed that, over the period from January 2003 until December 2013, investing in design-centric companies yielded returns 228% greater than investing in the S&P 500 over the same period of time (Figure 5.4).

Support for an evolutionary model of product development can be found in Berlyne (1971, and Section 10.7 of this volume), Christensen (1997, and Section 10.10 of this volume), Coates (2003), Crilly and colleagues (2004, and Section 10.11 of this volume), Jordan (2000, and Section 10.18 of this volume), Loewy (2011), Rogers (1995, and Section 10.25 of this volume), and Woodring

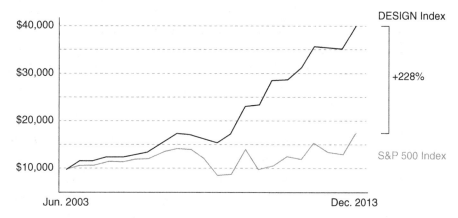

Figure 5.4 Investing in design-centric companies compared with investing in the S&P 500 (After Rae, 2014)

(1987, and Section 10.27 of this volume). The best starting points for a model of evolutionary product development can be found in the demographic models (Veblen, 1994, and Section 10.26 of this volume; Mitchell, 1983, and Section 10.21 of this volume; Foot, 1996, and Section 10.14 of this volume; Motivaction International, 2017, and Section 10.22 of this volume) and hierarchical structures (Maslow, 1976, and Section 10.20 of this volume); Woodring, 1987; Rogers, 1995; Pine and Gilmore, 1999, and Section 10.23 of this volume; Jordan, 2000). Several authors conclude that there is a certain hierarchy in the performance that users expect from products and that there is a certain, fixed pattern in the way this hierarchy is arranged (Woodring, 1987; Rogers, 1995; Pine and Gilmore, 1999; Jordan, 2000). Furthermore, Abernathy and Utterback (1975, and Section 10.1 of this volume), Anderson and Tushman (1990, and Section 10.3 of this volume), Bijker (1990, and Section 10.8 of this volume), and Christensen (1997) give descriptions of different types of innovations. Abernathy and Utterback speak of a fluid pattern, followed by a transitional phase and a specific phase. Anderson and Tushman distinguish eras of ferment or radical innovation, which start with a technological discontinuity, followed by eras of incremental change, which start when a dominant design is accomplished. Bijker speaks of innovations "outside the technological frame" of the product (or the material) and innovations "inside the technological frame." Outside the technological frame usually means that many directions of product innovations and improvements are tried and that the products brought to the market are very different. Inside the technological frame means that current technology, tacit knowledge, and existing engineering practice can be used to (further) develop the product. Christensen gives a description of a phenomenon called "disruptive innovation" that appears similar to the description of Rogers (1995) with regard to products that are attractive to people he calls "innovators." What Bijker calls "inside the technological frame" is in Christensen's study called a sustaining innovation. The first phase of evolutionary product development usually starts with a product "outside the technological frame" or a "disruptive innovation" to slowly transform into a "sustaining innovation inside the technological frame." The theory of Foot (1996) and the models of Mitchell (1983) and Motivaction International (2017) offer starting points with regard to target groups, based on, among other things, demographic models and the wishes that users have with regard to products.

Some research directions, like the "numeric aesthetics" of Bense (1954, and Section 10.6 of this volume), and research regarding appreciation of design and works of art (Boselie, 1982, and Section 10.9 of this volume; Hekkert, 1995, and Section 10.17 of this volume), have been abandoned since they seemed, with regard to the evolution of products, to lead to a dead end. To give an impression of this kind of research, and of ideas of the past, a few of them have been included in Chapter 10.

From Deterministic to Evolutionary Models

It is interesting to note that, at the end of the twentieth century, a deterministic starting point has slowly been supplemented with an evolutionary one in a number of disciplines. Examples are economics and economic history (Nelson and Winter, 1982; Freeman and Louçã, 2001), technological developments (Ziman, 2000), psychology (Gaulin and McBurney, 2004), and processes of cultural change (MacDonald Dunbar and Knight, 1999).

One example is the neoclassical equilibrium model from theoretical economics. The character of this model is deterministic. The model predicts that markets will reach an equilibrium between the economic subjects and the available means if all the sellers who want to sell at or below a given price sell to all the buyers who are willing to buy at or above a given price (among others, see Yang, 2001). The mechanism behind this equilibrium functions in the same way as natural selection does in an evolutionary model. Only those products will survive that offer a maximum of (economical) satisfaction against the lowest possible price. Being "adapted in the best possible way to the environment" is described in the neoclassical equilibrium model as "the highest possible benefit for the lowest possible price." Since, in the equilibrium model, competition runs completely blind, meaning that no individual subject can influence the result of the process, it is clear that the "natural selection" in an evolutionary model and the "completely blind" running in the deterministic equilibrium model perform the same function and work in the same direction.

If the two fundaments of the model (those of complete information for all subjects and complete homogeneity of the competing products) are not present, the model loses its deterministic character and starts to look more and more like an evolutionary process (Nelson and Winter, 1982; Ormerod 1994, 1998, 2005). Concepts such as "(partial) path dependence," "embeddedness," "technological lock-in," and "dominant design" cannot be explained by the neoclassical model and are therefore considered "anomalies." However, they can be explained if an evolutionary product development model is used as a framework. This constitutes an important reason to investigate in more detail the possibilities of an evolutionary perspective on product development and innovation. For both industrial design engineers and economists, the selection is the same, namely acceptance by the market. This principle cannot be used only in evolutionary economics, but also in evolutionary product development.

It is possible to conclude that the performance of a new product shortly after its introduction will be low and that, at the start of its evolution, it is not yet clear what configuration will offer the best chances for survival and improvement of this performance (among others, see Bijker, 1990; Rogers, 1995; Christensen, 1997). It can therefore be expected that different configurations will be introduced and tested on the market. The introduction of a new product will generally be based on a strategy that appears to be similar to trial-and-error and that will therefore have a lot in common with biological evolution. After a time, one or more configurations will become successful in the market. Competitors will often respond by copying the successful products, either by launching it onto the market for a lower price or by improving it. Some of them will probably be successful because they do not have to earn back the original research and development costs. The competition at this stage of the marketing product life cycle (M-PLC) of a product will be based on performance with the strategies either being copying or slightly improving the successful products. And so successful know-what and know-how will accumulate and the less successful variants will not. After a while, it will become clear that some variants can be improved more easily than others. More and more competitors will use this variant, thereby taking the first step toward a "dominant design." It is still possible to improve the performance, but the steps that can be made decrease gradually. The consequence will be that new innovations will not only be aimed at the performance of the product, but also at the production and distribution. The dominant activities in this phase will be optimization of the product, the production, the distribution, the service, etc.

After a while, this strategy will also lose its effectiveness. The profits that can be made will become smaller when it is no longer possible to improve the margins by means of improved performance or an improved process. The only remaining strategy to keep or enlarge the market is to introduce the product on different markets. In this phase, the product designer will start to concentrate his activities on segmentation. The products will be increasingly attuned to the target groups, as a consequence of which the submarkets will become smaller. The final result may be a market segment with one customer or, in other words, individualization (Prahalad and Ramaswamy, 2004, and Section 10.24 of this volume). However, individualization is not possible for some products. An example is fuel for cars (petrol, diesel). Someone who needs fuel generally stops at the nearest petrol station without worrying about the brand being offered. This has led to two strategies. On one hand, customers are offered an additional reason for choosing a brand, for instance, by means of saving systems, which are quite popular in the Netherlands, or via a shop that offers other products (food, drinks, small souvenirs, etc.). The other strategy is "corporate communication." The importance of this communication, and the power that consumers have, was shown by the consumer pressure on Shell because of its decision to sink the drill platform Brent Spar in the ocean after negative press publicity.

As an alternative to the existing deterministic approaches to product development, an evolutionary model is proposed. This model is described in the following sections.

5.5 Product Phases

As mentioned in Section 5.2, a well-known method for analyzing the different phases of development of a product is the marketing product life cycle (M-PLC). In this life cycle, the turnover of a product is measured against time. Although the M-PLC is a key concept in product development and marketing, questions can be raised about its predictive value. If no unexpected events occur, the level of turnover may be predicted for a couple of years, but it is impossible to make predictions about the nature of product renewal or about users' demands and wishes. However, with the help of "product phases," it is possible to make overall predictions as to the functionality, the design, the pricing, and the production of a product, as well as the level of service and the social behavior of a company.

This chapter summarizes the phenomena that appear during the phases of a product's life. These phenomena apply to, among other things, the market (is the product new to the market, or are there a lot of competitors?), the functionality (is it possible to improve the functionality or has it reached a high degree of perfection?), and the ergonomics (has enough attention been paid to the product's ease of use or is there scope for improvement?). The regularities that were found have been analyzed and described, and this led to the description of six product phases: performance, optimization, itemization, segmentation, individualization, and awareness. The six phases are placed in a chronological order so that any predictions about new or future products can be made. This can be done by positioning a product, based on its product phase characteristics, in one of the product phases. When developing a future product, a designer can add the product phase characteristics of the next product phase, thereby creating added value for the intended user. In this way, the product phases can help a designer to create the next generation of a product. The six product phases are described in more detail in Section 5.7.

5.6 Product Phase Characteristics

The product phases are described by means of so-called product phase characteristics. A product phase characteristic is an example of an item (see Section 1.6). Each product phase can be described in terms of 10 product phase characteristics, of which five apply to the product itself and the others to its market, its production technology, the services that accompany it, and the ethical aspects of the product in question. The 10 product (phase) characteristics are:

1. Newness;
2. Functionality, reliability, safety;

   3. Ergonomics, user interface (UI);
   4. Product development;
   5. Styling;
   6. Pricing;
   7. Simplicity vs. complexity;
   8. Production and assembly;
   9. Service;
  10. Ethics.

5.7 Description of the Product Phases

We assert that each of the six product phases displays a typical pattern of product characteristics. In this section, the product characteristics are explained for each product phase.

Product Phase 1: Performance

New types of products – that is, products that provide a new basic function – normally suffer from teething troubles for some time when they first appear on the market. By implication, improving the basic function (i.e., the primary purpose of the product) is the most important aspect of product development in this phase. New products often start as status symbols, and usually perform worse than the existing alternatives. The product characteristics of the product phase "performance" can be summarized as follows. Technically speaking, the product is new and often results from a "technology push." The performance of the product is often poor (i.e., the performance of the basic function is still poor). Product development is primarily aimed at improving performance. Design in the limited sense of "overall form giving" is unimportant and product aesthetics are, therefore, of minor concern. The product is often launched into the market by a monopolist or a small number of heterogeneous oligopolists, so competition is low. As a consequence, the price per unit can be relatively high. The product is frequently produced by standard equipment, it often has more parts than the minimum amount technically feasible, and assembly is mostly done by hand. In terms of adoption of innovations (Rogers, 1995), the product is bought only by the innovators, a type of user willing to take risks with new types of products, and to adopt technologies that might ultimately fail.

Summary

   1. The product is new to the market and results from a "technology push."
   2. The performance of the product is poor.

3. Ergonomics is often poor; user interfaces are based on the possibilities of the technology used, not on the requirements of users.
4. Product development is aimed at improving the performance.
5. Form giving is not very important, and therefore matching form giving with different parts of the product is poor (sometimes leading to a product that is not very aesthetically pleasing).
6. The price per unit is relatively high; the number of competitors is low.
7. The product is often constructed from standard parts; the complexity of the product can be quite high.
8. The product is designed for production using standard machining, usually has many parts, and is often assembled by hand.
9. There is no organized service organization. (This does not mean that there is no service, since start-up companies often offer a lot of service and support.)
10. The social behavior of the company or organization behind the product is of no concern to the customer.

Product Phase 2: Optimization

In the second phase, product development is broadened to include ergonomic aspects and issues of reliability in use and safety. The "optimization" product phase is characterized as follows. Although the product is technically speaking still new, consumer awareness of the product is starting to develop. The performance of the product is reasonable, but product development is still aimed at improving performance. Other aspects, like increased reliability, improving ergonomics, and safety aspects, are becoming serious considerations. The price per unit is still relatively high, but increasing competition creates a tendency toward lower prices. In this and the following phase, it can be advantageous to involve clients in the product development process to improve the performance and ergonomics.

Summary

1. The product is new to the market or there is some consumer awareness. It often results from a "technology push."
2. The performance of the product is reasonable.
3. Ergonomics is reasonable, but there is room for improvement.
4. Product development is aimed at improving performance, better reliability, improvement of ergonomics, and safety.
5. Form giving is not very important, and therefore matching form giving with different parts of the product is sometimes poor.
6. The price per unit can still be relatively high, although there is more competition.
7. The number of parts (needed for the basic function) is decreasing.
8. The product is designed for production with standard machining, the product usually has many parts, and assembly is often done by hand.

9. There is no organized service organization.
10. The social behavior of the company or organization behind the product is of no concern to the customer.

Product Phase 3: Itemization

When producers have improved their product to the point that they satisfy generally accepted standards of functionality and reliability, the edge of competition shifts to convenience. Buyers will prefer those products that are the most convenient to use and – especially in the business-to-business market – sellers that are convenient to deal with. Often in this phase there is a dominant design. Sometimes there are more dominant designs, e.g., in the case of shavers: wet shavers and electric shavers, based on either rotating or vibrating knives. Mass-produced products make personal selling impossible. The market grows less and the number of competitors increases. As the product range grows, prices fall and promotion costs increase. Endeavors are made to develop extra features and accessories, including special editions of the product that are developed for different trade channels and target groups. Design becomes more important, and product aesthetics become a major concern. The number of product parts of the basic (cheapest) products decreases, but accessories or extra features can cause an opposite effect, namely an increase in the number of parts. Mechanic and/or automatic assembly also becomes more important. If needed, well-organized service organizations are set up to support the product.

Summary

1. There is some consumer awareness of the product; often there is a dominant design.
2. The functionality and reliability of the product are good; the product is safe.
3. The ergonomics and human interface are acceptable.
4. Product development is still aimed at improving performance, reliability, ergonomics, human interfaces, and safety. Endeavors are made to develop extra features and accessories, including special editions of the product that are developed for different trade channels and target groups.
5. The matching of the form giving of different parts (integration of form giving) with the product is good.
6. Prices start falling.
7. The number of product parts (of the basic product) decreases. However, the development of extra features and accessories (see: 4) can cause an opposite effect.
8. Automation, both in production and in assembly, becomes more important.
9. There is a well-organized service organization to support the product.

10. The social behavior of the company or organization behind the product is of very little or no concern to the customer.

Segmentation, Individualization, and Awareness

In the original study, based on five retrospective case studies and a classification by experts (Eger, 2007a, 2007b), it was proposed that the product phases follow one another. Based on additional studies, it can be concluded that the last three phases often exist simultaneously and that one or two of these phases are sometimes not suitable for the product or product group (Eger, 2013). A good example of the phenomenon that the last three product phases – segmentation, individualization, and awareness – often coexist can be found in the fashion world. More than 3,000 fashion brands currently exist in Western countries. Each of them launches new collections onto the market, sometimes twice a year, sometimes four times, and, in the case of some brands, even more often. As a consequence, the chances are very small that you will meet someone wearing the same clothes. Moreover, consumers can create their own combinations. Therefore, the need to individualize clothing is not that strong for most consumers. In addition, it has been possible, for a long time now, to have your clothes custom made. The fashion brand 50/50 was successfully introduced in the Netherlands in 2003. Clothing collected by the Salvation Army was reused and redecorated and brought to the market "as new" – a good example of the product phase of awareness. It can therefore be concluded that the last three phases coexist in this sector. There are also products and markets in which there are hardly any possibilities to further segment or individualize a product. Companies in these sectors do not have much choice and often choose the awareness phase. Oil companies are a good example. Most gasoline stations offer five kinds of fuel, namely two types of gasoline, two types of diesel, and LPG (liquefied petroleum gas). Adding an extra product to this assortment is almost entirely impossible. All gasoline stations would have to install an extra pump and extra facilities to be able to offer the product. This would require huge investments, and it is very questionable whether consumers are interested in this extra choice. The next option would be individualization: the possibility of mixing one's own fuel at the petrol station. A concept like that will be fraught with problems: first, the investment in special equipment to mix the fuels at the station; second, to find an advantage that the consumer will understand and appreciate; and finally, the consumer must be convinced to gather the necessary knowledge to carry out the necessary activities. The chances of such an innovation being successful seem small. It is therefore no coincidence that some oil companies pay attention to environmental problems and communicate about them. An example was given by BP with its "Beyond Petroleum" campaign adopted in 2001 to emphasize the company's commitment to moving the world's energy infrastructure away from fossil fuels. The slogan became dubious in 2010 in the light of the massive Gulf of Mexico oil spill and allegations that BP cut corners to save costs representing anything but a real commitment to move beyond petroleum. To encourage consumers to choose and stay loyal to their brand, other oil companies, for instance in the Netherlands, initiated savings systems (with cards or stamps) or built shops and coffee corners in their stations.

Product Phase 4: Segmentation

In the first three product phases (i.e., performance, optimization, and itemization), the focus was on improved functionality, reliability, ergonomics, and safety. An attempt to add extra features and accessories in order to differentiate the product from its competitors takes place somewhere in the third stage. However, this kind of development comes to an end. Indeed, there comes a time when the performance offered is actually greater than the performance required. For relatively uncomplicated products, such as furniture and trinkets, the possibilities for adding features or accessories are limited. Moreover, products become less attractive to innovators and early adopters during the latter product phases. The market share is such that the product is considered "accepted." Owning the product is no longer distinctive, as it does not offer any form of status. Adding emotional benefits to a product is now possible. Research (Candi et al., 2010) has shown that involving customers in the design of emotional benefits (experience design) does not improve the success of the product.

Characteristics of the product phase "segmentation" are that the product is part of the daily life of almost all members of the target group. As the product, technically speaking, has entered the domain of some "dominant design" (or, a limited number of "dominant designs"), product development is aimed at adding extra features and accessories, including special editions of the product for different trade channels and target groups. Design has reached a stage of complete integration of the different parts of the product into a completely unified and recognizable form and the design focus shifts from form giving proper to expressive features, aimed at increasing emotional benefits. The market approaches perfect competition.

Summary

1. The product is part of the daily life of a majority of people; nearly everybody knows the product, including people outside the target group.

2. The functionality and reliability are good; the product is safe. The customer has plenty of choice thanks to the broad product range.
3. Ergonomics and human interface of the product are good.
4. Product development is aimed at extra features and accessories, including special editions of the product for different trade channels and target groups.
5. The matching of the form giving of different parts (integration of form giving) with the product is good. Form giving becomes more expressive (styling) and is aimed at adding emotional benefits.
6. Since competitors' prices are low, it is almost impossible for a company to lower its prices even further. By adding emotional benefits, the company can realize better prices.
7. The number of product parts (for the basic function) is at its minimum. However, the development of extra features and accessories (see: 4) can cause an opposite effect, and make the product very complicated.
8. Production and assembly are highly automated.
9. There is a well-organized "service organization" to support the product.
10. The social behavior of the company or organization behind the product is of little or no concern to the customer.

Product Phase 5: Individualization

Extrapolation of segmentation (continuous fine-tuning of products on ever-smaller target groups) ultimately leads to a product that is properly attuned to one individual. The developments in information and production technology make this kind of individualization even more possible. These developments imply the following changes in characteristics in the "individualization" product phase. Product development is geared to mass customization and cocreation, allowing the customer to influence the final result. The market starts to shift from a homogeneous polypoly into a heterogeneous polypoly. Although prices approach average technical production costs of the dominant design, cocreation and mass customization offer possibilities to realize higher prices. Interactive media are used to customize the product to the needs of the individual customer.

Summary

1. The product is part of the daily life of a majority of people; nearly everybody knows the product, including people outside the target group.
2. The functionality and reliability are good; the product is safe. The customers have the possibility to adjust the product to their taste.
3. Ergonomics and human interface of the product are good, and they can often be adapted to the wishes of the user.
4. Product development is aimed at mass customization or cocreation, allowing the customer to influence the final result.

5. Form giving becomes more expressive (styling) and is aimed at adding emotional benefits, and the customer is offered the opportunity to influence the appearance of the product.
6. Cocreation and mass customization can offer possibilities for realizing higher prices. Interactive media are used to customize the product to meet the needs of the individual.
7. The number of product parts (for the basic function) is at its minimum. However, individualization can lead to extra parts that offer individualized functions.
8. Production and assembly are highly automated.
9. There is a well-organized "service organization" to support the product.
10. The social behavior of the company or organization behind the product is becoming more and more important to the customer.

Product Phase 6: Awareness

Marketing-related research on the importance of ethics in influencing consumers' purchase decisions shows contradictions (Schäffer, 2014). If consumers are asked if they are willing to pay a higher price for ethical behavior, the results are positive. According to this kind of motivation research, this group is growing (Witte et al., 2013). But when the purchase decisions are observed, it shows that these consumers still buy products from unethical firms if the price is lower (Marylyn Carrigan, 2001; Sandhu et al., 2010; Thøgersen et al., 2012). These researches show what is called the "citizen-consumer paradox": as a citizen, one finds sustainability important, but as a consumer, one does not always take sustainability into account in purchases (Witte et al., 2012). The purchase motivations of consumers who buy sustainable products also show that the personal motivations of consumers are more important than ethics: the trigger for consumers to purchase sustainable goods is rather their own interest than the public interest. For consumers who find sustainability important in their purchase decisions, this is especially the case when they benefit from it personally. This becomes apparent from how the number of consumers who find sustainability important differs per product type. For products where sustainability leads to cost savings such as white goods, cars, energy, and electric products, this is 60%. For food, this is 50%, with motives such as health, taste, or animal welfare. In contrast with products that have a high impact on the planet but fewer personal benefits, products such as household and personal care products, mobile phones, clothes, and flights, only 30% to 40% of consumers find sustainability important (Witte et al., 2012).

From this research, it can be concluded that a substantial proportion of the consumers is willing to contribute to a better environment and to help solving societal problems by changing their consumption patterns, but only if this can be done without much effort, and only if it does not lead to decrease in consumer satisfaction and a too big increase in the financial burden. Most people expect companies to play an active role in solving common societal problems. A company can successfully tempt a small group of consumers by offering them the possibility of showing their ethical involvement by acquiring products that in some way claim to be more environmentally or socially beneficial than their competitors.

Awareness Target Group

An awareness product phase usually starts with an awareness target group. To serve this target group, pioneering companies are established with the purpose to solve an environmental or social problem with their products or services. These products have features that contribute to an issue in society, such as product safety, child labor, human health, animal well-being, or energy saving. The relation between the product and the issue can be made visible through product design, packaging, and product information. Because in most cases it concerns an innovation, the product is often more expensive, for instance because the "true" environmental or social costs are included in the product.

Awareness Pressure Group

The fact that users of awareness products are willing to pay extra for the related issue shows that they are very involved in it. Therefore, they sometimes form pressure groups to either force companies to stop their unwanted behavior or to force governments to create regulations or legislation that stimulate or enforce change in the unwanted behavior. Examples are Nike (child labor, pressure group), child safety seats in cars (DANA, Drivers Appeal for National Awareness, safety, pressure group, see Chapter 8), energy labels of washing machines (regulations, governments), or the worldwide ban on incandescent light bulbs (legislation, governments, see Chapter 7). If an awareness pressure group is successful, the awareness item becomes a standard for all products and the awareness phase disappears. If no pressure group arises or the pressure group is not successful, the awareness product phase may remain as a segment of the market (as a part of the segmentation product phase). Sometimes this can lead to a substantial part of the market; examples can be found in the food industry: Tony's Chocolonely (chocolate) and Ben & Jerry's ice cream (both use "fair trade" ingredients).

Awareness Product Characteristics

A lot of companies communicate about their corporate responsibility on their websites or in their annual reports, but do not make this explicit in their products. However if they do, this leads to changes in the characteristics of the last product phase, "awareness." Aspects that are taken into account are the use of environmental-friendly and nontoxic materials, recyclability, energy use both of the product itself and during its production, emissions during production and use of the product, working conditions in the company, and by its suppliers, etc. The addition of extra features and accessories, including special editions of the product for different trade channels and target groups, has not stopped, but becomes a secondary concern. Design may still be focused on the enhancement of expressive features, aimed at increasing emotional benefits, however, when these benefits start to include ethical concerns, this can lead to a sudden leap into ascetic and sober forms. This tendency is reinforced even more by product claims on societal and environmental issues. The producing company explicitly communicates company ethics in its promotion campaigns. The ethical behavior of the producing company does influence – to some extent – consumers' choices. Sectors exist where companies and governments seem more concerned than the consumers, which may lead to measures forced by regulations or taxes. Examples are the energy use of cars, regulations regarding emissions, or the banning of incandescent lamps.

Summary

1. The product is part of the daily life of a majority of people; nearly everybody knows the product, including people outside the target group.
2. The product conforms to new standards, which are related to issues in society, such as environmental labels, legislation for lower energy consumption, fairness, banishing of harmful ingredients.
3. Ergonomics and human interface of the product are good.
4. Product development is aimed at addressing the product's impact on people, on the environment, and on the planet, during its whole life cycle.
5. The matching of the form giving of different parts (integration of form giving) of the product is good, but in this phase, that sometimes means a rather sober design to emphasize the product's environmental friendliness.
6. New ways are found to reduce costs, such as recycling, energy saving, or the use of product-service systems. New forms of ownership like product sharing are introduced.
7. The number of product parts (for the basic function) is at its minimum. However, segmentation and individualization can lead to extra parts that offer individualized functions.
8. The production process is optimized to minimize its environmental impact. In the assembly process, working conditions and environmental impact play an important role.
9. The service can head in different directions: it may be aimed at making the product available without ownership by the consumer, or the company may involve societal issues in its service.
10. The social behavior of the company or organization behind the product is a major concern to the customer. The organization communicates the ethics of the company concerning the society and the environment.

Product phase characteristic	Aspects	Short description of the present situation	Solution space for future products
Newness	Technology push Dominant design(s) Product is part of daily life	The product is not ensued from "technology push"	Only minor improvements are possible
Functionality	Poor performance Reliability Safety	The product's functionality and reliability are good The product is safe	No action intended No action intended
Ergonomics	Handling Comfort User interface	The product is easy to handle and meets the ergonomic demands	No action intended
Development	Assortment Emotional benefits Mass customization Individualization	The product does not offer much choice The product does not offer the user possibilities to influence the product's functionality Interactive media could be used to adjust the product to the individual user	There is room for segmentation Individualization can be promising Individualization or mass customization
Styling	Not very good Integration of form giving Expressive styling Emotional benefits Sober	The styling of the parts of the product (integration of form) is good The styling is neutral and does not distinguish from the dominant design	Not much chances here The styling could be more expressive or meaningful
Pricing	High Under pressure Low Customized	The unit price can become variable by adjustment of the product to the individual user	Individualization
Complexity	Number of parts Extra features/accessories	The number of parts is at its minimum	Keep it that way
Production	Assembly Manual Automated Outsourced	Production of the product is automated to a high level Assembly of the product is outsourced to low-wage countries	No action intended No action intended
Service	Not organized Organized Involves societal issues	The product has a well-developed service organization	No action intended
Ethics	Sustainability Working conditions Energy saving Animal welfare Nontoxic materials Recyclability	The user might become more interested in the company's behavior regarding the environment	There is room for attention to the company's ethics

Figure 5.5 A fictional example of the use of the model to determine the solution space for future products based on the product phases and the product phase characteristics (Source: authors)

	Performance	Optimization	Itemization
Newness	The product is new to the market and results from a "technology push"	The product is new to the market or there is some consumer awareness. It often results from a "technology push"	There is some consumer awareness of the product, often there is a dominant design
Functionality, reliability, safety	The performance of the product is poor	The performance of the product is reasonable	The functionality and reliability of the product are good; the product is safe
Ergonomics, user interface	Ergonomics is often poor; user interfaces are based on the possibilities of the technology, not on the requirements of users	Ergonomics is reasonable, but there is room for improvement	The ergonomics and human interface are acceptable
Product development	Product development is aimed at improving the performance	Product development is aimed at improving performance, better reliability, improvement of ergonomics and safety	Product development is aimed at improving performance, reliability, ergonomics, and safety. Endeavors are made to develop extra features and accessories, including special editions of the product, for different trade channels and target groups
Styling	Form giving is not very important, and therefore matching form giving with different parts of the product is poor (sometimes leading to a product that is not very aesthetically pleasing)	Form giving is not very important, and therefore matching form giving with different parts of the product is sometimes poor	The matching of the form giving of different parts (integration of form giving) is good
Pricing	The price per unit is relatively high; the number of competitors is low	The price per unit can still be relatively high, although there is more competition	Prices start falling
Simplicity vs. complexity	The product is often constructed from standard parts; the complexity of the product can be quite high	The number of parts (needed for the basic function) is decreasing	The number of product parts (of the basic product) decreases. However, the development of extra features and accessories (see: product development) can cause an opposite effect
Production and assembly	The product is designed for production using standard machining, usually has many parts, and is often assembled by hand	The product is designed for production with standard machining and usually has many parts; assembly is often done by hand	Automation, both in production and assembly, becomes more important
Service	There is no organized service organization. (This does not mean that there is no service, since start-up companies often offer a lot of service and support.)	There is no organized service organization	There is a well-organized service organization to support the product
Ethics	The social behavior of the company or organization behind the product is of no concern to the customer	The social behavior of the company or organization behind the product is of no concern to the customer	The social behavior of the company or organization behind the product is of very little or no concern to the customer

Figure 5.6 An overview of how the 10 product phase characteristics describe the six product phases (Source: authors)

	Segmentation	Individualization	Awareness
Newness	The product is part of the daily life of a majority of people; nearly everybody knows the product, including people outside the target group	The product is part of the daily life of a majority of people; nearly everybody knows the product, including people outside the target group	The product is part of the daily life of a majority of people; nearly everybody knows the product, including people outside the target group
Functionality, reliability, safety	The functionality and reliability are good; the product is safe. The customer has plenty of choice thanks to the broad product range	The functionality and reliability are good; the product is safe. The customers have the possibility to adjust the product to their taste	The product conforms to new standards, which are related to issues in society, such as environmental labels, fairness, banishing of harmful ingredients.
Ergonomics, user interface	Ergonomics and human interface of the product are good	Ergonomics and human interface of the product are good, and they can often be adapted to the wishes of the user	Ergonomics and human interface of the product are good
Product development	Product development is aimed at extra features and accessories, including special editions of the product for different trade channels and target groups	Product development is aimed at mass customization or cocreation, allowing the customer to influence the final result	Product development is aimed at addressing the product's impact on people, on the environment, and on the planet, during its whole life cycle
Styling	The matching of the form giving of different parts (integration of form giving) with the product is good. Form giving becomes more expressive (styling) and is aimed at adding emotional benefits	Form giving becomes more expressive (styling), is aimed at adding emotional benefits and the customer is offered the opportunity to influence the appearance of the product	The matching of the form giving of different parts of the product is good, but in this phase, that sometimes means a rather sober design to emphasize its environmental friendliness
Pricing	Since competitors' prices are low, it is almost impossible to lower the prices even further. By adding emotional benefits, the company can realize better prices	Cocreation and mass customization can offer possibilities for realizing higher prices. Interactive media are used to customize the product	New ways are found to reduce costs, such as recycling, energy saving, the use of product-service systems, or product sharing are introduced
Simplicity vs. complexity	The number of product parts (for the basic function) is at its minimum. However, extra features and accessories (see: product development) can cause an opposite effect and make the product complicated	The number of product parts (for the basic function) is at its minimum. However, individualization can lead to extra parts that offer individualized functions	The number of product parts (for the basic function) is at its minimum. However, segmentation and individualization can lead to extra parts that offer individualized functions
Production and assembly	Production and assembly are highly automated	Production and assembly are highly automated	Production and assembly are optimized to minimize the environmental impact. Working conditions play an important role
Service	There is a well-organized "service organization" to support the product	There is a well-organized "service organization" to support the product	The service can head in different directions: e.g., aimed at making the product available without ownership by the consumer, or involving societal issues
Ethics	The social behavior of the company or organization behind the product is of little or no concern to the customer	The social behavior of the company or organization is becoming more and more important to the customer	The social behavior of the organization is a major concern. The company communicates its ethics concerning the society

Figure 5.6 (cont.)

5.8 Conclusion

The phenomena that appear during the phases of the life of a product have been described. The regularities that were found have been analyzed and described. This has led to the six product phases: performance, optimization, itemization, segmentation, individualization, and awareness. The six phases are placed in chronological order in such a way that any predictions about new or future products can be made. This can be done by positioning a product, based on its product phase characteristics, in one of the product phases. When developing a future product, a designer can add to the product phase characteristics of (one of) the next product phase(s), thus creating added value for the intended user. In this way, the product phases can help a designer to create the next generation of a product.

For each separate product phase characteristic, a short description has to be made of the present situation. The summaries in the previous section can function as a checklist for these descriptions. Based on the present situation and the product phase characteristics of the next product phase (or product phases), intended actions can be formulated. From these possible actions, a choice has to be made. If making such a choice gives problems, selection methods such as described in Eger and colleagues (2013) can be used. Figure 5.5 gives a fictional example of the use of the model in the way suggested earlier.

Overview

Figure 5.6 gives an overview of how the 10 product phase characteristics describe the six product phases.

6 Retrospective Case Surveys Based on Product Phases

In this section, in multiple retrospective case surveys, the history of five products is analyzed. This was done by means of a literature study and with the aid of interviews of people involved with the products, such as directors, marketing managers, product managers, and designers. The following products were analyzed: electric shavers, mobile phones, bicycles, working-class housing, and traveling. The shaver was chosen because it is an example of a durable consumer product that has gone through a long period of product development. It is supposed that emotional benefits are not as important as they are with products like a mobile phone or a bicycle, since for friends and acquaintances, it is invisible, as a shaver rarely leaves the confines of a bathroom. The mobile phone was chosen as an example of a product that developed very quickly in a very short period of time. Moreover, it is a product with a lot of exposure. The bicycle was chosen because it is a product that people usually use for a very long time (often 10 years or more) and because it has had a long history so that it seems likely that the last two product phases, individualization and awareness, have played an important part in this product.

Working-class housing and holidays were selected to show that the theory of product phases is also suited for architecture and services.

Den Hertog and Van Sluijs (1995) describe the research methods that are available for research into the effectiveness of innovations. They distinguish five groups of methods: experiment, survey, case study, action research, and ethnography. For this subject, the retrospective case study and the survey are the most suitable. In a retrospective case study, many aspects of one case are studied. In a survey, a few aspects of many cases are studied. The comparative (multiple) retrospective case survey, a method between the survey and the case study, seemed the best choice – a few cases are studied based on a number of aspects. The study described in this chapter therefore exists of five retrospective case surveys; in the following chapters, three more case studies are elucidated: the compact fluorescent lamp (CFL), the child restraint system (CRS), and the basketball shoe. According to Eisenhardt (1989), between four and 10 cases are usually sufficient for most surveys. In Eisenhardt's paper, she advocates choosing cases that are very different from one another, leading to better insight into the applicability of the theory. A disadvantage of a retrospective case survey is that the cases are analyzed by someone who has to know the theory of product phases. If not, this person cannot judge if the studied case meets the formulated criteria. This means that there is a risk that the researcher may (unwittingly) fit the results of his or her research into the theory of product phases. Another disadvantage is that consulted experts have to rely on their memory.

These problems were addressed in a second study (Eger, 2007a, 2007b, 2013) that was carried out in two parts: a pilot study and a main study. The pilot study tested whether the formulations of the product phase characteristics were clear to the subjects and if the method used (attaching stickers with statements to a field (a large piece of paper) with indications of the time the product was on the market and the market penetration of the product) was appropriate. The statements that described product phase characteristics were printed on stickers. The statements were sorted by the product phase characteristics and collected in 10 folders. These folders were then offered to the subjects in random order. Within the folders, the statements were also randomized. The subjects were then asked to attach the statements in a historic way, meaning that they had to position the statements in the order they expected them to take place during the course of a product's life cycle. On the experiences in the pilot study some small improvements were made. For the main study, subjects were selected from a population of experienced industrial designers, design managers, and marketing managers, because it was expected that they had enough knowledge of the life cycle of products and were therefore able to work with the statements about the product phase characteristics. Based on the classification by the experts, it can be concluded that the product phase characteristics describe the product phases with mixed results. The first two product phases were described very well. There were 49 statements describing the product phase characteristics. From these statements about the product performance phase, a value of 93% was confirmed by the experts. For optimization, this percentage reached 85%. The next four phases are described in less detail. Itemization had the lowest score, as only 56% of the statements were confirmed by the experts. For segmentation, the percentage was 67%, for individualization, it was 62%, and for awareness, it was 57%. Note that the experts denied only one of the statements, and that any other statements that were not confirmed, were not denied either (for a detailed description of this research, see Eger, 2007 and 2013).

6.1 Electric Shaver

Until the beginning of the twentieth century, shaving was a task carried out by hairdressers. Only after the invention and introduction of disposable razor blades in 1903 did shaving slowly become an activity carried out in the home. Even though they were originally called "safety razors," they still often caused cuts. The lack of safety and the fact that not every home was equipped with running water were the reasons to develop dry shaving. Around 1910, the first ideas of a dry shaver were born. They came from Jacob Schick, who, after he retired from the US army, started digging for gold in Alaska. In the extreme cold, it was quite unpleasant to use water when shaving. It was then that he hit upon the idea of dry shaving with a shaving head powered by an external motor. When World War I broke out, Schick returned to the army, so it took until 1919 before he picked up his idea again. It would take until 1928 before he filed his patent (Figure 6.1). In 1929, Schick was the first company to introduce an electric dry shaver (van Nifterik, 2013).

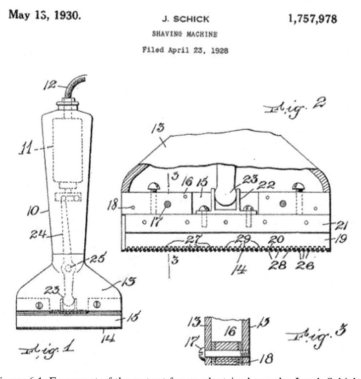

Figure 6.1 Fragment of the patent for an electric shaver by Jacob Schick (Source: US Patent 1721530)

The Performance Product Phase

The dry shaver that Schick brought onto the market in 1929 was what is referred to as the vibration type, consisting of small knives that moved to and fro behind a grid. Its price was $25 (if corrected for inflation in 2014, this would mean $347.12; if the labor value[1] is calculated, it would mean about $1,300); it sold – probably also due to the Great Depression – only 3,000 units in its first year. Ramakers (1984) wrote the following about the first shavers: "The skin was heavily irritated and the appliances continuously pulled out beard hairs." In the years that followed, the shaver was gradually improved. In 1935, the Schick Model S was introduced; two years after its introduction, almost 2 million copies were sold. In the meantime, the first competitors appeared on the market. One of the first was the Viceroy nonelectric dry shaver (patent application filed in 1937) that was driven by a friction motor and external hand crank. It was quite difficult to use as two different movements were needed simultaneously: guiding the shaving head and cranking the lever. Another one was Remington, which entered the market in 1937. In December 1938, in *Life* magazine an advertisement appeared for the Casco "75," probably the first shaver with rotating cutting blades (van Nifterik, 2013). Soon a number of competitors of the vibration-type shaver appeared on the market, to name a few: Champion Electric Dry Shaver, Fleetwood, Gillette (Model G Dry Shaver, 1938), Elgin (Model V, 1938), Minute-man, Packard Lifetime Lektro (1937), Sunbeam, Tack (1938), and Zephyr (Anon., 2013b). It is quite clear that these products typically fit into the performance phase.

In the Netherlands, Philips was the first producer of electric shavers. In 1937, Alexandre "Sacha" Horowitz (1904–1982), head of Philips Laboratories for Appliances, was assigned the task of developing an electric shaver. Horowitz started by analyzing the electric shavers that were on the market at that time. In 1939, Philips introduced its first Philishave at the annual spring exhibition (Voorjaarsbeurs) in Utrecht (The Netherlands). The Philishave had a circular shaving head with slots that pointed inward, behind which three bronze knives rotated and cut the hairs. In contrast to what many people think, Philips did not invent the rotating system. The first rotating shaving technique was patented by H. Westendorp, even before the first Chick was introduced (US patent 1114322). The design of the first products was not very distinctive. The black, Bakelite housing was more or less in line with shaver construction up to then, being a cylinder shape with, at one end, a chromed steel shaving head with a diameter of 17 mm and the electrical cord at the other end. The shaver was soon nicknamed "the cigar." Between 1940 and 1955, product

---

[1] The price of a good or service determined by the total amount of labor required to acquire it.

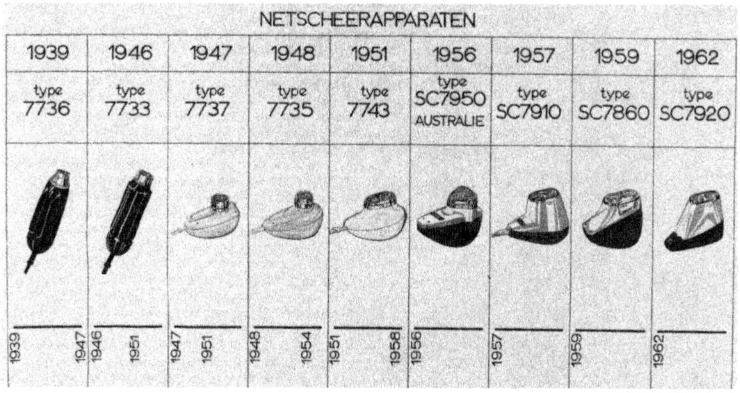

NETSCHEERAPPARATEN								
1939	1946	1947	1948	1951	1956	1957	1959	1962
type 7736	type 7733	type 7737	type 7735	type 7743	type SC7950 AUSTRALIE	type SC7910	type SC7860	type SC7920

Figure 6.2 The development of the Philishave between 1939 and 1962 (Source: Philips)

development focused mainly on improving performance. In 1940, the shaving result was improved with the introduction of a skin tensioner. Shortly after that, the shaving speed was improved by increasing the number of knives from three to six and by replacing the bronze knives with steel ones that did not break as quickly. In 1946, a new appliance, with a larger shaving head and a stronger motor, was introduced under the name "Steel Beard" (Staalbaard), but the product was still far from perfect. Shaving took about 20 minutes, and many people still experienced problems with irritated skin.

The Optimization Product Phase

For Schick, the optimization product phase started shortly after the introduction of the first shaver. By using a smaller motor, it was possible to reduce the size of the shaver, which made the handling easier. The price of the shaver could be decreased to $15. The competition also grew in this period, which ultimately led to a price of $7.50 in the late 1930s. Around 1940, the manufacturers of oscillating cutters started increasing the number of shaving heads and adapting their form to improve the performance.

It took nearly 10 years, until after World War II, before more attention was paid to the styling of the Philishave. In 1947, a white, kind of egg-shaped shaver with the shaving head on one side, designed by famous American industrial designer Raymond Loewy, was launched onto the market. This appliance, which was developed for the US market, where Philips owned the Norelco brand, was still made of Bakelite. Its successor was introduced just one year later. It had an ivory color and was made using urea formaldehyde (Figure 6.3). Bakelite was considered old-fashioned by that time. In the design of these two shavers, physical ergonomics started to play a role

Figure 6.3 Type 7735, the egg-shaped device made by Philips (1948) (Source: Philips)

for the first time. The designers were instructed to develop a shaver that fit exactly into the palm of the hand. The slogan used was: "As if your hand invented it."

Even though styling had now started to play a role, product improvements were still possible and necessary. Around 1940, Philips started setting up a network of dealers to help sell its electric shavers. These dealers received sales instructions and organized demonstrations (Dijkstra, 2005). In 1951, both the speed of shaving and the quality of the result had been significantly improved through the introduction of a double shaving head with corrugated shaving slots. In 1956, a shaver with three shaving heads was introduced. However, this three-headed shaver was introduced only in Australia and New Zealand. For reasons that are not known, it was decided to continue the development of the two-headed shaver. In 1957, this appliance was equipped with a so-called flip-top cleaning system. The shaving head can be removed to be cleaned by a simple push of a button. In 1959, another important improvement was introduced, namely spring-driven shaving heads, which followed the contours of the face better and were even larger (22 mm) (Ramakers, 1984; Van Oost, 2003). These improvements marked the beginning of the optimization phase.

The Itemization Product Phase

It would take until 1966 before Philips introduced the three-headed shaver worldwide, which had been tested 10 years earlier. After some styling and color adjustments in 1975, Philips again introduced a complete redesign: the

Figure 6.4 The TH design (telephone head) by Philips/Norelco (1975) (Source: Philips)

so-called TH design (telephone head). The shaver could stand (Figure 6.4), and the shaving heads were positioned at an angle of 90°. After 1975, the light color and rounded forms of the Philishave disappeared. Instead, the colors became metallic in combination with black. The product styling became more angular.

Another important improvement was introduced in 1980 in the form of a "double-action" system. The system was equipped with two knives placed in close proximity to each other. The idea was that the first knife would lift the hair a little, after which the second knife cut it off. The goal was, of course, a better shaving result. Real innovations and improvements then became rarer, and the time between the introductions increased.

Although Philips had already introduced a battery-operated, two-headed shaver in 1952 and one with rechargeable batteries in 1966, it would take until the 1980s before shavers with rechargeable batteries became a success. This was because it was only then that the technique was advanced enough to make it possible (Figure 6.5). During the same decade, the shavers were equipped with displays showing information on the amount of energy left in the battery and the amount of time the shaver could still be used. Most of these features can be considered "extras" and therefore belong in the itemization product

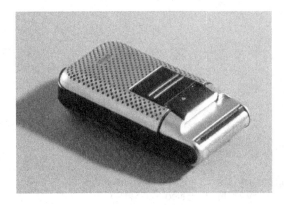

Figure 6.5 An electric shaver from Braun in which special attention was paid to tactile aspects. The shaver was equipped with rechargeable batteries for wireless shaving (around 1980) (Source: authors)

phase. In 1998, Philips introduced the "Cool Skin," a shaver that applied an emulsion to the skin during shaving. This caused a sensation reminiscent of wet shaving. The shaver was particularly successful in the United States, where, up to then, around 75% of men still shaved wet.

The promotional activities changed between 1950 and 1970 from providing personal information and demonstrations to the involvement of celebrities. The two-headed shaver can be seen in the movie *The Long Wait*, and commercials were made with Buster Keaton.

The introduction of the first shaver in 1939 showed that Philips had already realized that women were an interesting target group for its products, which, at the time, were solely aimed at men. The manual included a short explanation for women. However, it would take until 1951 before a shaver for women appeared on the market. It was called "The Beautiphil." The technical differences from the Philishave were small. The slots in the shaving head were somewhat wider, and the space in which shaved hair was (temporarily) stored was a little larger. The most important difference was in the packaging of the ladies' shaver (Figure 6.6). It would take until 1959 before Philips introduced a special design for ladies, which was known as "The Lipstick" (Figure 6.7). In its design, a clear link is made to cosmetics. Contrary to what had been done with regard to the styling of the men's shaver, the technical elements were hidden wherever possible. Some of the measures were quite extreme. For example, the product even had a small cushion with perfume to suppress the smell of the oil in the device. In 1960, Philips changed to a vibrating system for ladies' shavers (the system used by its competitors, Braun and Remington). In 1967, production moved to Klagenfurt (in Austria). It was at around that time that segmentation really started. The styling of the machines for men became more angular and the shavers were available in different colors. The ladies' shavers became more cosmetic. While the technological features were emphasized in the men's shavers, in the ladies' shavers, such features were hidden wherever possible.

Figure 6.6 The Beautiphil, the first Philips shaver for women (1951) (Source: Philips)

Figure 6.7 "Lipstick" (1959) (Source: Philips)

The Segmentation Product Phase

The segmentation phase had now been reached. Nearly everybody in the Western world knew what an electric shaver did and how well it functioned. The number of manufacturers was reduced to three major companies: Braun, Philips/Norelco, and Remington, with Philips/Norelco being the biggest with a market share of 60% in 1978. In this period, they all had different techniques. Philips had the rotating heads, Braun the rounded, oscillating head, and Remington the straight, oscillating heads. The manufacturers tried to reach different target groups and lifestyles using styling. Braun introduced a shaver in which a lot of attention had been paid to the tactile experience. Black, plastic bumps stuck through a metallic housing, which gave a pleasant feeling in the hand (Figure 6.5). Since 1985, Philips also focused on young men, and styled a model named Tracer for them. An important reason for doing this was that research had shown that men who start using an electric shaver are most likely to continue doing so for the rest of their lives. In this phase, nearly all electric shavers had rechargeable batteries, meaning that the user did not have to have an electric socket close to hand.

Advertising activities were becoming more common. Besides commercials on radio, on television, and in magazines, sportsmen were also sponsored by Philips. In the movie *Die Another Day* (2002), James Bond uses a Philishave. Philips's intention is clear. The expectation was that using famous sportsmen and movie stars would cause consumers to identify with them and therefore choose the Philips brand.

In 2003, 60 products were on display on the Philips website (Personal Care). Half of them related to electric shavers: Cool Skin (six different devices), Sensotec (7) (Figure 6.8), Super Reflex (4), Quadro Action (6), Micro+ (3), Turbo Vac (2), and two beard trimmers. The other half consisted of components such as shaving heads or accessories such as cleaning sets or gel (for the Cool Skin shavers).

The Individualization Product Phase

It is difficult to realize an individualization product phase for electric shavers. For example, a mobile phone is something people carry on their person and it therefore has a significant "expression value" (anyone can see it, or you can show it to anyone). However, the electric shaver remained (and has remained) a bathroom product. Although it is technically feasible to mold a shaver to a customer's hand in a shop, such service is not yet expected.

The Awareness Product Phase

The awareness product phase has, however, been more or less realized by manufacturers in the past. An example is an action of Braun at the end of the twentieth century, where used shavers were taken back. These kinds of activities not only offer users an extra discount, they also solve the problem they have with throwing away a product that still functions perfectly well. In the process, it is important that the company makes clear that the

Figure 6.8 Philips Sensotec, available in several colors, with rechargeable batteries for wireless shaving (2003 range, photo courtesy of Philips Design)

collected shavers are dealt with in a responsible way (e.g., by recycling). For years, Philips has been active in profiling itself as a responsible company. According to the Dow Jones Sustainability Index, Philips was the market leader with regard to environmentally responsible entrepreneurship in both 2004 and 2005.

Conclusion

The development of the electric shaver follows the theory very closely. During the individualization and awareness product phases, some of the product characteristics are only partially fulfilled. With regard to "product development," this means that new product development is aimed at different target groups, but not at individuals. As far as "pricing" is concerned, this means that there is a lot of competition on the basis of product price.

Through segmentation, a price range for electric shavers is realized that varies between €10, for the cheapest available shavers, up to more than €500, for the top range of Philips/Norelco. The awareness product phase has been reached for leading manufacturers such as Braun and Philips, but the efforts made to minimize the environmental impact are not communicated via the products, only in the mission statements of the companies, e.g., on their websites.

6.2 Mobile Phone

The mobile phone has a short history compared to the bicycle and the electric shaver. The principle of the phone itself is much older and dates back to 1876, when Alexander Graham Bell filed his patent (Bell, 1876). In cooperation with Thomas Watson, he created a commercial product by the end of the nineteenth century (Casson, 1910). It would take until the second half of the twentieth century before nearly every household in the Western world had one or more domestic phones.

The mobile phone was accepted much faster. The concept was introduced in 1947 by Bell Laboratories under the supervision of Dr. Martin Cooper (Anon., 2004; Anon., 2005a). However, the development was not continued because, at that time, the Federal Communications Committee (FCC) made so few frequencies available that a maximum of 23 phone calls would be possible simultaneously per service area. In short, the FCC did not believe in the possibilities of mobile phones. It would take until 1968 before the FCC reconsidered its decision and was prepared to increase the number of frequencies, subject to technological improvements.

MTS (Mobile Telephone System) was the first car phone system, introduced by Bell in 1946. A year later, AT&T (American Telephone and Telegraph) launched the first commercial radio-telephone system – called "Highway Service" – between New York and Boston. The products consisted of a receiver, a transmitter, and a logic unit, with a dial and handset connected to it. They were very heavy and very expensive, so only a few people could afford them (Lacohée, Wakeford, and Pearson, 2003). The first signal for mobile phones was an analog radio signal. During the First World War, AT&T developed this system as an assignment from the US Army Signal Corps. The first radio contact between an airplane and a ground station was established in 1917. This led to portable military AM radio telephone sets in that same year (Van Kessel, 2013). These phones are considered the first walkie-talkies; they were used to communicate between military vehicles. In 1956, Ericsson (Sweden) came on the market with the Mobile Telephone Service (MTA), with much smaller products. Ericsson's system differed from the others in that it was fully automatic; it did not require any manual control. In the 1960s, the car phones were provided with transistors; therefore, they required less power and became even smaller. An example was the Motorola Improved Mobile Telephone Service (IMTS).

The Performance Product Phase

In 1973, Motorola revealed a portable telephone in the United States, which it called the DynaTAC, but it would take until March 6, 1983 before the mobile phone was introduced commercially. In that year, the Motorola DynaTAC 8000X (Figure 6.9) was to be the first "FCC-approved portable cellular phone." Until then, Motorola had worked for 15 years on the project and spent $100 million. The DynaTAC (DynaTAC stands for Dynamic Adaptive Total Area Coverage) weighed nearly 1 kg (870 grams to be precise), measured 33 x 9 x 4.5 cm, and had an LED display. It could be used to make phone calls for up to one hour, and its standby time was eight hours. It took 10 hours to recharge the batteries. The phone had a memory that could store 30 phone numbers. Despite the price of $3,995.00, there was a waiting list shortly after its introduction of many thousands of consumers who wanted to buy the product. The phone had very limited options. The necessary infrastructure was far from ready. So there were only a few places from where it could be used. It is quite clear that the first products fulfilled the criteria of the performance product phase. Rudy Krolopp, one of the members of the team who developed the Motorola DynaTAC, said the following:

> In 1983, the notion of simply making wireless phone calls was revolutionary and it was an exciting time to be pioneering the technology at Motorola. Marty (Dr. Martin Cooper) called me into his office one day in December 1972 and said, "We've got to build a portable cell phone," and I said, "What the hell's a portable cell phone?" (Anon., 2005a)

Although the FCC authorized AT&T Bell Laboratories in 1977 to install the first cellular telephone network – called 1G – with 10 base stations in Chicago, because of the size of America, soon Europe and Japan could take over the lead. In 1969, the Nordic Mobile Telephone group (NMT) had been set up in Denmark, Finland, Sweden, and Norway to develop a cellular network. It was introduced in 1979, two years after the American system. In 1981, in Sweden alone, there were already 20,000 mobile phone users (van Kessel, 2013). Japan started its network in 1979. It was set up in Tokyo by NTT (Nippon Telegraph and Telephone) and had 23 base stations. The 1G networks became such a great success that countries all over the world started their own cellular networks.

Figure 6.9 Motorola DynaTAC 8000X, the first commercially available mobile phone (Source: authors)

The Optimization Product Phase

In 1991, the second-generation network (2G) was launched in Finland. This global system of mobile communication (GSM) was the first digital transmission network. It made communication much faster. In a few countries, the analog 1G and digital GSM network used the same frequencies, which resulted in a very quick replacement of the 1G network by GSM. A new possibility of the GSM network was text messaging, which in no time became extremely popular. The first text message was sent on December 3, 1992, then still from a computer, in the UK. The first personal text message was sent the next year in Finland (Agar, 2003). The first handheld GSM phone was brought to the market by Motorola in 1992. Nokia soon followed with its 1011, the first mass-produced mobile phone that also set the dominant design: the so-called candy bar.

Until the beginning of the 1990s, the developments with regard to mobile phones focused on product improvement. Special attention was paid to reliability, weight reduction, miniaturization, and completing the infrastructure. The developments took place in rapid succession (Figure 6.10). The 1011, for example, introduced by Nokia, weighed 470 grams and measured 19.5 x 6 x 4.5 cm (Figure 6.11). In that same year, Ericsson introduced the GH 198, which

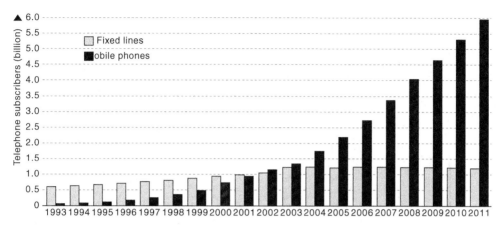

Figure 6.10 Growth (worldwide) of the number of mobile phones compared to the number of fixed lines (Based on data from: ITU, International Telecommunication Union, URL: itu.int)

weighed 330 grams and measured 14.7 x 6.6 x 3.1 cm. In this period, three cell phone companies dominated the market. Motorola with its "flip phones," which had a hinged section that could be flipped open when the phone was going to be used. Motorola launched the Motorola 5080 (1993), 5200 (1994), and 7200 (1994). Nokia presented the 2110, the first phone with a musical ringtone. Nokia improved its phones gradually with the 110 (1993), 232 (1994), 2110i (1994), 2140 (1994), and 2010 (1994). The third company, Ericsson, introduced the Jane models: EH237 (1994), GH337 (1994), and PH337 (1994) (van Kessel, 2013). The "candy bar" and "flip phone" existed together, the first being the dominant design. In 1995, 1 million people in the world owned a cell phone.

The Itemization Product Phase

The first really handy mobile phones appeared on the market in the mid-1990s. In a few years, the Nokia 2100 series sold 20 million units. (Anon., 2005b). In 1995, Ericsson introduced the NH237 (at the moment of introduction, it was the smallest mobile in the world). This phone remained on the market until 1997. By now, mobile phones weighed about 200 grams and measured about 15 x 6 x 2 cm.

In an article in *Design Engineering*, it was concluded that competition between manufacturers was mainly based on price, size, and lifetime of the battery.

Manufacturers of modern digital cellular telephones compete principally on the basis of price, size and battery lifetime. ... Typically, an existing amplifier

Figure 6.11 Nokia 1011, introduction 1992, measured 19.5 x 6 x 4.5 cm (Source: authors)

in a digital cellular telephone is 35% efficient, with 65% of the power wasted as heat. This gives a typical talk time between battery charges of 2hr.

(Anon., 1997)

The Segmentation and Individualization Product Phases

In a later study (Karjaluoto, 2005), a change in these criteria was found that suits the segmentation product phase. According to this research among students in Finland, the most important criteria are: price, brand, user interface (UI), and (technical) features. The design, that is, the styling of the phone, also plays a – less important – role.

The product phases follow one another in a short period. This can be explained by the rapid acceptance of the product. The reason for this is most likely that the product is in fact not really new. It can be regarded as an important improvement of an existing product, namely, a telephone that is not mobile because it is wired. As early as in 1996, mobiles were launched onto the market with characteristics of the segmentation phase. For example, Ericsson introduced the GH388, which was aimed at the business-to-business market. A comparable product that was aimed at the consumer market was available in three colors, namely, green, blue, and grey. This phone was the one on which the GF388 was based. It had a flap that covered the buttons. Separate flaps were introduced as accessories with prints by famous artists, such as Keith Haring, Roy Lichtenstein, Chagall, Picasso, and Moholy-Nagy.

In 1994, the "candy bar"-shaped mobile phone without visible antenna became one of the dominant designs. Nokia also offered different covers to customize the phone. Of its 3210 model, more than 160 million units were sold. In the same year, Nokia introduced the 7110, which had the first wireless application protocol (WAP) that enabled users to browse the Internet on their phones. Also in 1990, Nokia introduced the 5210, which was marketed as a very durable and shock-proof phone. To accentuate this feature, the phone had a kind of bumper on its cover. In that same year, Motorola introduced the L7089 Timeport, which could switch between the three GSM signals so that the phone could be used all over the world. The product became a success for (business) people who travel a lot and therefore need to switch between the available networks. Samsung came up with the first phone with an MP3 player.

In her paper, Srivastava (2005) provides some interesting examples of segmentation. For example, LG Electronics introduced a telephone with a built-in compass onto the market. This feature allowed Muslims to find Mecca for their obligatory prayers five times a day.

A mobile phone became a status symbol, especially for young people.

> A lot of young people show off their mobile phones to each other. The ringtones they use and the number and quality of messages stored on their mobile phones enhances their social status. ... In Japan, mobile users personalize their mobile phone with stickers and colorful beaded accessories. Fashionable wallpaper can be downloaded to enhance the look of the mobile. If that's not enough, "designer mobiles" have appeared on the market, with everything from embedded precious stones to leather or fur covers for every occasion and mood.
> (Srivastava, 2005, 115)

> Young people use the mobile primarily to sustain and enhance their social networks. It allows them to maintain their status, in terms of age, gender, class, peer group and so on.   (Srivastava, 2005, 121)

In 1999, the segmentation phase had clearly been reached. Ericsson, for example, introduced the A1018s series in three basic configurations, each with several variations:

- the A1018s Art, with six exchangeable design flaps,
- the A1018s TwinColor, with canvas belt holster and two exchangeable flaps,
- the A1018s Business, wine red, with portable hands free.

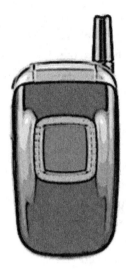

Figure 6.12 The Lady Phone of Samsung (2002) (Source: authors)

At the end of the 1990s, developments took place extremely quickly. Brands such as Nokia introduced more than 12 new models each year. In 2002, Samsung launched the Lady Phone (Figure 6.12). This red mobile phone with a consumer price of €499 has a clock on the front surrounded by fake little diamonds. These light up in different colors so that the owner can see who is calling. Furthermore, the Lady Phone has a mirror and a menstruation calendar to predict the owner's fertile days. In 2004, the Lady Phone was also introduced in blue, white, and gold.

In 2000, at the start of the new millennium, Ericsson launched the R380, which is equipped with a touch screen. It was marketed as "Smartphone," which set the product type name for the later dominant design after the introduction in 2007 of the iPhone by Apple. Ericsson also introduced the T36, which could be linked to other devices in the neighborhood by Bluetooth. Bluetooth was invented in 1994 by Ericsson. It is a wireless technology that uses short wavelength radio signals to create a network within a distance of 50 meters (van Kessel, 2013).

The cell phone now had become such a widely used product that the 2G network was becoming overloaded. Therefore, the 3G (third-generation mobile) network was started in 2001. The first phone that used this network was the P2101 V of Matsushita, which has a camera and makes it possible – thanks to the 3G network, which has a higher bandwidth – to make video calls. In the first years of the new millennium, there were three much sold designs on the market: the "candy bar," the "flip phone," and the "clamshell." The first of these remained the dominant design.

From the beginning of the twenty-first century, it has been hard to keep up with all the developments in the mobile phone market. There are a lot of different products and companies. In its May 2001 issue, the Dutch *Consumer Guide* (*Consumentengids*, 2001) reviewed 50 mobile phones from 13 different manufacturers. It does not only indicate which phone is the best and which phone has the best price-quality ratio, but also the best economic choice. This shows that a new distinction can be made in the mobile phone market: a difference between "normal phones" and "budget phones." In 2002, the company Research in Motion (RIM) launched its first phone, the BlackBerry 5810. Later, RIM changed its company name to BlackBerry. The Quark 6210 is considered the first "real" cell phone from BlackBerry, because, in contrast to the 5810, it can be used for calling without a headset. BlackBerry improved its series with the 7210, which is its first phone with a color screen. Another newcomer is Danger Hiptop. Because of its Internet capabilities, this phone is regarded as a predecessor of the smartphone. The successful PDA manufacturer Palm also entered the market with its Treo 180, which runs on its own operating system. Sharp brought the Mova SH251iS, the first phone with a 3D screen. Sprint introduced the Sanyo 5300, the first (clamshell) camera phone with a digital camera and flash. In 2003, Nokia tried – in vain – to compete with the then popular gaming computer "Game Boy advance" with a cell phone that looks like a gaming computer, the N-Gage. The same year the Nokia 7600 was launched, a 3G phone with a remarkable new design (Figure 6.13). In 2004, Motorola brought a revolutionary design to the market, the Razr V3, a super-thin clamshell mobile phone that became a very popular fashion item. In four years' time, Motorola sold 110 million units of the Razr V3 (Figure 6.14) and its successor, the V4. Vertu, a spinoff of Nokia, created luxurious mobile phones for the rich. These phones were made from precious metals, like gold and platinum, decorated with precious stones, and covered in leather, and came with prices that went up to €20,000. In 2006, Samsung launched the first camera phone with a 10-megapixel camera. In 2007, LG introduced a sleekly designed phone, the KE850, also marketed as the Prada phone. The phone won the prestigious Red Dot Design award for "Best of the Best." That same year, the first phone from Apple was introduced: the iPhone.

In a study into the social consequences of the introduction of the mobile phone by Srivastava, it was concluded that the design and use of the mobile phone have huge consequences for the individuality of the users.

> The highly personalized nature of the mobile phone has meant that its form and use have become important aspects of the individuality of a phone user. Banking on this trend, many manufacturers are embedding the latest fashion trends into their mobile handsets, and providing a wide array of services for users, personalizing their phones (e.g. mobile wallpaper, ring tones, coloured phone covers, etcetera)   (2005, 112)

> Moreover, the extent and nature of the personalization of the telephone is now essential to individual identity, particularly among the youth.   (p. 115)

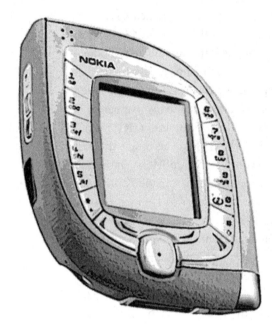

Figure 6.13 Nokia 7600 (2003)
(Source: authors)

The Awareness Product Phase

An article in the Dutch newspaper *De Volkskrant* (Didde, 2004) showed that mobile phones had also reached the awareness phase. The article described the collecting of used mobiles by the company Recell. For each mobile phone collected, Recell donated a sum of money to a charity. In 2003, Recell collected more than 35,000 mobiles. Considering the number of unused mobile phones, this number is not that high. According to the same article, 14 million mobiles were in use in the Netherlands in 2004, while another 15 million were lying unused in drawers or cupboards. Recell repaired the collected mobiles (if necessary) and then exported them to countries in Africa or Asia. The company recognized that it was also exporting a waste problem. It tried to organize a collecting structure in the countries to which it exported the products, but that produced almost no response. In 2009, Motorola introduced the Renew, the first carbon-neutral mobile phone. Its casing was made of recycled water bottles (van Kessel, 2013).

A New Dominant Design

An interesting development is the appearance of a new dominant design, with Apple's introduction of the iPhone. This smartphone distinguished itself from the competition because of its intuitive interface design, its multi-touch screen – which allows the use of two fingers at the same time, for instance to enlarge a

Figure 6.14 Motorola Razr V3 (2004) (Source: authors)

photo by moving two fingers apart – and the use of "apps" (applications for features like calling or for using iTunes). While, until 2008, the focus of different mobile phone brands was on emphasizing the differences between the mobile phones (segmentation), the phones that came after this introduction – now called smartphones – started to look more alike (Figure 6.15). The most prominent differences between the brands are now found in the user interface (UI) and operating system (OS). The new dominant design that appeared provided much new functionality compared to the mobile phone. For smartphone users, "making phone calls" appears not to be the dominant use (once the basic function) anymore, which underlines that a new type of product emerged (van Ammelrooy, 2005). In order to distinguish between the brands, one has to look at the user interface.

Conclusion

In a short period of time, the mobile phone passed through all the product phases and fulfilled almost all the product characteristics. However, because of the quick development of the market and the enormous number of products

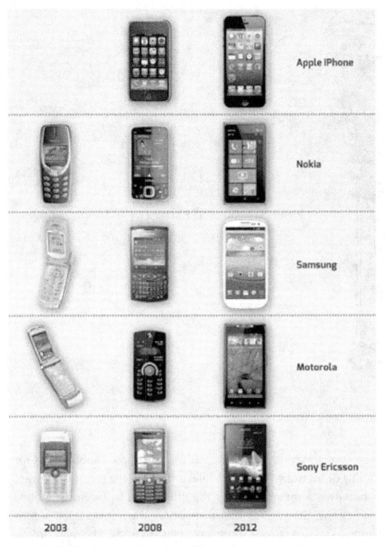

Figure 6.15 The introduction of the iPhone led to a new dominant design for mobile phones (smartphones) (Source: authors)

sold in a short period of time, the mobile phone does not meet the product characteristics for "production" in the optimization product phase. In an earlier study (Eger, 2007a, 2007b), it was mentioned that the market was dominated by five competitors (Nokia, Motorola, Samsung, LG, and Sony Ericsson), however, after the introduction of the Apple iPhone in 2007, a big shift took place. In 2013, there were only two big competitors, Samsung, with a worldwide market share of 29.6% and Apple, with 15.3% (Andrianto, 2013), followed by eight competitors with a market share between 3.5% and 4.5%. According to Millward (2014) and Triggs (2014), the number of smaller brands is growing fast. Millward describes 15 Asian smartphone manufacturers "hoping to crush Samsung and Apple." In an overview of the state of the smartphone industry in the third quarter of 2014, Triggs concludes:

> Overall shipments are up, but it is the smaller brands that are growing the fastest. The last quarter, particularly, has seen more OEMs than before surpass the 5 million units shipped per quarter mark.

6.3 Bicycle

For some time, it has been suggested that the first design of a bicycle was created by Leonardo da Vinci. In 1965 in Madrid, a drawing dating from 1493 was discovered that showed a design of a bicycle. Nowadays, however, there are strong doubts about whether this sketch can be accredited to Da Vinci. Lessing (1997) even argues that it is impossible that the drawing was made by him. The next serious candidate to be the first bicycle is the Draisienne, a "running machine" built in 1817 by Karl Drais (Karl Friedrich Christian Ludwig Freiherr Drais von Sauerbronn). The first bicycle with a system of pedals and bars, used to drive the rear wheel, was designed in 1839 by Kirkpatrick MacMillan.

The Performance Product Phase

The Frenchman Michaud was the first to fix the pedals directly to the front wheel. In the beginning, his bicycles were made of wood. In 1866, however, he put a bicycle on the market that was completely made of steel, and that, after an exhibition in Paris in 1869, became quite successful. Riding a Michaud bicycle was not comfortable at all and required a lot of force and skill. For the first bicycles, participation in exhibitions, like Michaud did in Paris, and free publicity were the most important promotional activities. The pioneers of the bicycle attracted so much attention by simply riding their own bicycles in public that publications in papers and magazines, both positive and negative, followed "of their own accord." In 1871, James Starley introduced his "Ariel," a bicycle that would become very successful under the names "High Bi" (Figure 6.16) and "Ordinary." The "Ariel" was the first bicycle with spokes. It had solid rubber tires, a front wheel with a diameter of 125 cm, and a rear wheel of 35 cm. In the beginning, the bicycle was mainly a product for upper-class and higher-middle-class youngsters, and was used for sports (competitions) and tourism. Riding a high bicycle was not without danger: the center of gravity is located quite high, near the axle of the big front wheel, which means a great risk of toppling over. Moreover, in the course of time, the front wheel was made even bigger to allow faster cycling, which increased the risk.

Figure 6.16 A so-called High Bi or Penny-Farthing from 1875 (Source: authors)

In order to enlarge the market, a lot of manufacturers tried to solve the problem of toppling over that bewitched the High Bi. In the beginning, designers sought – and found – solutions in building cycles with three or four wheels. That these efforts were indeed to some extent successful is illustrated by the Stanley Show in 1883, where 289 tricycles were shown against 233 bicycles. Another solution was sought in trying to move the saddle toward the rear wheel. As a result, two cycles became very successful: the "Facile" from Ellis & Co (1874) and the "Xtraordinary" from Singer (1878) (Figure 6.19). Another design strategy in these days consisted of the development of totally new cycles that were driven at the rear wheel and with the saddle near to the rear axle. Well-known examples are the American "Star" (1881) with a small wheel in the front and a bigger one behind, and "Lawson's Bicyclette" (1879) (Figure 6.17). The latter was the first bicycle driven by a chain on the back wheel. In 1885, John Starley introduced the "Rover Safety Bicycle" (Figure 6.18), generally considered the last step in the evolution of the bicycle into the dominant design we know today.

A Nonlinear Development

In his thesis "The Social Construction of Technology," Bijker (1990, and Section 10.8 of this volume) poses that in historical, philosophical, and economic studies of technology, often a linear model of technological development is assumed, as if the technological development followed an orderly and rational path. Based on an extensive study of – among others – the bicycle between the end of the eighteenth and the beginning of the twentieth century, he concludes that the path for the bicycle was not linear, and that Lawson's Bicyclette (Figure 6.17), the bicycle that in retrospective studies is supposed to be the

Figure 6.17 Lawson's "Bicyclette" (1879) (Source: authors)

Figure 6.18 "Rover Safety Bicycle" (1885) (Source: authors)

"first modern bicycle," was, in the commercial sense, a complete failure. Other bicycles – Bijker mentions the "Star" and the "Geared Facile" (see Figure 6.19) – did much better, but were written off by historians "into the margins of the linear story."

In his description, he comes close to an evolutionary model:

> This suggests that trial-and-error models, often cast in evolutionary terms, have specific advantages over models that stress the goal-oriented rational character of technology development   (1990, 20–21)

In the period between 1850 and 1900, a lot of different designs were created and brought to the market (Figure 6.20) (Bijker, 1990; Van Nierop et al., 1997). It is remarkable that in the beginning of this period, the two-wheelers with direct

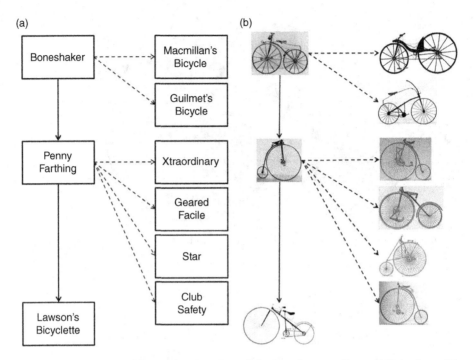

Figure 6.19 The quasi-linear development of the bicycle according to Bijker; the solid lines indicate "success," whereas the dashed lines indicate "failure"; left: the names of the bicycles, right: what they looked like (Source: authors)

transmission (on the front wheel) were much more successful than the two-wheelers with indirect transmission. Even some three- and four-wheelers (with indirect transmission) were more successful than the two-wheelers that we nowadays call bicycles. To explain the success of the first direct-driven two-wheelers, Bijker – a sociologist – looked at what he calls "social groups" (in industrial design terminology "target groups" and "stakeholders"): the producers, the users, and the nonusers.

The Producers

In 1869, the Coventry Sewing Machine company started producing direct-driven two-wheelers. Until then, the company had produced sewing machines. Most likely the reason to start this new activity was a declining demand for the sewing machines it produced, which was in its turn probably caused by the Franco-Prussian War of 1870–1871, which had a negative impact on the export to Europe. In the beginning, the two-wheelers had been produced by carriage builders, but new inventions and production methods, such as wire spokes, tubular frames, and special castings, required different specialisms and facilities, facilities that were closer to the production methods of this builder of

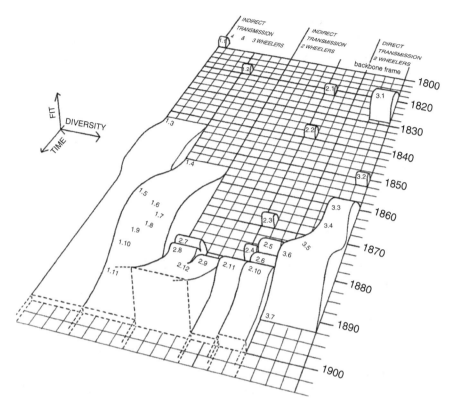

Figure 6.20 The evolution of the bicycle between 1800 and 1900 according to Van Nierop and colleagues (1997) (Source: Van Nierop)

sewing machines. The company changed its name to Coventry Machinists. So the first social group – the producers – started because it needed a new product to compensate for its stagnating market. It was so successful that it soon needed a bigger factory and got a lot of competitors:

> The city of Coventry soon saw a variety of former watch makers, ship engineers, cutlery shop workers and gun makers starting small workshops to build velocipedes. (Bijker, 1990, 41)

The Users

Probably in 1871, James Starley and William Hillman introduced their new, direct-driven two-wheeler, which they named the "Ariel" – the first bicycle with spokes – in an effort to establish a new record. They succeeded in riding from London to Coventry in one day, a distance of nearly 100 miles (96 to be precise). This ride drew a lot of attention and enhanced the already existing image of the bicycle as a "sport machine." Cycling turned out to be an activity of "heroic," daring young men. Everything about cycling was difficult and dangerous. It was not easy to mount and dismount the two-wheeler, neither was it easy to keep cycling on it and to make a turn. Because the center of gravity was located quite high, near the axle of the big front wheel, there was a great risk of toppling over, going "head over heels." And because the two-wheelers were very expensive – the laborer who would have liked to use the machine for his transportation to work could not afford one (Bijker, 1990, 47) – its riders were "young, athletic and well-to-do."

The Nonusers

Because you had to be both wealthy and healthy to ride an Ordinary – that had become the common name of the Penny-Farthing, Ariel and similar two-wheelers – there were a lot more nonusers. There were those who would want one, but were physically not able to ride it or who could not afford it. But there were also a lot who actively opposed the bicycles. As reasons for opposing the Ordinary, Bijker mentions that the riders of the high-wheelers were (literally) looking down on people walking in the streets, from their elevated positions. There were numerous reports in newspapers of accidents between cyclists and pedestrians. And for women, it was often considered undignified to ride one.

Success or Failure?

It is interesting to see that the bicycle that comes closest to our present "two-wheeler with indirect transmission," Lawson's Bicyclette, was a failure, whereas the Ordinary, a type of bicycle that has completely disappeared, was a great success. And this not only in England, as described in the previous section, but also "on the Continent." For instance, in 1865, in France, Pierre Michaud already produced 400 velocipedes per year. Four years later, he opened a new plant where he employed 500 workers who manufactured about 200 bicycles per day. Bijker poses the following question:

> Is the Ordinary a non-working machine because it was highly dangerous and very difficult to master? Or was the Ordinary bicycle a well-working device because it displayed so nicely the athletic skills of the young upper class and because it dealt so effectively with the bumps and mud pools in the roads?
>
> (1990, 83)

This very well illustrates the evolutionary principle of "survival of the fittest." As the circumstances changed, the selection criteria also changed. The

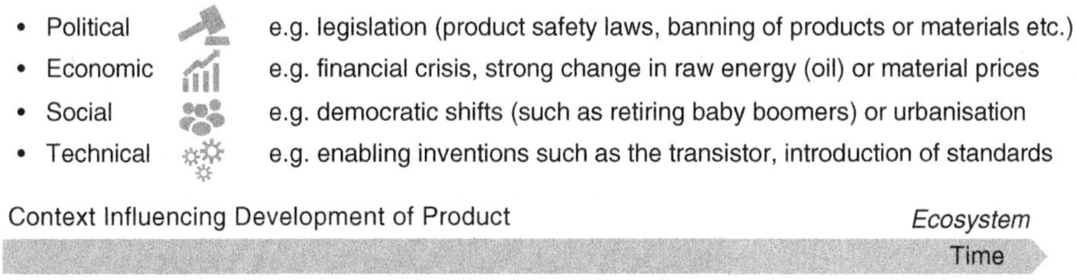

- Political   e.g. legislation (product safety laws, banning of products or materials etc.)
- Economic   e.g. financial crisis, strong change in raw energy (oil) or material prices
- Social   e.g. democratic shifts (such as retiring baby boomers) or urbanisation
- Technical   e.g. enabling inventions such as the transistor, introduction of standards

Context Influencing Development of Product   *Ecosystem*

Time

Figure 6.21 Using a time-mapped PEST analysis to depict drivers of product evolution (Source: authors)

Ordinary was mainly used for touring and for racing. As we will see in the next sections, the indirect-driven two-wheeler was improved in such a way that the direct-driven two-wheelers dramatically lost every race. The Ordinary was no longer a successful racing machine and quickly lost its attraction. Bijker shows that this development resembles an evolutionary process that goes in different directions with variations, solutions, and resulting products. Variation can be found in the problems selected to be solved. (Manufacturers do not try to resolve all problems, but first deal with the ones that they consider the most important.) Next are the solutions generated for these problems. Again there are usually several possibilities (variation) and again the entrepreneur makes a choice (selection) resulting in a new product. The feature/product is successful if customers buy it (selection). If then a next standard is set, a new dominant design emerges and a period starts of incremental change, elaborating the captured know-what and know-how (retention). Once circumstances – the ecosystem – change, as described in Chapter 4, products have to be adapted again to the new context.

Bijker refers to "social groups" as actors who influence the development of technology, a process he refers to as the "social construction of technological systems" (1990 and also Sections 1.4.2 and 10.8 of this volume). Examples of such social groups are target groups, competitors, or manufacturers. Changes in relations between these social groups, e.g., an increasing number of competitors, will affect (the speed of) change in products. Obviously, these changes among social groups can be depicted on the S-part of the PEST analysis (Figure 6.21).

Another thing that Bijker found with regard to the development of the bicycle is that a product – or the improvement of a product – sometimes is successful because of a quality developed to solve a totally different problem. This was the case with the air tire developed by John Boyd Dunlop. The air tire was supposed to be a solution for the vibration problem. In the first advertisement, which appeared in 1888, the claim was made that the air tire made "vibration impossible." However, for the main target group – the young, well-to-do, upper-class men – vibration was not a problem on their high-wheelers. But when the air tires were mounted on a low-wheeler with indirect transmission, they raised "sweeping victories" over the high-wheelers. Two things happened: the direct-driven high-wheeler lost its attraction to the sporting and racing cyclists, and the low-wheeler became a product that was interesting and useful to new, much bigger target groups, such as tourists, elderly, and women (Figure 6.22). The "anti-vibration device" had become a "high-speed device." Note that the new target groups were not interested in this high speed, but in the safety it offered them to ride the bicycles they were mounted on.

> The using practice of the social group of "young men of means and nerve" – i.e. racing, showing off and impressing the ladies – constituted the "Macho machine," while the using practice of the social groups of women and elderly men – i.e. touring, falling off and "breaking limbs and bones" – constituted the "Unsafe machine." The "Macho machine" led to a design tradition with larger wheel radius and the "Unsafe machine" gave rise to a variety of designs with, for example, smaller wheels, backward saddle or the smaller wheel in front. Thus, different using practices may bear upon the design of artefacts, even though they are elements of technological frames of non-engineers.   (Bijker, 1990, 122)

In their paper on the "Evolution of the Bicycle," Van Nierop and colleagues (1997) show this evolutionary character of the development of the bicycle in the nineteenth century. They use a three-dimensional diagram with on the x-y plane the product variations (which they define as "diversity") and the time, and vertical (in the third dimension) something they call "fitness" (or FIT in Figure 6.20). According to Van Nierop and colleagues, this fitness depends on the selection criteria that matter at that time (such as safety, vibration, and speed, Figure 6.22) and on the competing products that are available. For each criterion there can be several solutions, especially in the early phases of product development (the "era of ferment," according to Anderson and Tushman (1990, and Section 10.3 of this volume), whereas later in time, when a dominant design has emerged, the number of solutions will often be much smaller and an era of "incremental change" starts.

In their "landscape," Van Nierop and colleagues distinguish four- and three-wheelers (that most of the time have indirect transmission) and two-wheelers with direct and indirect transmission. In 1.1 (in Figure 6.20; see also Figure 6.23), they describe a few examples from before 1800. According to their research, the first human-powered vehicles date back to carnival carts in medieval Italy. The picture shows "Docteur Richard's four-wheeler." The doctor steers his vehicle with reins while his servant does the (probably heavy) pedaling. Number 3.1 in Figure 6.20 (top right with a peak around 1820) shows the first successful product: the walking or running machine (also

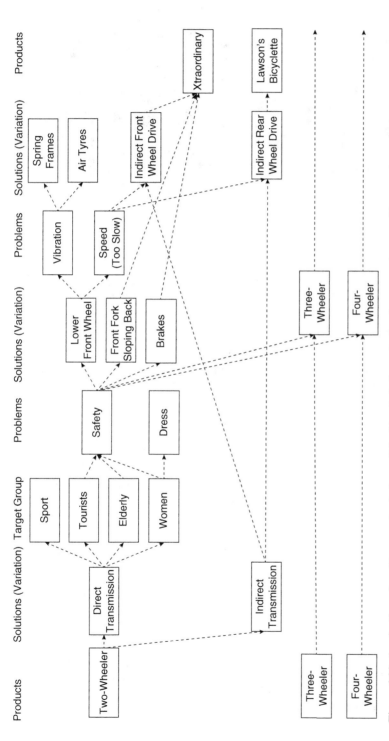

Figure 6.22 A selection of problems and solutions of the bicycle in its early development phases to illustrate its evolutionary character. Note that this overview has no pretention to be complete (Based on Bijker, 1997) (Source: authors)

Figure 6.23 Docteur Richard's four-wheeler (1669) (Source: Van Nierop)

known as the Draisienne) invented by Karl Drais (Figure 6.24). The success was short-lived and ended by 1820. Most examples in the fitness landscape from before 1850 are "one-offs." The landscape clearly illustrates that the success of the three- and four-wheelers comes first, followed by the direct-transmission two-wheelers. The success of the indirect-transmission two-wheelers – the dominant design we know until today – only starts at the end of the nineteenth century, from about 1880.

In their conclusions, Van Nierop and colleagues argue that product development is nonlinear; designers and manufacturers look for opportunities to improve (on earlier failures) and copy earlier successes. They further conclude that – in the evolution of the bicycle – both innovations and failures were beneficial to the development. The process seems comparable with the natural process of evolution, with one important difference: an engineer or designer can profit from both previous successes and failures.

The Darwinian Analogy

In the case of the bicycle, some similarities with biological evolution can be found. Steadman postulates that fitness in nature can be found in many attributes:

> In an animal being better fitted for finding food, better fitted for moving about, better camouflaged to evade predators, more attractive to possible mates, more fecund – any quality which contributes to the animal's success in avoiding early death and producing offspring.   (2008, 73)

Figure 6.24 Draisienne (1818) (Source: Van Nierop)

He continues by stating that fitness is not an absolute quality, but relative to the environment. When compared to product development, this means that "being better fitted" can be realized only with the available materials, production methods, and tools. In the case of the bicycle, the materials and tools changed, for example, wheels with spokes, tubular frames, and air tires appeared. But the environment (ecosystem) changed as well: the target group "young men of means and nerve" disappeared and a new target group who used the bicycle for transportation and recreation appeared. The air tire, developed to solve the – for the old target group nonexistent – vibration problem, unexpectedly improved the low-wheelers for the new target group. This phenomenon has some similarity with the variation (random mutation) of Universal Darwinism.

Division of the Market

It is striking that in this beginning period of bicycle production, the division of the market between competitors resembles the present situation. There were the mass-produced bicycles made by the big manufacturers; however, there were also a lot of small workshops where bicycles were locally produced, making use of the components that were also used for the mass production. Finally there were the custom-built bicycles that were produced by the small workshops as well as by special departments of the larger manufacturers.

The Optimization and Itemization Product Phases

In the performance product phase, bicycles were exclusively used for sports and tourism. In the later phases, the transportation function slowly crept in. Bicycles enabled people to move to cheaper houses, further away from their work. An important development for the bicycle was the already mentioned invention of the pneumatic tire in 1888 by John Boyd Dunlop. In 1890, about 98% of all tires were solid, while four years later, in 1894, the market share of pneumatic tires had grown to nearly 90% – a clear indicator that a new dominant design for the subsystem tire had emerged. According to Baudet (1986), it was then that the bicycle reached its final stage: until the early 1890s, technical improvements (tires, bearings, transmission, steering, etc.) were quite important, sometimes even of fundamental interest. The bicycle as we know it now reached its form around the year 1895. Fundamental technological innovations, like there were in the early stages of development, were not realized after that. The fact that the dominant design of the bicycle was realized around the end of the nineteenth century does not imply that it was completely impossible to realize further technical improvements on the bicycle after that time. Van der Wal (2005) mentions:

- The development of the aluminum bicycle by Frenchman Rupalley (1895).
- The introduction of the three-speed hub gear by Sturmey & Archer (1902).
- The invention of the derailleur in the 1930s, only becoming a success after World War II.
- The introduction of the drum brake (1937).
- The development of synchronously operating brakes (1960).

But, overall, during the first half of the twentieth century, the basic design of the bicycle remained unchanged. Men's bicycles had a "diamond frame," while women's bicycles had, because of the long skirts of their riders, a so-called lady's curve, nowadays in Holland known as the "grandma bike" (*omafiets*). Virtually all bicycles were black. It was not until after World War II that, due to the increasing competition of the new motorized bicycle (moped), new models were introduced: so-called sports bicycles. These cycles did not look like the present sports bikes at all, but compared to their contemporary bicycles, they looked quite dynamic: sporting smaller wheels (66 cm instead of 71 cm), a shorter wheelbase, and narrower tires. They were furnished with color striping and chromium parts and could be equipped with many accessories: decorated gear cases, white grips, special rear lights, saddles and handle bars, etc. From the 1920s on, production of bicycles became increasingly mechanized. Manufacturers invested in automated lathes and specialized production halls with functional layouts. Despite that, still a lot of handwork was needed for assembly.

The Segmentation Product Phase

Once entering the segmentation phase, the product has gone through some optimization already and now starts to differentiate toward different types of users (segments of the market) in order to further gain competitive advantage. For bicycles, the 1960s and 1970s marked such a period of change in bicycle design toward different segments. The "general" market had been well served, and competing manufacturers started looking for new niches. Examples are the introduction of the "Moulton bike" (1962), a bike with aluminum parts and small wheels designed by Alexander Moulton, and the all-terrain bike (ATB) or mountain bike, mainly developed in California.

This process of segmentation resembles speciation, as we know it from evolutionary biology. The first-generation product became a "mother product" (referred to as "base" in Chapter 4) that set the dominant design and marked the beginning of a (product) family, in this case, the product family of bicycles. Then new products based on the "mother" are formed that specialize in niches or segments in the market. The root and branches form a product family tree (PFT) that can be drawn to map the historic development of the product family. Figure 6.25 shows such a PFT as drawn by Bakker (2013). The PFT depicted shows how the main trunk develops from walking frames (end of the 1700s) toward the Rover Safety Bicycle in 1885. According to this author, segmentation starts after the Rover Safety and then peaks between 1970 and 2000. He distinguishes eight market segments: folding bicycles, E-bikes, city bicycles, tour bicycles, BMXs, hybrids, mountain bikes, and racing bicycles.

The 1980s saw the introduction of special bicycles for nearly every purpose: shopping bicycles, children's bikes, recumbent bicycles, racing bikes, touring bikes, etc. New materials and production methods gave designers more freedom to vary in the design of frame constructions. In this way, the bicycle slowly transformed from a mere means of transportation into a fashion and lifestyle product. Two examples are described next: the folding bicycles and the mountain bikes (BMX, ATB).

Folding Bicycles

The first design for a folding bicycle dates from 1878 and can be found in a patent by William Grout. However, it is debatable if this bicycle can really be considered "foldable," since it only had a folding front wheel and the frame had to be taken apart (Bakker, 2013). The first folding bicycle that would become successful was built in 1892 by Charles Morel, a wealthy French industrialist. A year later, a French army lieutenant by the name of Henry Gérard filed a patent for a folding bicycle that didn't work. Morel saw possibilities to sell folding bicycles to the army and made an agreement to produce his bicycle

126

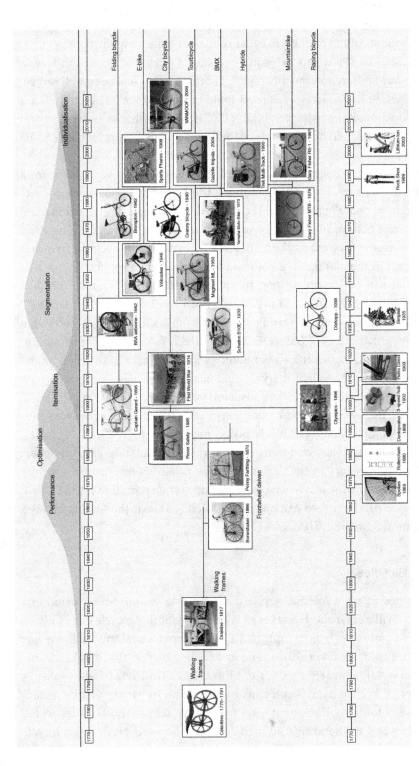

Figure 6.25 Product family tree of bicycles. On top the product phases. In the middle the product family tree. On the bottom the introduction of several subsystems. (Source: Bakker, 2013)

under Gérard's name, who was, because of the success of the folding bicycle in the army, promoted to the rank of captain. The bicycle was then named the "Captain Gérard." It became the first folding bike produced in relatively large numbers (Anon., 2013a). The 1960s marked a new interest in folding bicycles, exemplified by the introduction of the "Moulton bike," a bicycle that, because of its aluminum parts, its frame construction, and its small wheels, paved the way for folding bicycles such as the Brompton and Dahon.

BMX, ATB, Mountain Bike

The BMX (Bicycle Motor Cross) is inspired by motorcycles: they have fat tires, rounded shapes, and wide handlebars. The first recorded bicycle of this type – not yet known as BMX – was the Schwinn B-10E from 1933. These bicycles were very robust and kids started to cross the country with them. Yamaha was the first to pick this trend up and designed the Yamaha Moto-Bike in 1973 (Bakker, 2013). The BMX developed into the now well-known mountain bike or ATB (all-terrain bike).

Price Development

Around 1890, in the Netherlands, the price of an average bicycle equaled several months (three up to six) of an average workman's salary. Despite the rising price level during the first decennia of the twentieth century, prices of bicycles fell dramatically. Around 1935, they reached a minimum in absolute terms. At that time, in nominal terms, a bike would cost approximately 14% of its price in 1890, which is in real terms about 10% of its price in 1890. After the mid-1930s, prices started to rise again, until an average-quality bicycle in 1970 would cost (in nominal terms) the same as in 1890, which still means that in real terms (i.e., correcting for changes in the general price level), its price in 1970 was 15% of its 1890 price. Stated in other terms, in 1890, an average Dutch workman had to work three to six months to raise the money for a bicycle. In 1935, this had dropped to one month, and in 1965, to half a month. Between 1960 and 1970, bicycle prices could vary between €90 and far above €500 (i.e., a range of 1.39 times the average), due to segmentation. Since then, the price range of bicycles has increased even more.

Individualization and Awareness Product Phases

Due to the basic design (a frame as a basis to which all other parts and accessories are attached), the bicycle reached the individualization phase soon after its segmentation phase: the typical layout made it very easy to vary

parts and to remove, add, or change accessories, and by doing so to individualize the bicycle. Since about 1985, completely custom-made bicycles have
been widely available. Bicycles entered the awareness phase somewhere
around 1980, but for slightly different reasons than the theory of product
phases predicts. In this period, the bicycle was rediscovered as a healthy and
environmentally friendly alternative to the "unhealthy and polluting" car.
However, these qualities were not deliberately developed by manufacturers,
for instance by using environmentally friendly materials and production
processes or by committing themselves to social responsibility. These qualities were simply inherent to the product itself and would have come to the
surface anyway, even if manufacturers had no environmental conscientious-
ness at all.

Conclusion

The bicycle follows the theory of product phases to a great extent. The first
three phases are passed through in accordance with the theory. Despite that,
the history of the bicycle is, at some points, at odds with the product phases
theory, which can partly be explained by its long and special history. Of
course, the development of the bicycle was influenced by historical developments, but in this case, this statement could also be reversed in some respects.
The process of suburbanization became possible, among other factors, due to
the bicycle (and later, to a greater extent, also due to the introduction of the
car). Thanks to the bicycle, people could live further away from their work.
Some other interference with the theory can be attributed to the lack of
materials caused by the Second World War and the introduction of the car
and the moped.

6.4 Working-Class Housing

This section describes a retrospective case survey of working-class housing
in the UK, Belgium (*Sociale woningbouw*), and the Netherlands
(*Volkshuisvesting*).[2] The UK was chosen because the problem – housing
large numbers of people who came to the cities after the Industrial
Revolution – started there. Belgium was chosen because Richard Foqué
lives there, and the Netherlands were chosen because the author lives
there, which means that the information was easy to access. The assumption
is that the history in other countries will not differ much, but this has not
been verified.

---

[2] An earlier version of this case was published in *Bringing the World into Culture, a "Liber
Amicorum" for Richard Foqué* (Eger, 2009). This explains the chosen countries.

The Performance Product Phase

One of the conditions of the theory of product phases is competition. Before the Public Health Act of 1848, working-class housing was left to the free market in line with the doctrine of *laissez-faire*. Tarn (1973) describes the situation in the cities in England as follows.

> England led the industrial revolution, its towns were larger and uglier than those of any other country, they were filled with great mills and factories belching forth acrid smoke and fumes. ... Now, for the first time, they constituted a separate recognisable and articulate class, living together in well-defined ghettos either newly run up by speculative builders around the gates of the works, or in old courts taken over and over-occupied ... to leave the town was like escaping from hell itself.   (1973, xiii)

By the middle of the century, towns were places of poverty, ill health, disease, inadequate water supplies, and nonexistent drainage and garbage collection. The severity of the situation is reflected in an official account by a city missionary.

> On my district is a house containing eight rooms ... the parlour measures 18 ft. by 10 ft. ... in this one room slept, on the night previous to my enquiry, 27 male and female adults, 31 children, and two or three dogs, making in all 58 human beings breathing the contaminated atmosphere of a close room.   (Hansard, 1851)

An Example of an Early Awareness Product Phase

The large quantity of houses built in England during this period resulted from speculative developments that were, in most cases, totally uncontrolled. Before 1850, there were a few examples of public concern, financed from philanthropy and often fostered by a sense of guilt. An example was the Bagnigge Wells estate, built by the Society for Improving the Conditions of the Labouring Classes. These examples were the first steps toward an early awareness product phase. The following optimization and itemization phases became possible only because of the pressure of these awareness groups and the legislation they enforced.

The history of public housing (*Volkshuisvesting*) in Belgium started halfway through the nineteenth century. Cities were growing rapidly due to the Industrial Revolution. The number of inhabitants of Brussels (and its environs) grew from 260,000 in 1850 to 760,000 in 1900 (De Pauw, 2006). The consequence was an enormous housing shortage. In 1868, a group of private persons started a charitable organization – the Société Anonyme des Habitants Ouvrières dans l'Agglomération Bruxelloise – that built working-class housing in Sint-Gillis, Anderlecht, Vorst, Molenbeek, and Schaarbeek (Figure 6.26).

Figure 6.26 Linthoutwijk, Schaarbeek (1870). (Source: De Pauw, 2006)

The first Public Housing Act was passed in 1889. This law made it possible to borrow money at a low rate of interest and led to the construction of 60,000 quite basic homes in Belgium between 1890 and 1914.

In the Netherlands, public housing started to be developed after the passing of the Housing Act (Woningwet) of 1901. This Act was a response to the miserable situation in working-class areas at the end of the nineteenth century (Anon, 2001). The Act was motivated primarily by public hygiene issues. At first, only small changes were made in the new houses. Rooms without fresh air, such as alcoves and box beds, were no longer permitted. In the first few years after the Act had been passed, only a small number of houses were built. Whether it was possible to build often depended on the personal efforts of civil servants or statesmen. The houses were sober and traditional in appearance.

The fact that product performance was often poor and prices were relatively high meant that working-class housing followed the product phases theory. One can even say that it resulted from a "technology push," although this did not come from the building industry, but from the Industrial Revolution itself. The demand for housing was so high that any square meter could be used and the people renting them could be (and were) exploited.

On March 30, 1847, Lord Morpeth introduced the first version of the Public Health Act in the UK. The bill had clearly been prepared in haste and underwent a rough passage. The government withdrew it on July 8. On February 10 the following year, Morpeth introduced a revised bill intended to have – among others – the following effect: to build public sewers, to require owners or occupiers to provide house drains, to cleanse streets, to cleanse, cover, or fill up offensive ditches, to provide sufficient supply of water, to alter drains, privies, water closets, and cesspools built contrary to the Act, to make by-laws with respect to the removal of filth and the emptying of privies. The battle for the passage of this bill was as great as in the previous year. During the debate, the following, rather shocking passage appeared in *The Economist*.

> In our condition, suffering and evil are nature's admonitions; they cannot be got rid of; and the impatient attempts of benevolence to banish them from the world by legislation, before benevolence has learned their object and their end, have always been more productive of more evil than good.   (1848)

The Optimization Product Phase

Although the bill was passed, it should be emphasized that the degree of success was minor. Until 1875, most buildings for working-class housing that were "better" in the sense that they were well built, had good ventilation, drainage, and an ample supply of water and had sometimes been designed by an architect, were (personal) charity initiatives or initiatives by organizations like the S.I.C.L. C. However, in 1890, Tarn speaks of houses with a "variety of types and standards of accommodation . . . on the ground floor were shops with living accommodation arranged in the rear around small yards" (1973, 101). The buildings became more visually attractive and there were experiments with the façades. For instance, cast-iron balconies were constructed to avoid the monotonous regularity of the barrack-like buildings of earlier decades. After 1905, some architects adopted a modified classic style in an attempt to get away from the rather ponderous and oppressive quality of the earlier housing blocks.

The 1920s were the most important years for working-class housing in Belgium. In this period, garden quarters were built, such as Logis-Floréal in Watermaal-Bosvoorde (Figure 6.27), Cité Moderne in St. Agatha Berchem, and Kapelleveld in St. Lambrechts Woluwe. However, cheap, compact buildings were also built in city centers. From 1926 onward, the rate of building slowed because the construction of garden quarters was considered too expensive and to take up too much space. Another reason was that the liberal government wanted to promote private ownership of houses (De Pauw, 2006).

In the Netherlands, housing construction stopped almost completely during the First World War. When the construction of buildings restarted, the government exerted a lot of influence. Typical projects were large-scale building blocks. Examples are the Berlage buildings in Amsterdam, Van Elmpt in Groningen, and the first Amsterdam School buildings. The most important aspect was not the floor plan, but the façade and the way it matched its surroundings. During the

Figure 6.27 Floréal, Watermaal-Bosvoorde. (Source: De Pauw, 2006)

depression, the number of projects decreased, but two important developments started, namely row building and multistory building. Although both developments were continued after the war, the poor quality of these buildings meant that many were demolished or thoroughly renovated.

The Itemization Product Phase

It would appear that a "dominant design" became discernible in England at the beginning of the twentieth century, namely a cottage with two levels, three bedrooms and, in the case of the larger types, a bathroom.

> Development continued until 1911, but latterly the demand was for smaller houses for rents which the poorest class could afford, since private enterprise catered very adequately for the artisan who could afford a normal house with three bedrooms.   (Tarn, 1973, 138)

In the Netherlands of the 1950s, the emphasis was increasingly put on building quickly and cheaply, as well as building as many houses as possible. The key words were "increase in scale" and "standardization." Complete residential neighborhoods were set up, including playgrounds and parks for recreation. This tendency continued in the 1960s. In this period, large-scale projects such as the Bijlmermeer (Amsterdam) and Hoog-Catharijne (Utrecht) were developed

(Anon, 2001). The result was uniformity. Architects started to break with this trend by trying to create – within the limits postulated by the Dutch rules – variations by designing unusual housing types, by creating public gardens, and by adjusting the plan of the area to the existing situation.

The Segmentation Product Phase

Even in 1885, there was some awareness of segmentation. Tarn (1973) mentions a publication that says: we must take the working class as consisting of various degrees: the upper, middle, and lower of the laboring classes. In the 1970s, the attention "on the Continent" shifted to more attention on the individual. The development projects became smaller. The Dutch government made funds available for experimental building. In the field of social housing, experiments were carried out with the design and use of materials. Examples are Kasbah (in Hengelo) and the Bolwoningen (in 's-Hertogenbosch) (Figure 6.28). Suitable housing was developed for elderly people, for singles, and for small families. In Belgium, the quantity of working-class (social) housing seems to have remained low, although it is difficult to find detailed information (De Meyer and Smets, 1982) (Figure 6.29).

Figure 6.28 Spherical houses ("Bolwoningen") built in 's-Hertogenbosch in 1985. Architect: Dries Kreijkamp (Source: authors)

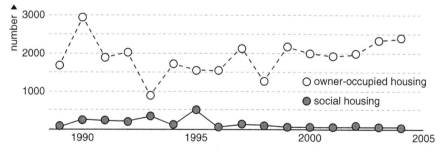

Figure 6.29 The number of owner-occupied houses compared to the number of social houses built in Brussels between 1989 and 2004 (Based on data from: De Pauw, 2006)

(a)

(b)

Figure 6.30 a) Two (originally identical) housing blocks in Enschede b) and what people did to individualize them (Source: authors)

At the end of the nineteenth century, the first signs of individualization could already be perceived.

> The identity of the individual had been lost in a Georgian terrace behind reticent, similar façades, designed to produce a harmonious street or square, rather than to glorify the separateness of each house. The rising class who possessed the money to own and build such houses were now no longer content with this reticence; they required that their social advancement should be more ostentatiously paraded by a showy individualistic house.   (Tarn, 1973, 153)

The Individualization Product Phase

In the 1980s and 1990s, more attention was paid to architecture in the Netherlands. The consequences of the energy crisis of the 1970s had an effect on building projects. In many projects, both private and social housing were built to create a good social mix of residents. The rising costs of the social tenement houses was compensated for by the benefits of the private housing. A new development was the building of shells that enabled the inhabitants to influence the plan of their future home. It looks like there was almost a century between

Figure 6.31 Example of *Het Wilde Bouwen* in Roombeek, Enschede (Source: authors)

individualization in England and in the Netherlands. Figure 6.30 shows very clearly the wish to individualize one's home.

In recent years, "random building" (*Het Wilde Bouwen*) was introduced in the Netherlands. "Anything goes" in certain areas, as long as people stick to the legal regulations concerning construction, ventilation, insulation, etc. Roombeek (in Enschede) is an example of such an area (Figure 6.31).

The Awareness Product Phase

As already mentioned, the energy crisis led to renewed requirements in house building, for example due to insulation and other energy-saving measures. In the last decade of the twentieth century, special "green building" quarters (*Milieuwijken*) were developed in the Netherlands. Examples are the Ecowijk in the Westerpark district of Amsterdam and Oikos in Enschede.

Conclusion

The market for private and social housing is different in several ways from the market for products. First of all, there is the location of the house. This is an aspect that is not relevant to products, but is very important for houses. It means, for instance, that people sometimes do not have much choice unless they are willing to accept traveling long distances to and from their work. In addition, there are more governmental rules and regulations for housing than for most other products. And these rules and regulations (legal system) tend to differ significantly per country and thereby affect housing styles. Finally, it is easy to individualize a house, usually easier than to individualize a product. Despite all these differences, it can be concluded on the basis of this limited study that it looks like product phases also apply to working-class housing. As is the case with most products, the findings reveal that it is difficult to draw a fine line between the end of one product phase and the beginning of the next, and that some product phases overlap one another for long periods of time.

6.5 Traveling (Tourism)

This section describes the development of tourism. Types and trends of tourism are studied against the background of their evolutionary development. Traveling in the classical world and during the Middle Ages is mentioned; the discussion includes the so-called educational journeys that were considered useful for the education of people (mostly youths). Traveling for business is excluded. Most of the international information is based on the work of Gyr (2010). The information of the Dutch situation in this section is based to a significant degree on interviews with Ferdinand Fransen and Rob Admiraal,[3] on documentation that they made available, and on the personal archive of one of the authors of this book.[4]

Early "Tourism": The Performance Product Phase

The earliest forms of recreational and educational travel can be found in Egypt, under the pharaohs, and in Greece and Classical Rome (Gyr, 2010). In this period, traveling for amusement and recreation was possible only for the wealthy. In Classical Rome, traveling grew due to the development of an infrastructure of around 90,000 kilometers of main roads and 200,000 kilometers of local roads in the year AD 300. The well-off Romans visited seaside resorts or took a "summer health retreat" in luxury thermal baths, sites that originated from health care, but turned into locations for pleasure and entertainment.

From the twelfth century on, traveling more and more became a component of education. In the beginning of the sixteenth century, traveling even became an obligatory part of education. These trips could last up to four years and were, due to the circumstances of that time, not without risk: not every student attending the "university of life" returned from his trip. Over time, leisure and pleasure became increasingly important. Countries that were visited often were France and Italy; popular cities were London, Paris, Amsterdam, Madrid, Munich, Vienna, and Prague. In the eighteenth and

---

[3] F. G. Fransen and R. Admiraal were interviewed on February 14, 2006. Fransen started his career in 1944 in "Reis- en Passagebureau Arke," of which he became the owner in 1975 (the name was then "Arke Reizen"). Admiraal became the public relations manager of Arke Reizen in 1973. In 1994, Arke Reizen was sold to the German travel agency TUI.

[4] Between 1959 and 1970, the father of Arthur Eger ran a travel agency. Part of the archive of this agency is in his possession.

nineteenth centuries, the educated middle class started to copy these educational travels, although the trips grew shorter and the destinations less far away. Also the reasons for traveling changed from education to visiting luxury spa towns where the most important activities were bathing, balls, horse races, and gambling.

The structure of the present forms of tourism developed in the period between the beginning of the nineteenth century and the end of World War II. In this period, the way to mass tourism was prepared, starting in the upper middle class.

> The development progressed episodically and built upon a number of changing social conditions and factors. The most important undoubtedly include not only the advance of industrialisation, demographic changes, urbanisation and the revolution in transportation, but also the improvement of social and labour rights, the rise in real income and the resulting changes in consumer demand.
>
> (Gyr, 2010, section 13).

It would take until the end of the nineteenth century before the lower middle class and working classes could go on holiday. In the beginning, these trips consisted of short-stay and day trips by, for instance, train or ship. In the same period, the publication of travel guidebooks started. The German Karl Baedeker (1801–1859) was one of the most successful writers. He founded his own publishing company in 1827 and produced a series of reliable, well-researched books. The attractions he mentioned soon became touristic "must sees."

The first "travel agency" was created by Thomas Cook (1808–1892). On July 5, 1841, he arranged a trip from Leicester Campbell Street Station to a rally in Loughborough. He arranged for the rail company to charge one shilling per person, which included rail tickets and food for the journey. He received a share of the fares charged to the travelers. For all we know, this was the first privately chartered excursion by train. During the following years, Cook planned and conducted several more trips, until in 1844, the Midland Counties Railway Company offered him a permanent arrangement. This success led him to start his own company, running rail excursions for pleasure, and making his money by taking a percentage of the railway tickets. Cook introduced many innovations in the traveling industry that are still used today, such as guided holidays abroad, inexpensive all-inclusive holidays, and vouchers for hotels.

Growth of Tourism: The Optimization and Itemization Product Phases

The development of tourism really took off after World War II. The dominant motifs for traveling after 1900 were relaxation and recreation. Gyr (2010) calls

	Persons travelling, in millions							
	1950	1960	1970	1980	1990	2000	2007	2008
World	25.3	69.3	165.8	278.2	436	683.6	904.2	921.8
Europe	16.8	50.4	113	177.5	262.6	392.5	487.3	487.9
Asia and Pacific	0.2	0.9	6.2	23.6	55.8	110.1	181.9	184.1
North, Central and South America	7.5	16.7	42.3	62.3	92.8	128.2	142.9	147.2
Middle East	0.2	0.6	1.9	7.5	9.6	24.9	47	55.6
Africa	0.5	0.8	2.4	7.3	15.2	27.9	45.1	47

Figure 6.32 Numbers of persons traveling between 1950 and 2008 (Source: World Tourism Organisation (UNWTO): Tourism Highlights 2008 Edition, World Tourism Barometer June 2009)

	Revenues of tourism in billion U.S.-dollars							
	1950	1960	1970	1980	1990	2000	2007	2008
World	2.1	6.9	17.9	106.5	273.2	479.2	855.9	944
Europe	0.9	3.9	11	63.7	145.6	231.6	433.4	–
Asia and Pacific	0	0.2	1.2	11.3	46.7	90.4	188.9	–
North, Central and South America	1.1	2.5	4.8	24.7	69.3	131	171.1	–
Middle East	0	0.1	0.4	3.5	5.1	15.6	34.2	–
Africa	0.1	0.2	0.5	3.4	6.4	10.6	28.3	–

Figure 6.33 Revenues of tourism in billion dollars between 1950 and 2008 (Source: World Tourism Organisation (UNWTO): Tourism Highlights 2008 Edition, World Tourism Barometer June 2009)

the period between 1915 and 1945 the "development phase." The growth in this period was related to the regulations in more and more countries of holidays as part of employment conditions. Gyr mentions that of 100 Swiss companies in 1910, only 11.9% gave their employees paid holidays, while by 1944, this number had risen to 87.9%. Figures 6.32 and 6.33 give an impression of the enormous growth of tourism after the Second World War.

The Situation in the Netherlands

There is a major difference between selling vacations and organizing them. Tour operators or travel organizers assemble and organize the vacation. Travel agencies, operating as agent or as go-between, sell these vacations to the consumer. The introduction of direct selling, mainly via the Internet, has changed this process. Because the different activities are not always strictly separate, attention is paid in this section to both activities.

In the Netherlands in 1934, Frits Arke and Jan ten Barge started "Reisbureau Twente." They borrowed money from their families and had a bus body built on an Opel chassis. The tasks were separated. One day one partner would drive the bus and the other partner would take care of maintenance, and the next day they would change places. They were able to buy a second bus just one year later. Business went well in the quickly growing market and both the number of buses and the number of destinations grew. Although they started with trips lasting one day, they were soon offering longer trips to, for instance, Germany, Belgium, and France. Fransen's view on the number of competitors was that "There were a lot of companies that had buses and offered trips. Almost every city had a few companies."

World War II brought a temporary halt to the growth. At the beginning of the war, Reisbureau Twente owned 19 buses. Out of fear of confiscation, 12 of them were dismantled and hidden. In 1943, the Germans ordered that all vehicles that could still be used would become *sichergestelt* (seized). Another three buses were immediately dismantled, meaning that only four buses were still operational at the end of the war. However, they were not used to any great extent. As Fransen explained, "Most money was earned by selling coal that was used to power the buses." Gasoline was no longer available, so the remaining buses were powered by coal gasifiers. The first few years after the war were quiet in the travel sector. The borders were still closed. However, after a few years, things started to develop very quickly. In the beginning, the destinations were still close to the Netherlands with the popular ones being Belgium, Germany, Austria, France, Italy, and Switzerland. Short trips to the Belgian Ardennes and along the river Rhine were also offered.

After a conflict between the initiators Arke and Ten Barge, a new agency was started, namely "Travel and Passage Agency Arke" ("Reis- en Passagebureau Arke"). Competitor OAD, founded in 1942 as a consequence of a merger between three small bus companies, introduced its first travel guide in 1952 (Figure 6.34). In this brochure, six afternoon excursions in the direct vicinity (the Province of Overijssel), 24 day trips, 10 two-days trips, five three-days trips, and six longer trips, varying from eight to 10 days, were offered (De Haan and Van der Vliet, 2005).

In the optimization phase, there still was, as was the case in the performance phase, enormous growth in the number of travel agencies. There were specialized agencies that offered scheduled service airline tickets, ship passages, and train tickets, and there were bus companies offering day and holiday trips. However, tobacco shops were also selling holiday trips. The trips were not aimed at a target group, and it seemed that any trip could be sold. A small classified ad in a journal and a stenciled brochure were often enough to entice

Figure 6.34 The first travel guide of OAD (Source: OAD)

new clients (Figure 6.35). Travelers were inexperienced and they did not know what to expect, so it was not hard to satisfy their needs. Comparing prices was very difficult because the propositions were very different. However, over time, the agencies' documentation was improved. Information was provided about the hotels, apartments or campsites, about the area and the facilities. The facilities themselves were also improved.

Arke designed its first brochure in 1950. Besides trips by bus, train trips and car trips were also offered. The latter was the market that A. Eger & Zoon targeted from 1958. The destinations were further away every year. The first trips by boat to Morocco were offered. In the early 1960s, when competition started to grow and more and more people went on holiday in their own car, Fransen (who was one-third owner of Arke by then) succeeded in convincing

(a)   (b)

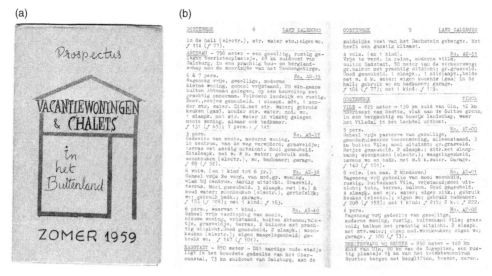

Figure 6.35 The travel guide of A. Eger & Zoon from 1959, a stencil duplicated brochure suffices (Source: authors)

his partners to get involved in air travel. The first air travel to Mallorca was organized in 1965. As Fransen explained: "It took a six-hour flight to Mallorca, one of the destinations where sun was guaranteed. For the time being, that was the furthest destination because traveling any further would involve an expensive stopover having to be made." Although the first flights were loss-making for Arke, from 1968 onward, destinations such as Costa Blanca and later Costa del Sol (Figure 6.36) became very profitable. Soon after that, Arke introduced separate guides for car, train, bus, air, and youth vacations (Figure 6.37).

The demand for vacation trips was still much greater than the supply, especially in the main season (July and August). Every year, demand grew for hotel and apartment complexes in the popular "sun destinations." First they demanded advanced payment of rooms and apartments for one year, then for two years and after that even for five years. Tour operators did not have much choice; if they did not accept these conditions, they did not have anything to let. Fransen therefore decided to build his own, large-scale complex of apartments and bungalows in Barbacan on Gran Canaria in 1978.

In the 1958 A. Eger & Zoon travel guide, prices vary between 80 and 200 guilders per week (corrected for inflation in 2013, this would be between €550 and €1,370) for between four and eight people. In the off-season, period prices were 25% lower. More than 10 years later, in 1970, the prices had risen to between 150 and 450 guilders (in 2013, this would be between €300 and

Figure 6.36 Arke travel guide of 1972 (Source: Arke / TUI)

€900). Off-season prices varied between 75 and 150 guilders. This may give the impression that the prices had gone up; however, after correction for inflation, this is not the case. Having said that, the off-season prices were indeed lower.

The Segmentation Product Phase

In 1970, going on holiday was no longer an exclusive activity, and most people could afford to take a trip abroad. In addition to the usual car, train, bus, and airline vacations, the big tour operators also offered vacations for young and elderly people and to cities. Often they had specialized guides for different destinations, such as Spain, Portugal, and Greece or for special occasions like winter sports. The most important developments of the 1990s are intercontinental vacations.

Besides the big tour operators, a niche market had started with small tour operators that specialize in a target group or an often exotic destination (Figure 6.38). They organize special vacations for their target groups:

Figure 6.37 The "winter sun" and "faraway destinations" guide for the season 1981–1982 (Source: Arke / TUI)

adventure travels, cultural travels, city travels, etc. In the segmentation phase, the corporate identity becomes more and more important: the interior of the office, the quality of the brochures, or even the building where the agency is situated need to have an atmosphere appreciated by the target group.

The Individualization Product Phase

For a travel agency, the individualization phase is easy to realize. The consumer can decide for himself where he wants to go, for how long, in what kind of accommodation, and which sights he wants to visit. Many of the agencies, which were initially small, specialized in this niche market and often organized individual travels. A search of the Internet on February 29, 2012 for "individual

Figure 6.38 Facade of the "China shop King Ape" in Amsterdam in 1993; then a small travel agency specializing in China, Vietnam, and Cambodia, nowadays an agency with many "faraway" destinations (Source: authors)

tours" produced 218,000,000 results. These results included many small, specialized agencies, as well as many big tour operators. In 2006, according to Admiraal, there were about 1,200 big and small travel agencies in a small country like the Netherlands.

The Awareness Product Phase

In the world of tour operators, the awareness phase became relevant more than 30 years ago. Consumers became more and more critical with regard to supply. Criticism concerned damage to nature because of ski pistes, damage to Egyptian graves because of the moisture that the enormous number of visitors brings in, and the risk that some kinds of turtles would die out

Figure 6.39 Holidays that don't cost the Earth (Source: Elkington / Hailes)

because the beaches they used to lay their eggs were filled with sunbathing tourists. The book *Holidays That Don't Cost the Earth*, published in 1992, gives a clear description of this kind of problem (and tries to offer solutions) (Elkington and Hailes, 1992) (Figure 6.39).

In this same period, the familiar notices appeared in hotels asking you to help protect the environment by throwing used towels onto the floor (or into the bathtub) if you want them changed for clean ones, or by leaving them on the rack if you want to use them again.

Europe

Since 1945, tourism has become an important economic factor for modern, industrial nations (Gyr, 2010). Factors that influenced this enormous growth were rising prosperity, increase in mobility, first by train and boat, then by road (bus, car, and caravan), and finally also by air, and growing communication facilities (advertising, brochures, Internet). From 1960 onward, competition increased, which led to cheaper offers, but also to new destinations and modes of holidaying. In 1955, the first "holiday club" appeared: "Club Méditerrané," followed by, among others, "Club Soleil" (1966), the "Robinson Club" (1970), and "Club-Aldiana" (1973). The number of travel agencies and tourist organizations grew strongly, although there still was a big difference between countries. Around 1975, 70–80% of the Scandinavian population went on holiday, while in the UK, Switzerland, and the Netherlands, this figure was 60% and in Italy, only about 25% (Gyr, 2010).

Conclusion

The history of the travel agency sector also largely follows the theory of product phases. The product phase characteristics of production were not considered. The documentation and presentation were studied for information on the characteristic of styling.

7 Retrospective Case Study of General Lighting Solutions and the Compact Fluorescent Lamp

7.1 Introduction

This section explores the historical development of electric lighting technologies in general and, in particular, the evolution of the *general lighting solution* (GLS) product class, zooming in on the *compact fluorescent lamp* (CFL) in a retrospective case study. Electric lighting is one of the key applications that sparked the demand for electricity and, as such, is an important factor in electrification. Electric lighting developed into three technology families: incandescent, gas discharge, and solid state. Each of these lighting technologies families is based on different physical functional principles leading to different technological solutions to generate light. Each family represents complex development paths producing a plethora of products.

The incandescent family was the first to produce a highly successful product that became known as the general lighting solution (GLS). The GLS became the dominant design for electric lighting products and is based on a lamp using a screw base as the standard interface and is roughly the shape and size of a pear. GLS developed into a product class when lamps based on other technologies started to provide the same interface and basic function. The case illustrates that superior economic and environmental performance is not always enough to oust an incumbent dominant design. It appears that the evolutionary path of products is influenced by many factors like consumer preferences, legislation, and technology from other domains.

The case study starts by drawing a picture of electrification, the technology transition that was part and parcel of the evolution of electric lighting. Next, it explores the rise of three different lighting technologies. After that, the development of the CFL is explored in more detail.

7.2 Electrification and the Rise of Electric Lighting

Electric lighting played an important role in electrification, a technology transition that modernized our world from the mid-1880s through to around 1950. The roots of electric lighting go back to the start of the nineteenth century. The invention of the battery by Alessandro Volta in 1800 provided the first practical source of electricity. Soon that would lead to the discovery of incandescent light by Humphry Davy in 1802, who first observed a platinum strip illuminate light as it heated up due to the electric current conducted through it. Around the same time, Davy also demonstrated that light could be produced from an electric arc. The gas lamp, powered by coal-gas, had been invented a decade before, leading to the first public street lighting in 1807, in London. The gas lamp proved a more practical illumination solution than candles and oil lamps. During the following decades, gas illumination spread to other countries like France, the United States, and Russia. However, open fire and toxic fumes associated with gas lamps imply an intrinsic hazard. The gas lamp made the world receptive for a safer and more practical form of artificial light provided by the incandescent lamp described in Section 7.3.1. Electric lighting, however, required an infrastructure that provided electricity to the point of use, which was not yet available. Once a practical electric lamp was invented, the infrastructure developed over time, shaped by an intense battle of standards and technologies in which was revealed that "the details of the timing of small historical events could have important and lasting consequences" (David and Bunn, 1988). In this era of ferment (Anderson and Tushman, 1990), the foundations were laid for today's electric network standards that roughly divide the world into 110 Volt and 220 Volt regions. Together with electric networks and electric lighting, many more products using electricity were developed and distributed throughout the world. Electric motors were soon being used in manufacturing, thereby ousting steam engines that once powered the Industrial Revolution. Electrification not only enabled electric light; it changed the world.

The evolution of electric networks is a case example of path dependence in development that caused technological solutions to become locked in. Once the (110 or 220 Volts) networks had been laid, it became nearly impossible to change them due to the costs involved. And a change would not involve only the networks; the installed base of products based on these standards would also be affected.

7.3 Electric Lighting Technology Families

Since its conception, wide ranges of competing lighting technologies have been developed (Figure 7.1). The CFL can be regarded as a precursor to

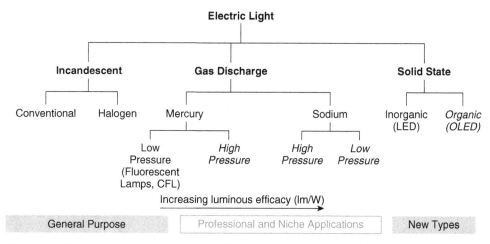

Figure 7.1 Electric lighting technology families (note: the number of lighting types mentioned between brackets is not exhaustive, and only those discussed in this section are included) (Source: authors)

energy-efficient lighting products that mark the current transition to energy-efficient societies. The CFL is part of a group of lighting technology families, the development paths of which are complex and interconnected. It is therefore interesting to study how new types of products come about and develop into families of more advanced versions. This section explores how three technology families evolved and all produced a product that became part of the general lighting solution class.

7.3.1 Incandescent

In 1879, both Joseph Wilson Swan in the UK and Thomas Alva Edison in the United States applied for a patent for a carbon filament incandescent lamp and started to produce it soon after. In the product evolution diagram (Figure 7.2), this is marked as "[A]," the new branch of carbon filament lamps with Swan's lamp (Figure 7.3). However, Friedel and Israel (1985, 91) mention no fewer than 19 inventors of incandescent lamps prior to Swan and Edison. All these inventors experimented between 1838 and 1879 with different filament types (carbon, platinum, and platinum/iridium) and atmosphere types in the enclosure (vacuum, air, nitrogen, and hydrocarbon). Those inventors built on the prior work of Humphry Davy, who, in 1802, discovered the principle of electric light by incandescence when he used Volta's newly discovered batteries to drive a large electric current through a platinum strip. Nearly eight decades of development by pioneering predecessors was required for the roots of incandescent lamps to accumulate into the first commercially available product.

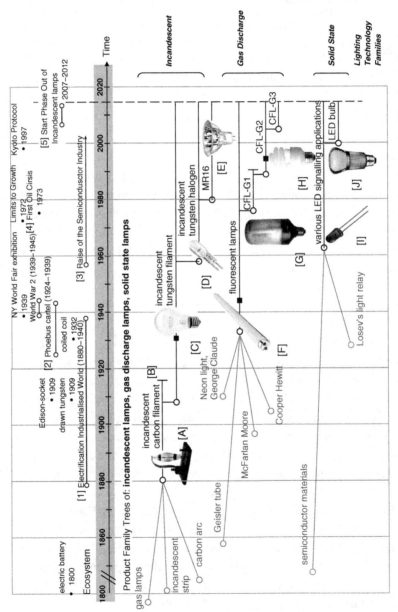

Figure 7.2 Product evolution diagram of most common types of electric lighting technologies (Source: authors)

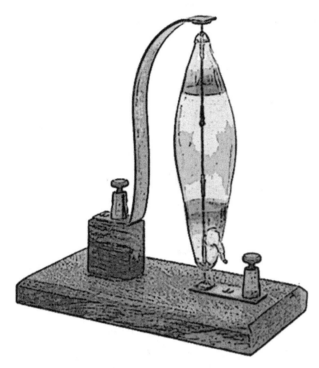

Figure 7.3 The first incandescent lamp by Joseph Wilson Swan (1879) (Source: authors)

Basalla (1988) described how Edison developed electric lighting as a system inspired by the existing gas lighting infrastructure, and as alternative to the carbon arc lamp that produced a light too intense for domestic use. Edison understood that, in order for electric lamps to become successful, electric networks had to be developed to power them. Companies commonly referred to as the utilities started producing and distributing electricity. Others started to develop and manufacture products using electricity. The introduction of electric lighting gave the impetus for the development of a whole range of new industries targeted at generating and transporting electricity as well as products that used it. The process of electrification had started (marked "[1]" in Figure 7.2).

The incandescent bulb was the first source of electric lighting embraced by the consumer market. It has been the dominant lighting technology for domestic use for more than a century, although more efficient types of lighting technology have been invented since it first appeared on the market (Menanteau and Lefebvre, 2000). It was also one of the first major applications to use electricity. Due to its relative safety, it outcompeted gas illumination, which constitutes an inherent fire hazard.

Initially, incandescent lamps used a carbon filament, which had a lifespan of about 40 hours, and produced a yellowish light due to the relatively "low"

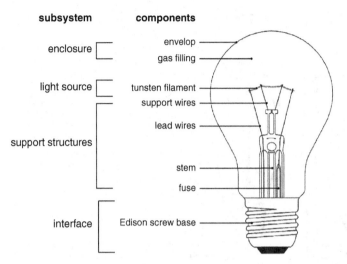

Figure 7.4 The incandescent lamp system diagram (Source: authors)

operating temperature. They needed to be replaced very often. To make them easy to replace, a screw base socket (see also Figure 7.4 and "[C]" in Figure 7.2) developed by Edison in 1909 was used. This subsystem became the interface standard for mounting incandescent lamps in North America and Continental Europe (Wikipedia, 2011). In the UK, and many countries associated with the British Empire, the bayonet socket became the interface standard. In order to produce a whiter light, the lamp needed a higher operating temperature, which reduced the lifespan. These conflicting demands resulted in a technology cycle in subsystems filament and enclosure. Experiments with all kinds of filament materials and different gas mixtures led to a wide range of different types of incandescent lamps.

Finally, experiments using metals with high melting points led to the invention of drawn ductile tungsten filaments in 1909 by General Electric (GE) employee William David Coolidge (Brittain, 2004) that combined well with a nitrogen atmosphere. Soon afterward, this new and improved type replaced the carbon filament lamps and they ceased to exist as a common form of lighting. In Figure 7.2, this is marked "[B]," as a dead end in the product family tree (PFT) of incandescent lamps. Note, however, that the carbon incandescent lamp did not completely disappear. Carbon filament lamps are still available on a very small scale for nostalgic reasons. Similarly to steam engines, these carbon filament lamps did not die out or disappear completely, but lost their socio-technical relevance.

The tungsten filament evolved from straight to coiled and then double coiled, further improving its luminous efficacy. Since then the basic design of the incandescent lamp has remained the same (Figure 7.4). The

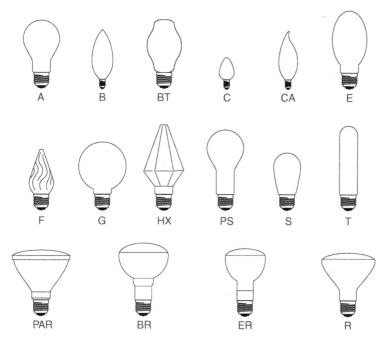

Figure 7.5 A selection from the range of envelope shapes and sizes offered for incandescent lamps (Source: authors)

incandescent light bulb is a non-directional lamp that became the dominant design for electric lighting and has since been referred to as "general lighting service" (GLS) or "general service lamp." The operational lifetime for GLS incandescent lamps increased to 1,000 hours. This lifetime was allegedly capped by the Phoebus cartel ("[2]" in Figure 7.2), which operated from 1924 to 1934. Over the years, a series of incandescent lamp variants emerged, each designed for different types of use in a variety of fixtures or lampshades. The most common variant is marked with an A in Figure 7.5. The GLS has become associated with this most prolific variant, also referred to as the type-A or the A-bulb.

In terms of product phases, the incandescent lamp entered the performance product phase in 1879, when Edison and Swan started producing the first incandescent lamps with carbon filaments. From the end of the 1880s until the turn of the century, the electric lamp was in the optimization product phase, and many experiments led to variants being produced in order to improve their lifespan and efficiency and make them suitable for different types of use. Metals like platinum, tungsten, molybdenum, and tantalum, and even ceramics, were used to make more robust filament types, thereby increasing the lamps' lifespan. In the 1890s, the electric lamp entered the itemization product phase. Many different types of lamps designed for different purposes became available on the market.

These included very small lamps for use in microscopes and focus lamps for use in projectors.

After 1910, the electric lamp entered the segmentation phase. The drawn tungsten filament, the Edison screw base (1909), and the coiled coil filament, invented by Philips in 1932, provided the incandescent lamp with its final architecture. Evolution in the various subsystems of the lamp finally led to the *general lighting solution* or *GLS* that remained stable for nearly a century as the dominant design of the product that provided electric lighting to consumers. The many variants of the incandescent lamp displayed in Figure 7.5 cater to different segments of use. In recent years, a new variant referred to as the "GLS halogen incandescent lamp" has been added as an energy-efficient new member to this family.

7.3.2 Gas Discharge

German glassblower Heinrich Geissler invented a proto gas discharge lamp in 1857 that became known as the Geissler tube and that produced a strong, green glow on the walls near the cathode end. This first version of a gas discharge lamp was very inefficient in terms of light production and had a short operating life. Various decades of experiments led to two- to three-meter-long tubular nitrogen-based gas discharge lamps, made by Daniel McFarlan Moore (USA) in 1895 that enjoyed some commercial success. Although the lamps were much more complex and expensive to install, they were considerably more efficient and produced a more natural light than their incandescent competitors at that time, which still used carbon filaments. Cooper Hewitt (USA) invented the first mercury vapor lamp, which was marketed in 1901. An improved 1903 version was widely used for industrial lighting (*Encyclopædia Britannica*, 2013). Inspired by Geissler and McFarlan, George Claude (France) produced a neon tube light in 1910, which became widely used in advertising applications.

Decades of experimenting with various forms of gas discharge lighting in pioneering predecessors led to the modern fluorescent lamp that uses phosphorous coatings to convert UV into visible light. The key components for modern fluorescent lamps became available at the end of the 1920s. These are the ballast required to control the electric current, long-lasting cathodes (using ductile tungsten wire, here an *enabling technology* that earlier was invented to improve the incandescent lamp), reliable electric discharges, mercury vapor as a source of UV radiation, fluorescent phosphorous coatings to convert UV to visible light, and cheap glass tubing. In 1934, General Electric in the UK experimented in its laboratories with fluorescent lighting. Soon GE (from the USA) copied the experiments in its Nela Park laboratories. Bijker (1997) describes how the emergence of the fluorescent lamp technology was shaped by a power struggle between lamp manufacturers who competed with new products and electricity producers who feared their electricity sales would be damaged. Consumers allegedly did not play a significant role in this. Although fluorescent lamps were superior in terms of efficacy from the outset, this appeared not to be enough to oust the incumbent incandescent lamps.

Sales of fluorescence lamps ("[F]" in Figure 7.2) commenced in 1938 and the New York World Fair exhibition in 1939 used fluorescent lamps for illumination, thereby making them popular among the general public. Wartime manufacturing required large quantities of artificial lighting, boosting the further development and production of fluorescent lamps. Fluorescent lamps were developed in many types, of which the tubular lamp became the most commonly used. The shape and size of the fluorescent tube lamp or TL proved less practical than the compact bulb used for incandescent lamps, and incompatible with the compact screw base sockets that had become a widely available interface standard in lighting infrastructure. Furthermore, fluorescent lamps produced a type of light that was perceived as cold and unpleasant because they did not produce the full spectrum of light visible to the human eye and thereby display colors faded. This made them less popular, particularly in markets that first adopted electric lighting and had grown accustomed to incandescent light, which is perceived as more pleasant by the human eye. These disadvantages restricted application and therefore the growth of the fluorescent lamp market. Incandescent GLS lamps remained the lamp of choice for consumers. In public and commercial spaces, fluorescent lamps had a stronger position as their higher efficiency and longer lifespan resulted in a lower total cost of ownership (TCO).

Decades after gas discharge lighting was introduced, a new era in lighting was triggered by societal developments that demanded energy-efficient technologies. In 1972, the Club of Rome, a global think tank that deals with a variety of political issues, drew considerable public attention with its publication "The Limits to Growth" (Meadows et al., 1972). It stated that economic growth could not continue indefinitely because of the limited availability of natural resources, in particular oil. Shortly after, the first oil crisis (marked as "[4]" in Figure 7.2) was set off in 1973 by an embargo of the Organisation of Arab Petroleum Exporting Countries (OAPEC), leading to a spike in oil prices. These events encouraged major lighting manufacturers to start searching, with government backing, for more efficient forms of electric lighting (Roy, 1994). GE and Philips laboratories developed a more conveniently shaped version of the tubular fluorescent lamp using the widely adopted GLS interface standards (screw base or bayonet) that could be used as a retrofit energy-efficient alternative to incandescent lamps. In 1981, the compact fluorescent lamp (Figure 7.6 and marked as "[G]" in

Figure 7.6 The Philips SL 18 (556 gram; 165 mm) compared with the incandescent GLS (33 gram; 95 mm) and modern CFL (46 gram; 90 mm) (source: authors)

Figure 7.2) appeared on the market, marking the beginning of the awareness product phase for electric lighting. The introduction of the CFL created a product class for GLS lamps. Now products using different technologies to generate light could be used as substitutes for each other in the screw base sockets. CFLs have a significantly longer lifetime than incandescent lamps, according to the manufacturers ranging from 5,000 up to 15,000 hours, which means they need to be replaced less often. However, in practice, this promised lifespan is not achieved very often. Frequent on/off switching is a known cause of CFL failure. What is more, high temperatures building up in lamp enclosures are known causes for reducing the lifespan of the electronic components used.

In the early 1990s, CFLs had captured only about 2% of sales by volume in the domestic market and had achieved higher penetration only when they were specially promoted or subsidized (Roy, 1994). The utilities, which feared a drop in electricity sales after the introduction of fluorescent lamps in the 1930s, changed their position at the end of the twentieth century. Some utilities in the United States initiated special programs to distribute CFLs for free to customers because saving energy consumption was a more economic option to building new power stations (Roy, 1994), which were needed to meet the ever-growing consumption of electricity.

Figure 7.7 shows how, over time, demand for CFLs slowly increased in the beginning. During the first decade after market introduction, only

Figure 7.7: Development of global CFLi production volumes as share of GLS demand (figure based on data by Waide, 2010) (Source: authors)

"innovators," who constitute the first 2.5% of the market share (Rogers, 1995, and Section 10.25 of this volume) adopted the CFL. During the second half of the 1990s, the "early adopters" and subsequently other customers followed.

7.3.3 Solid-State Lighting

Light-emitting diodes (Figure 7.8 and marked as "[J]" in Figure 7.2), commonly referred to as LEDs, were introduced by the semiconductor industry ("[3]" in Figure 7.2) that emerged at the end of the 1950s. LEDs are the first branch in the technology family known as solid-state lighting (SSL). SSL technology is currently enabling a technology transition (Geels, 2002) to significantly more efficient and versatile electric lighting. The rooting period for this lighting technology started in the nineteenth century when experiments by scientists like Michael Faraday and Ferdinand Braun led to the discovery of certain material properties that we currently associate with semiconductors. Oleg Vladimirovich Losev is regarded as the first to discover that diodes used in radio receivers emitted light when current was passed through them. He filed a patent in 1927 for a "light relay" and published the first article on the matter (Losev, 1927) in a Russian journal and later in German and English journals as well.

A wide range of LED lighting types are currently entering the market, offering a combination of high efficiency, robustness, and long lifetimes (according to manufacturers, ranging from 20,000 up to 50,000 hours). Although the advertised lifetime of the LED bulb ("[J]" in Figure 7.2)

Figure 7.8 The light-emitting diode or LED (Source: Philips Lighting)

means it needs replacing 20 to 50 times less often than was common for incandescent GLS, it is still designed with a screw base so it can be used as a retrofit replacement in the same screw base sockets. The reason for this is convenience for the consumer and the large installed base of screw base sockets, not technical necessity. With the introduction of the LED bulb, the next competitor became available in the GLS product class.

Philips was the first to introduce a 60 W incandescent GLS equivalent LED bulb in 2009 (DOE, 2011a) (Figure 7.9). A few years later Philips (2012) introduced a LED bulb named HUE (Figure 7.9) of which the light color and intensity can be tuned via smartphone or tablet. Moreover, a range of software applications, controlled via smartphone or tablet, allows new functionality not available for the GLS product class or other consumer lamps before then. The development of LED lamps combined with other new types of products opened up completely new opportunities in both functionality and perception, giving them a competitive edge over other GLS types, and changing the way lighting is used. As LED lamps had only just entered the market at the time of writing of this book, further branching of the LED product family tree should be expected.

The introduction of the LED bulb and other LED-based lamps will disrupt the lighting industry for two reasons. First, the "conventional light" products (i.e., incandescent and gas discharge lamps) are replacement products requiring renewal every few thousand hours of operating time. Consequently, the conventional lighting industry produced mainly for replacement, which is why it was called a replacement industry. The very long lifespan of LED lamps means 20 to 50 times fewer replacements, thereby removing most of the market in the event that the level of light use

Figure 7.9 Left: the first 60 W bulb by Philips awarded the L-Prize in 2009 by the US Department of Energy; right: the Philips Hue introduced in 2012 (Source: Philips Lighting)

and the number of light points were to remain the same. Hence, a lighting industry producing LED lamps cannot be characterized as a replacement industry anymore. Second, the value chain for LED-based lamps is completely different to the one for conventional light. The conventional light industry is used to produce more or less all components in house from raw materials to finished products. Given the extremely high volumes produced, production mechanization is key to achieving high quality for low prices. An LED (light-emitting diode) is a semiconductor light source produced by semiconductor manufacturers. The diode is packaged with optical components used to shape the light radiation, and lead wires to connect to a printed circuit board. The lamp manufacturer acquires the LED as a component from another manufacturer (the supplier) and assembles it together with other subsystems (ballast, heat sink, optics, etc.) in a lamp. This process resembles consumer electronics manufacturing more than the process of producing incandescent lamps. Consequently, the industrial base used to mass manufacture conventional lamps does not suit the production of LED lamps. Change is therefore inevitable in this industry.

7.3.4 The Product Class of GLS Lamps

Section 7.3 has shown how three different lighting technologies evolved over time. The first of these technology families to evolve provided the incandescent lamp, patented twice in 1879. After three decades, what became referred to as the GLS incandescent lamp, emerged as the dominant design. This lamp remained the preferred type of electric light for consumers until the end of the twentieth century.

Half a century after the commercial introduction of incandescent light technology, the gas discharge light technology family experienced a break-through with the introduction of the tubular fluorescent lamp in 1938. This tubular fluorescent lamp (TL) was more efficient than GLS incandescent lamp from the onset. However, in markets where consumers first became used to light from the GLS incandescent lamp, these tubular fluorescent lamps were unable to oust the incumbent type. About six decades after the introduction of the GLS incandescent lamp, the compact fluorescent lamp (CFL) was introduced as an energy-efficient alternative.

In the beginning of the twenty-first century, the second alternative to the GLS incandescent lamp was introduced, namely the LED bulb. As the GLS incandescent lamp, the CFL, and the LED bulb all target the same type of use and apply the same dimensions, interface, and light distribution, they have together become referred to as GLS lamps. Being based on different lighting technologies but providing the same basic function, they are here defined as a *product class*.

7.4 Phase Out of GLS Incandescent Lamps

At the end of the twentieth century, evidence built up that the production of greenhouse gasses induces climate change. In 1997, the Kyoto Protocol was drafted, intended to set binding obligations for industrialized countries to reduce emissions of greenhouse gasses. Burning fossil fuels is an important contributor to the build-up of greenhouse gasses. Therefore, targets are set to reduce emissions by increasingly stringent efficiency targets for all major energy-using applications. With the CFL available as an alternative for the infamously inefficient incandescent lamp, governments around the world have deployed initiatives to phase out the GLS incandescent lamps ("[5]" in Figure 7.2) in recent years (Wikipedia, 2014). This policy has been a major support for the further rise of the CFL, which, since its introduction three decades earlier, has not been able to replace the incandescent lamps as the general service lamp of choice by consumers, despite being much more economical in use.

Although actual phase out took more than a decade to start after the Kyoto Protocol, Figure 7.7 shows a significant rise of CFL production volumes after 2000, which exceeded 25% of global GLS demand in 2007. The twenty-first century started as a new era for electric lighting in which halogen incandescent lamps, CFL bulbs, and LED bulbs will compete with each other to fill the screw base sockets left empty by the phased-out GLS incandescent lamps.

7.5 The Emergence and Development of a New Type of Product: The Compact Fluorescent Lamp

In 1976, both Philips and GE developed a compact fluorescent lamp, commonly known as CFL, based fluorescent tube lamp technology. The CFL was designed to compete with the GLS incandescent lamp, using similar dimensions and the same interface, allowing retrofit use in the same luminaires. In effect, the introduction of the CFL opened the GLS product class, providing the same basic function (general lighting) and used as a substitute (using the screw base socket).

Shortly after introduction to the market, it was assumed that CFLs would soon compete with the ubiquitous GLS incandescent lamps, first, because increasing energy consciousness resulting from the first oil crisis would lead to a growing interest in more efficient lighting sources; second, because progress in lamp technology had opened the way for more extensive miniaturization of fluorescent lamps (Bouwknegt, 1982). This proved rather optimistic as revealed by Figure 7.7. Consumers did not appear eager to convert to this new and efficient type of lighting. The CFL innovation diffused very slowly and first targeted the service sector and not the residential market (Menanteau and Lefebvre, 2000). It would take another decade of technological development to overcome a series of disadvantages before the retrofit CFL presented some sort of competition to the GLS incandescent lamp.

7.5.1 CFL Morphology

The CFL is essentially a folded-up version of the straight tube fluorescent lamp with miniature ballast mounted into the base of the lamp. This required the development of a new ballast, sufficiently compact to fit inside. It required new phosphorous coatings that could be used with the smaller tubes because it needed to withstand the "intense ultraviolet radiation occurring, for example, in lamps with a small diameter" (Bouwknegt, 1982). It also required new tube geometries providing compactness and sufficient length, including the required production equipment. Three different tube styles evolved for CFL, as depicted in Figure 7.10. GE worked on a spiral-shaped CFL (see also Figure 7.11), but abandoned the introduction because of the high investment needed to develop a production line. Philips used a simpler U-shaped tube

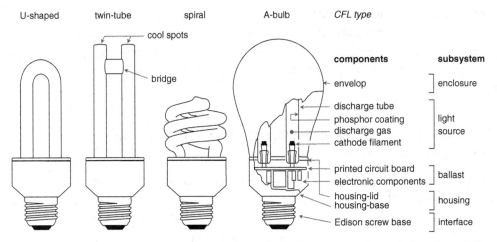

Figure 7.10 CFL system diagram. Three different CFL tube geometries evolved; if covered with a glass envelope they can be made to resemble the A-bulb incandescent GLS; the main subsystems and components are marked in this figure (Source: authors)

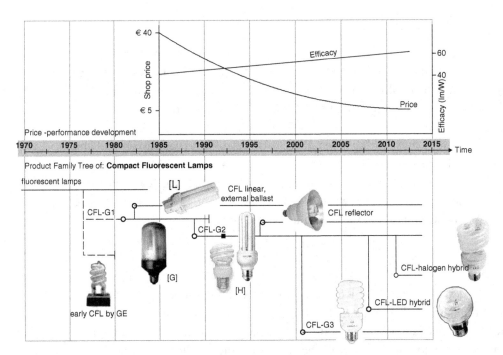

Figure 7.11 Product evolution diagram combining the CFL product family tree, showing standard and exotic types, as well as price and performance development (based on standard types only) (Source: authors)

design that was easier to produce and proceeded with production mechanization. The Philips SL18 (self-ballasted luminescent, 18 Watts) was the first CFL to be marketed in 1981 (Figure 7.6 and also marked as "[G]" in Figures 7.2 and 7.11).

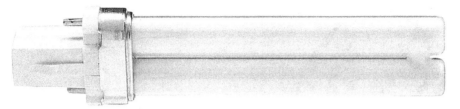

Figure 7.12 The external ballast CFL (Source: Philips Lighting)

CFLs come in variants with internal ballast, integrated between the discharge tube and screw base, often referred to as CFLi. CFLs are also sold with an external ballast (integrated into the luminaire), of which an example is shown in Figure 7.12 and in Figure 7.11 marked with "[L]." However, this section focuses on the CFLi that uses the same interface (Figure 7.13) as this version directly competed with the GLS incandescent lamp. From now on, the abbreviation CFL used in this section refers to lamps with integrated ballast. Over three decades, many variants of these three tube geometries have been developed to suit a variety of different market niches. Some include an additional envelope, which makes their contour resemble an incandescent lamp (A-bulb in Figure 7.10). Similar to the GLS incandescent lamp, the standard CFL is a non-directional lamp as the tube emits light in all directions. For directional use, there are CFL types that include a reflector (Figure 7.14) on the base side that turns them into a spotlight or floodlight. There are CFLs with a daylight sensor, which switches them on automatically between dusk

Figure 7.13 A standard CFLi with spiral tube (Source: Philips Lighting)

Figure 7.14 A CFL including reflector (Source: Philips Lighting)

and dawn. GE (2011) introduced a hybrid CFL-halogen lamp that provides instant bright light. OSRAM (2008) introduced the DULED hybrid CFL-LED lamp that has two modes: a first mode for normal use of the CFL source, and a second low-intensity light, using the LED source as an orientation aid in the dark (Consumentengids, 2012). Figure 7.11 contains a detailed product family tree of CFLs that shows many of the aforementioned CFL types.

7.5.2 Three Generations

The first-generation CFLs (CFL-G1) weighed 556 grams, included a prismatic glass cover to refract the light, and were bulky compared to incandescent lamps. This made the CFL-G1 incompatible with many situations in which conventional incandescent lamps were used. As a new type of product, the CFL-G1 started in the performance phase. The CFL-G1 used a magnetic ballast, did not produce a pleasant light color, took three minutes to warm up, produced a 50 Hz flicker, and could not be used with dimmers. Last but not least, the price of the CFL-G1 was factors higher than the price of the cheap incandescent lamps it competed with.

The ongoing miniaturization of electronic components produced enabling technologies that fueled a technology cycle in the subsystem ballast. At the end of the 1980s, the electronic ballast was introduced for CFLs, which was much smaller than the previous magnetic version. The second-generation CFLs (CFL-G2 marked as "[H]" in Figure 7.2 and Figure 7.11) marks the beginning

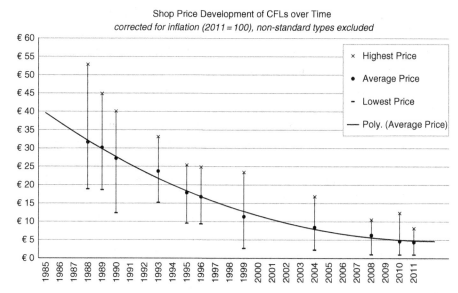

Figure 7.15 CFL shop price development over time in the Netherlands as published by Consumentenbond. Nonstandard types have been excluded to make the comparison as uniform as possible (*Consumentengids*, 1988, 1989, 1990a, 1993a, 1995, 1996, 1999, 2004, 2008, 2010c, 2011). Prices have been corrected for inflation with 2011 as the reference year using Consumer Price Index figures published by Statistics Netherlands (Source: authors)

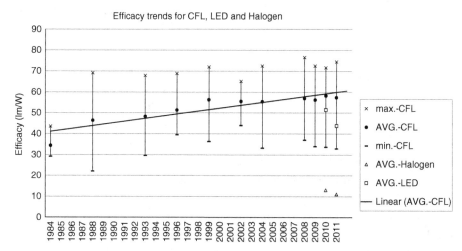

Figure 7.16 CFL efficacy development over time in which the last two years include the GLS halogen incandescent lamp and the GLS LED bulb (*Consumentengids*, 1984a, 1988, 1993a; 1995, 1999, 2004, 2008, 2009, 2010c, 2011) (Source: authors)

of the optimization phase. The CFL-G2 became substantially more compact and lighter, had none of the 50 Hz flickering, and was almost 10% more efficient. New mixes of components for phosphorous coating meant more and softer light colors could be offered. Consumers reacted positively to these technical improvements. Production volumes slowly increased from 1990 onward (see also Figure 7.7). Increased competition in the manufacturing base and cheaper electronic designs drove the cost price steadily down, thereby making the CFL suitable for larger markets. The CFL-G1 disappeared from the market as it could not match the CFL-G2 in price, performance, and compactness.

The evolving semiconductor industry provided cheap integrated circuits (ICs), an enabling technology that prompted the next technology cycle in the subsystem ballast. Using ICs meant the CFL could be operated more efficiently and it also worked with conventional dimmers commonly used for GLS incandescent lamps (NXP, 2009). This CFL is more efficient (up to more than 70 lm/W) and has a longer life (Waide, 2010). The third-generation (CFL-G3), also referred to as the Super CFL, is currently gaining ground.

It can be argued that the CFL entered the itemization phase in the mid-1990s. Many different companies around the world manufactured CFLs. Cheap manufacturers in low-wage countries like China and also in Eastern Europe and the availability of cheap electronic components caused prices to fall to below €10 (Figure 7.15). CFL prices steadily decreased and production capacity increased from 2000 onward, thereby offering policymakers the opportunity to phase out the GLS incandescent light bulb, as an alternative was readily available in the guise of the CFL. The CFL is now in the segmentation phase. The CFL became available in similar variants as displayed in Figure 7.5 for the GLS incandescent lamp.

7.5.3 CFL Price Performance Development

Many studies have investigated the development of the CFL market. Several studies also investigated CFL prices as an element of the barriers to adoption (Sandahl et al., 2006) or possible future price development (Iwafune, 2000). In this section, one resource is used, namely the *Consumentengids*, a publication of the Dutch consumer organization Consumentenbond, to analyze how price and efficacy have developed over nearly three decades. The comparative tests provide an independent and detailed overview of the technical performance of products and sales prices over time. These data were used to reconstruct the development of the average shop price and efficacy of CFLs over time. The prices analyzed are referred to as "shop prices" as they are common prices paid by consumers without the cost advantages of incentives from manufacturers (to gain market share), utilities or governments (to stimulate energy conservation). Only shop prices for standard CFL lamps with integrated ballast, which are also referred to as CFLi, have been used in this study (both magnetic and electronic). As only comparative tests from the Dutch consumer guide have been used, the products reviewed reflect CFL evolution in the Netherlands.

However, given that the Netherlands has been a lead market in CFL sales per capita (Menanteau and Lefebvre, 2000) and is the home market of Philips (a leading CFL manufacturer), and given that the same CFL technology is used throughout the world, with many lamps sold in the Netherlands being produced in different countries by many different manufacturers, the expectation is that the historical development analyzed is valid for most geographies.

Figure 7.15 shows the development of shop prices from an average of just over €30 in 1988 to below €5 in 2011. The prices have been corrected for inflation, using 2011 as the reference year. According to the International Energy Agency (IEA), the overcapacity that remained after the incandescent GLS replacement peak is expected to erode prices even further (Waide, 2010). The luminous efficacy of lamps is expressed in lumens per Watt (lm/W) and is used to define how much electric energy is converted into visible light. Figure 7.16 shows how the average CFL efficacy improved from below 40 to about 60 lm/W in 2010.

7.6 Competition among GLS Lamps

Christensen (1997, and Section 10.10 of this volume) noted that technology platforms with initially inferior price-performance ratios can develop over time and overtake the market shares of previously dominant types. For GLS lamps, this picture proved more complex. CFLs have quickly outperformed GLS incandescent lamps from the point of view of economics (Lefèvre, T'Serclaes, and Waide, 2006). However, they have struggled to gain a market share. It appears that technological properties of the fluorescent lighting technology were the factor that constrained consumer perception and so withheld CFL from ousting the incandescent lamp on economic merits. Moreover, the final breakthrough may be attributed to legislation, rather than superior economic performance. Three decades after the introduction of the CFL, the LED bulb was introduced as a new contender in the GLS product class. Although LED already existed as a technology before the CFL was introduced, it had not yet been applied to general illumination. It took many technology cycles in the LED industry until white light could be provided, power became sufficiently high, and prices low enough to allow useful application in the GLS product class. LED bulbs have developed since around the year 2000 with the first 100 W incandescent equivalent introduced to the market in the United States in 2011 (Switch Lighting, 2011).

LED bulbs are still expensive compared to CFLs, but the technology is evolving rapidly. In just a few years *Consumentengids* (2010a 2013a 2013b) changed its reflections from "waiting" to "encouraging." Prices for LED bulbs are going down because LED elements are becoming cheaper, as dictated by Haitz's law (Haitz et al., 1999). In addition, LED efficacy development is expected to continue for some time and eventually surpass that of CFL lamps by a factor of three (DOE, 2011b; Haitz and Tsao, 2011). Economic performance is advertised as an important argument for the adoption of energy-efficient lighting technologies. Institutional buyers are known to use rational total cost of ownership (TCO) comparisons. However, consumers behave less rationally. What is more, technical differences between available GLS lamp alternatives (halogen incandescent, CFL and LED bulb) mean that consumers at large are unable to calculate the economic benefits of new efficient lighting technologies. Besides that, differences in the definition of lifetime and testing protocols for GLS lamps make it difficult, at the very least, to make meaningful economic comparisons, even for institutional buyers.

It is clear that LED lamps provide functionality not offered by either incandescent or gas discharge lamps. Therefore, it can be expected that competition between incumbent light sources and LED will go beyond traditional competitive properties such as purchase price, lifespan, efficacy, and color perception. The evolution of lighting technology has entered a new era. Taking account of the fact that LED for general lighting purposes is only a recent phenomenon, it is clear that the evolution of electric lighting will not stop at the developments spanning more than two centuries described in this section. Further development of LED lighting, software applications used to control light sources, and expected introduction of new types of light sources, for example based on so-called OLED technology, will change the way we use electric lighting. Over time it might mean the end of the GLS product class, and most likely the introduction of new ones.

7.7 Conclusion

Section 7.2 elaborated on how a new type of product – the general lighting solution commonly referred to as the GLS incandescent lamp – came about and developed through time into a family of more advanced versions. Subsequently, two more types of product evolved with the same basic function and addressing similar types of use. Together these three products constitute what is defined here as the GLS product class. Because each of these lamps uses a different physical principle to generate light, they belong to different technology families. The development history of three different GLS lamps has been mapped in a product evolution diagram using three separate product family trees, and one mutual ecosystem.

The case study of GLS lamps clearly shows that major inventions, like the incandescent lamp, the CFL, and the LED bulb, do not just occur as stand-alone events, nor are they the work of a single genius. Major technological developments build on prior knowledge accumulation that provides a foundation built by many individuals and collectives over the course of many decades.

It is on this foundation that new types of products can emerge. The three examples reviewed in this section show that each required that same technological foundation, here referred to as the roots, before these new types of products could emerge. These root periods, which commonly require decades of experimenting with technologies, enable the "breakthrough innovations" that are instrumental in the conception of new types of products. Once a new type of product emerges, technology cycles characterize further development of the product and can be described as an evolutionary process in terms of *variation* (changes to product characteristics), *selection* (survival of best-adapted product variants), and *retention* (reproduction of product characteristics), at both the system (or product) and subsystem levels (Anderson and Tushman, 1990; Tushman and Murmann, 1998; Murmann and Frenken, 2006). Development into new types of products first focuses on the "what," addressing functionality, and later on the "how," addressing cost (Abernathy and Utterback, 1975; Eger, 2007a). For the case of the GLS incandescent lamp technology cycles in the subsystems of light source, enclosure and interface have been described here. The case of the CFL shows similar technology cycles in the subsystems of light source and ballast. The price and the performance development for the CFL have been visualized over time. Although it is tempting to view the battle between the different GLS products in price-performance ratios only, this case study shows that consumers greatly value other properties, like the extent to which lamps can reveal colors of illuminated objects, the start-up time, and the ability to be dimmed. It also transpired that differences in lifetime and testing protocols make it difficult to make meaningful economic comparisons, even for institutional buyers.

Furthermore, literature shows that in the cases of the incandescent lamp and CFL described here, the "breakthrough innovations" that led to the first commercially available products occurred not once but at least twice, more or less simultaneously on different continents and in like minds. The rise of the GLS incandescent lamp is inextricably linked to electrification, a large technological transition that Geels (2002) has described as an evolutionary reconfiguration process that unfolds on multiple levels. As described by Bijker (1997), GLS incandescent lamps became a main consumer of electric energy use that needed to be generated by companies referred to as the utilities. It was their fear of a reduction in electricity consumption that made the utilities influence the development of intrinsically more efficient gas discharge lighting technology toward higher illumination levels instead of higher efficiency in the 1930s. Four decades later, the perception of the availability of natural resources had changed drastically. With the need for energy-efficient products now apparent, the CFL was developed as a retrofit alternative to the GLS incandescent lamp. Although it was first assumed that soon after introduction the CFL would compete with the GLS incandescent lamp, it transpired that consumers still preferred the incumbent two decades later. It was only after climate change mitigation efforts discussed in the Kyoto Protocol that legislation was introduced that phased out the use of the GLS incandescent lamps. Selective pressures in the evolution of product are thus not only exerted by consumers and competing manufacturers; legislation can also play a decisive role.

The case of the CFL illustrates that the process of evolution in products cannot be understood if described in technology terms only. The ecosystem that constitutes contextual factors like societal change, economic development, and legislation has been shown to be part and parcel of the evolution of the CFL.

One can discuss to what extent the CFL is a successful product, or not. The fact that the CFL could not oust the GLS incandescent lamp based on consumer preference could be used as an argument to advocate it as a product that is at least partially unsuccessful or unpopular. However, the mere fact that billions of CFL lamps have been produced so far, and the role it has played in the transition toward energy-efficient lighting, are arguments for it being a successful product. Without having to answer the question, it can be remarked that investigating both successful and less successful cases probably contributes to the understanding of *how new types of products come about and develop through time into families of more advanced versions*. Although the CFL case was not chosen to explore an unsuccessful product, in retrospect it can be pointed out that it does make an interesting case to study because of its debatable level of success. This contrasts with cases that undoubtedly are regarded as successful (e.g., the GLS incandescent lamp) or those commonly regarded as failures (e.g., the unsuccessful development of a guided-transportation system in Paris as described by Latour (1993)).

8 Retrospective Case Study of the Child Restraint System

8.1 Introduction

This chapter analyzes the development history of child restraint systems (CRSs), also known as child car seats, as a retrospective case study. The CRS is a nested product that is used in another type of product: the car. It evolved from a product intended to restrain movement toward one intended to enhance child safety. The evolution of CRSs is inextricably linked to the evolution of cars and, in particular, car safety systems and safety perception and expectations. The changing perception of safety in cars is reflected in the changing function of CRSs, as will become clear in this chapter. The story of the evolution of CRSs is summarized in a product evolution diagram, from a child restraint seat into a family of advanced safety seats tailored to different segments and distinguished by age, weight, or length groups, as well as a variety of factors from the ecosystem that influenced its evolution.

8.2 Availability of Cars and a Niche for the CRS to Emerge

The presence of cars was a prerequisite for CRSs to emerge as a new type of product. The first cars with an internal combustion engine appeared in 1807. For about a century, cars still looked like horse carriages, but with an engine and no horse.[1] These predecessors of today's cars were highly exclusive products. The average young family could not afford them. There was little traffic, the average speed was low, and in-car safety was not a major concern. Consequently, there was no need for a product that provided safety to children traveling in cars. It took 100 years before large-scale production of cars started. The Olds Motor Vehicle Company opened the first production

---

[1] This is also referred to as the horseless carriage syndrome, an expression used to describe how new types of products first strongly resemble their predecessors. Time is needed for designs to evolve.

Figure 8.1 Development of car ownership in the United States and Western Europe (Sources: Davis, Diegel, and Boundy, 2003; Staal, 2003) (Source: authors)

line in 1902, soon followed by others, of which Henry Ford with the Ford Model T (T-Ford), which came onto the market in 1908, is the most famous. Figure 8.1 shows the development of car ownership in the United States and Western Europe.[2] The United States was the first market where large-scale car ownership developed, following the introduction of the T-Ford. In the 1930s, the level of car ownership in the United States rose to more than 200 vehicles per 1,000 people.

The mass production of cars meant that they became more affordable, and the number of cars on the road therefore increased, along with the problems we associate with cars today, such as congestion and accidents. Increasing car ownership dramatically increased our mobility and, with that, changed the way we organize urban and rural areas. Cars slowly became a standard feature of everyday life and this created a niche[3] for CRSs to emerge.

In Western Europe, it took four more decades to reach a similar level of car ownership as seen in the United States of the 1930s (Staal, 2003). This explains why the CRS models first appeared in the United States and not in Europe.

[2] The graph of car ownership development in Western Europe is based on averages of figures of car ownership development in Germany, France, Italy, the UK, and the Netherlands. The Western European countries show different car ownership development rates through time. However, compared to developments in the United States, all Western European countries show quite similar car ownership development rates.

[3] Geels (2002) also uses the term "niche" as a designation for the micro level on which radical innovations occur that eventually may lead to technological transitions that ultimately manifest on the macro level.

8.3 How the CRS Came About

8.3.1 The Root Period of CRSs

Today, parents are legally required to use child restraint systems (CRSs) if they carry small children in their car. This has not always been the case. The first known example of a product used for restraining small children in cars dates back to 1898 (Smith, 2008). According to Smith, "the device was little more than a drawstring bag that would attach to the actual car seat." The device did not look like the products that we know today. It was not intended to prevent injuries during accidents, but to restrain children and so keep them from falling or getting up from their seats when the car was moving. The first CRS products resembled existing child seats and rockers, commonly used to comfort babies at that time.

In the 1920s, car ownership rose to more than 100 vehicles per 1,000 people in the United States, and sources (Smith, 2008) refer to the production of CRSs. Patent files show that various inventors came up with ideas for CRSs. In 1928, a child seat was invented by B. Coleman Silver (Figure 8.2) that looked similar to the free-hanging CRSs still common in the second half of the 1960s and early 1970s. These products were intended to keep children from moving around. Child safety was not the main concern. Nevertheless, the product was brought onto the market by suppliers like the Bunny Bear Company, which started to manufacture CRSs in 1933. In the 1930s, car safety belts became more prevalent. Slowly but surely, safety in cars started to become an issue, but not yet as far as child passengers were concerned.

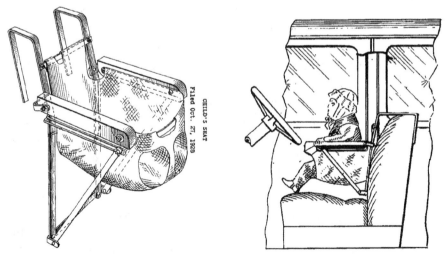

Figure 8.2 Child's seat invented by B. Coleman Silver in 1928 (Source: US Patent Office)

8.3.2 Introduction of Car Safety Features Influenced Child-Passenger Safety Expectations

The first safety belt patents date back to the nineteenth century. It was Swedish inventor Nils Bohlin who, in 1959, came up with the modern three-point seat belt that is now a standard safety device in most cars. Volvo introduced the lap-and-shoulder or three-point belt in 1959. As Volvo wanted to encourage the saving of lives, the company did support the idea of it becoming standard safety equipment for adults in the 1960s and therefore decided not to patent this belt (Kelley and Littman, 2005). Crash tests proved that these belts saved lives. However, they were met with resistance. Passive safety features such as three-point belts, self-applying belts, front- and side-impact airbags, plus active safety such as the anti-lock braking system (ABS) and electronic stability control (ESC) increased the level of protection for adults. These types of safety equipment became available from 1966 to 1995 (see also Figure 8.16). The crash safety performance of new cars was tested by the European New Car Assessment Programme (Euro NCAP) and was made transparent to consumers via a star rating system. Although the aforementioned developments cannot clearly be categorized as enabling technologies, these measures increased the safety consciousness and expectations of consumers and so paved the way for safety expectations for CRSs.

8.3.3 The First Safety-Focused Child Restraint Seats Appear in the 1960s

The first CRSs that were truly focused on safety were developed in the early 1960s. In 1962, an English couple named Jean Helen and Frederick John Ames invented a padded seat that was strapped against the rear passenger seat (Figure 8.3). The child was restrained by a five-point-belt harness that slipped over the head and shoulders and fastened between the legs. The CRS itself was anchored to the car seat with belts. According to the description in the patent, the object of the invention was "to provide a child's safety seat for vehicles which affords protection for the child comparable to that provided for adults by safety belts and harnesses" (Ames and Ames, 1964). With this definition, the basic function shifted from "restraining" toward "providing safety." The first safety-focused CRS was not a legislation-driven product. At that time, relevant legislation was simply not available. The inventors saw an opportunity to improve the safety of children in cars, which was not provided by the belts designed for adults or the CRSs available thus far. In the same decade, Bertil Aldman, a Swedish professor in biomechanics, was also working on child safety and became inspired by seats used in the Gemini space program that were shaped to distribute G forces evenly across astronauts' backs. Aldman first

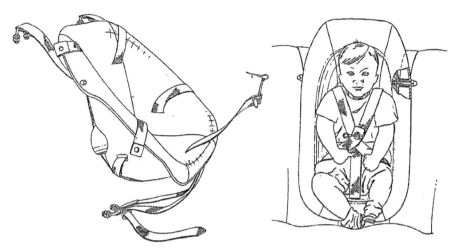

Figure 8.3 The Ames' "children's safety seat," patent application date: 22 November 1961 (Source: UK Patent Office)

Figure 8.4 Prototype of the first rearward-facing CRS tested in 1964 (Source: Volvo, 2014)

tested a prototype of a rear-facing CRS in 1964 (Figure 8.4). In 1972, the first rearward-facing CRS was launched in Sweden (Volvo, 2014).

In the United States, the Ford Motor Company introduced the Tot Guard in 1968 (Figure 8.5). *Consumer Reports* reviewed this product in 1972 as ACCEPTABLE-fair-to-good and the General Motors Infant Carrier (of which no pictures are available) as ACCEPTABLE-good.

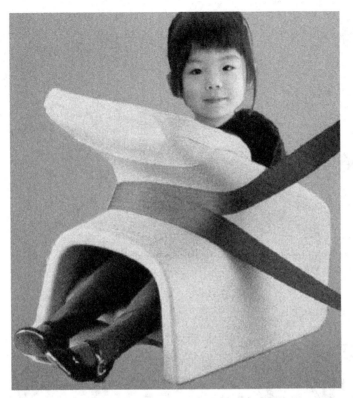

Figure 8.5 The Tot Guard introduced by the Ford Motor Company in 1968 (Source: authors, permission granted by Ford)

8.3.4 Unsafe CRSs Remain on the Market

In 1963, the German manufacturer Storchenmühle launched its first "Niki" CRS (Figure 8.6) onto the market. The product architecture was still the same as that of Coleman Silver's CRS from more than three decades earlier. The CRS was attached to the car seat by means of a hook. Obviously, this CRS would not remain in place in the event of a collision, and consequently the child passenger would be seriously hurt in the event of a crash. This CRS type was tested and found to be very unsafe during collisions in the 1970 issues of the Dutch consumer guide (*Consumentengids*, 1970). All nine CRS "hook over bench backrest" types were rated as "serious injury foreseeable" in the event of a slight collision. For that reason, the 1974 issue did not include this type in the test (*Consumentengids*, 1974). Nevertheless, it was still available on the market at the time. A second model marketed by Storchenmühle was a child restraint that was clamped between the backrest and the (rear passenger) seat (Figure 8.7). Similarly to the other Storchenmühle child seat, the child was not safely attached to the seat, nor was the seat securely attached to the car. Obviously it would not remain in place during a serious collision. Five CRSs

Figure 8.6 Storchenmühle CRS type "Niki" introduced in 1963 (Source: Dorel, 2005)

Figure 8.7 The Storchenmühle CRS "Jet SM 12," 1967 clamped between the backrest and seat (Source: Dorel, 2005 and *Consumentengids*, 1970)

"clamped between backrest and seat" types were rated as "injury foreseeable" in the event of a slight collision. *Consumentengids* featured this seat in tests in 1970 and again in 1974, when it was described as not providing sufficient protection. Finally, the guide advised against the use of this CRS type, describing it as unsafe due to the lack of anchoring to the car in the 1977 issue (*Consumentengids*, 1977). The perception of the product (and its basic function) began to change and the guide started to advise against unsafe types. In the United States, the test review by *Consumer Reports* rated 12 out of 15 CRS tested as not acceptable. Typically for the changing perception the article opened with the following line: "A restraint system for a child riding in an auto should not merely confine him so he cannot distract the driver; it should also protect the child in a crash, much as seat belts protect adults" (*Consumer Reports*, 1972, 485). Clearly the know-what (to make) regarding CRS changed as a result of a changing ecosystem. Consumer associations recognized early in the 1970s that, to be safe, a CRS needs to be anchored to the car. Such anchoring ensures that the CRS, and with it the child, remains in position during a collision and, furthermore, it benefits from the energy absorption system of the car. An interesting concept with anchoring was the CRS type of the Rimo brand (Figure 8.8). It consists of a belt harness connected to the car supported by an inflatable seat. In the 1970 issue of *Consumentengids*, this is the only CRS type for children aged up to two years (out of 17 tested) for which the test report mentioned that, if a child was belted into its seat, no injury would be expected during a collision (*Consumentengids*, 1970). Curiously, the product disappeared from the test a few years later and, as is assumed here, from the market as well. The 1970 test of CRS in *Consumentengids* describes 17 different CRS types for children aged up to two years and five CRS types for children between two and six years by a total of 17 brands. In 1977, this increased to 18 brands and 29 different types. The number of CRSs available on the Dutch market increased.

8.3.5 Consumer Guides Start Influencing Legislation

The increasing use of cars, the related increase in accidents, and the presence of CRSs that actually provided some safety created a climate in which legislation started to develop from the early 1970s onward. In the United States, articles in consumer guides also influenced CRS development. A 1972 issue of *Consumer Reports*, the American consumer guide published by the Consumers Union, states that most car CRSs that passed the FMVSS 213 legislation (which was the federal standard for CRSs enforced in the United States at that time) could not withstand crash tests (*Consumer Reports*, 1972). In 1975, this led to a proposal to revise the regulation issued in 1971. With the United States having a history as a single constitutional entity dating back to the end of the

Figure 8.8 Rimo belted harness with inflatable support (Source: *Consumentengids*, 1970)

eighteenth century and Europe still struggling to form one, it will come as no surprise that in car child safety, legislation was also harmonized in the United States earlier than in Europe. It would take until 1981 for ECE-44–01, the first European CRS legislation, to be introduced. Since then legislation, both from the European Union (EU) and the United States, has played a major role in requirements imposed on the design and use of CRSs.

The development of CRS legislation and CRS products is closely inter-twined. CRS legislation did not result in the invention of the first safety-focused CRS, but was developed after the products had appeared on the market. However, the continuous development of CRS legislation in both the United States and the EU set the scene for increasing legal requirements imposed on CRSs. Along with the development of CRSs as a product family, an increasing body of knowledge on (mis)use developed. Child passenger safety advocacy groups, consumer associations, and standardization programs

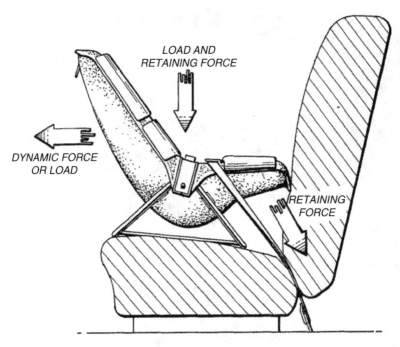

Figure 8.9 Baby carrier and car seat patent 4,231,612 filed in September 1978 by Paul K. Meeker (Source: US Patent Office); an earlier version was filed in 1977

have encouraged governments to continue renewing safety legislation. Four decades later, the resulting level sets a threshold for minimal safety function- ality for CRSs well above what was achieved by the best-performing CRSs in the early 1970s. CRS legislation coevolved with the CRS products.

8.3.6 Legislation Starts to Influence CRS Design

The legislative changes in the United States in 1975 led to heavy and therefore difficult-to-handle CRSs, and this prompted designer Paul K. Meeker to develop an easier-to-handle CRS (Figure 8.9). The resulting CRS was sold by Questor Corporation as the Infanseat 440 or the Dyn-O-Mite. The reclining seat could be used for different activities like sleeping, feeding, playing, and as a car seat. It was a rearward-facing CRS using the belt to secure it to the car seat. In 1977, Sjef van der Linden, a Dutch entrepreneur in baby articles, saw the Dyn-O-Mite in Macy's store in Manhattan while on a business trip to the United States (Dorel, 2005). Recognizing the potential of this product to fill the void in the European market, he started importing the CRS and selling the product in Europe. The first version was supplied by an Italian concession holder, Babymex Italiana. However, this product failed in crash tests at the Dutch contract research

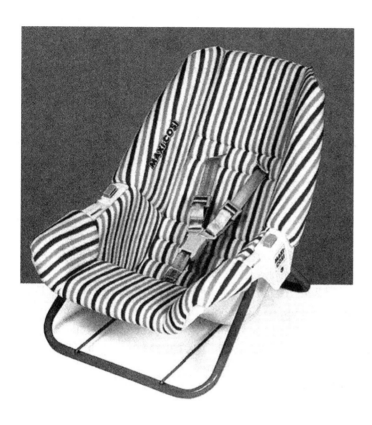

Figure 8.10 The Dyn-O-Mite was imported into Europe and sold as the first Maxi-Cosi. (Source: Dorel, 2005)

institute TNO. It turned out to be made from a different and more brittle type of plastic, which was permissible in Italy, where it was not used as a car seat. The plastic type was changed and the design improved with the help of a Swedish test institute and a Dutch designer. From 1985 onward, the product was sold in Europe under the name Maxi-Cosi (Figure 8.10). This signaled the start of the currently dominant design for CRSs in the Netherlands, targeting the baby segment, the youngest age group.

In a 1983 issue, the Dutch consumer guide observed that there was still no proper CRS for the smallest and youngest children (*Consumentengids*, 1983). The carrycot used for babies was described as a product that did not properly fulfill its safety function. In the event of collisions, the belt might cut through the thin sides of the carrycot. Besides this, any child who was not belted inside the carrycot would be slung so hard through the device that he or she would sustain injuries. In 1987, Consumentenbond (*Consumentengids*, 1987) published the first review that included the Maxi-Cosi and mentioned that CRSs were finally starting to become available that would really qualify as safety seats for babies. This took a quarter century from the invention of the first safety-focused CRS.

8.3.7 Types Come and Go

In the 1980s, *Consumentengids* continued to question the functionality of various CRS types. One issue (*Consumentengids*, 1983) described the belt harness as an outdated restraint type. In the event of collisions, children aged six years and older would slide into the lap part of the harness and might slip under it ("submarine"). This could cause severe damage to the liver, kidneys, and spleen of the child passenger. The arrival of a new, safer CRS type for children, the booster cushion, was welcomed as an improvement in child safety. This booster cushion is a seat type without a backrest that elevates the child in such a way that it can use the three-point belt. It is aimed at children in the 3–10 age group. The belt harness with its apparent unfavorable position in the competitive landscape disappeared from subsequent reviews in the *Consumentengids*. Reports like these helped increase consumer awareness of what makes a safe CRS and what does not. Consequently, they influenced sales and resulted in the ousting of this belt harness CRS type.

8.3.8 Perception of CRS Changes and Dominant Designs Emerge

Historic sources such as advertising by manufacturers and articles in consumer guides reflect changes through time of the perception of CRSs and how they should be used. Increasing safety requirements and the changing categorization are examples of this. The introduction of CRS categories marks the introduction of new dominant designs on the product (or system) level. As each category caters to a different segment in the market, it is a clear marker this product enters the segmentation phase. In the 1970s, *Consumentengids* only distinguished between child seats and child belts. The seats were for children up to three years old. Children aged between three and six were supposed to wear belt-type restraints. In the 1980s, the *Consumentengids* tests started to provide an overview of the different products, categorized into age groups. Following changes in legislation, the 1983 article on CRSs distinguished between the following age and product groups: up to nine months (cradles), about nine months to five years (seats), about three to 10 years (booster cushions), and finally about four to 12 years (the harness belts). The 1984 article on CRSs adds weight classes to these age groups (*Consumentengids*, 1984b). The article on CRSs published in the 1990 issue of *Consumentengids* mentions, for the first time, an age group system aligned with the ECE legislation (*Consumentengids*, 1990b). It uses four

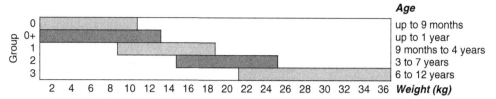

Figure 8.11 Overlapping age and weight groups (free after source: *Consumentengids*, 1993b) (Source: authors)

groups (0/0+, 1, 2, 3) with progressive weight groups and corresponding age classes (see also Figure 8.11). This weight and age classification system has been used for four decades. The same review states that the manufacturers of CRSs were trying to develop seats that could be used for longer and cover various continuous age groups. This approach did initially not prove very successful. Within a few years, the situation improved. Three years later, the guide (*Consumentengids*, 1993b) was more positive and stated that several manufacturers sold CRSs covering age groups 2 to 3 that functioned fairly well, although those targeted at covering age groups 1 to 3 still performed rather poorly.

As reflected previously, through time more names are being used for the family of CRS products, reflecting a changed perception of the basic function of the product (child car seat, child safety seat) as well as names becoming connected to segmentation, aimed at different age groups (cradle, infant safety seat, booster seat). Nevertheless, "child restraint systems" remains the designation for this family of products in the English language. This is a remnant of the fact that the origin of the product family is inextricably connected to the fact that car ownership first rose substantially in the United States, where the first use of the product was limited to restraining the movement of children in cars. In other languages such as German (*Kinderautositze, Autokindersitze*) or Dutch (*kinderzitje*), car ownership rose four decades later at a time when car safety technology also became available. Consequently, these languages do not use a direct translation of the default English-language designation for this product family (child restraint system). Instead they use versions semantically closer to the newer names that had also been introduced in the English language.

8.3.9 Coincidence Influences CRS Legislation

In 1994, three-year-old Dana Hutchinson from the United States was killed after being struck by an airbag deployed while she rode in a rearward-facing CRS in the passenger seat (Colella, 2010). During the investigation into why the CRS had not prevented fatal injuries, her relatives found out that the vehicle seating position and the CRS that was secured in it were incompatible. The case received huge attention in the United States, and resulted in the formation of a child-passenger safety advocacy group called the Drivers Appeal for National Awareness (DANA) Foundation by Joseph Colella (an uncle of Dana) and relatives. The goal of this nonprofit organization is to raise public awareness of incompatibilities and misuse, and to collaborate with manufacturers and regulators on simplifying the correct use of child restraints. DANA successfully advocated legislation changes, which made warning labels on CRSs and airbag cut-off switches for cars obligatory in the United States.

8.3.10 Focus Shifts to Details

In general, CRSs still provide less protection than was possible and desired in the early 1990s. One of the reasons is that they do not go together well with modern cars and standard seat belts. Cars sold from 1990 onward need to have safety belts available for the back seats. Once three-point belts had become common for rear seats, CRSs needed to adapt to this situation. Unfortunately, Dutch legislation of the early 1990s still allowed "unsafe transportation" of children. The use of a CRS was only obligatory if available. Children aged three to 12 could use belts if present, no matter whether those were lap belts or three-point belts and, if no belts were available at all, they were still allowed to travel on the back seat (*Consumentengids*, 1993b). In 1993, the Safe Fit belt adapter was sold as a CRS, which competed with booster seats (Figure 8.12). According to Consumentenbond (*Consumentengids*, 1993b), this belt adapter should never have received ECE-44 approval as it is unsafe. Consumentenbond requested clarification from the minister of traffic and road safety with regard to the assessment of approval for this particular belt adapter, and it subsequently disappeared from the market.

Once the dominant designs for CRSs started appearing in the 1980s, and car safety features improved, the focus of articles in *Consumentengids* shifted in the 1990s from descriptions of new and improved CRS types (basic function; providing safety) to an emphasis on comfort and proper use (supportive functions; providing comfort and ease of use). Features such as removable lining were added to make CRSs easier to clean. As studies show that more than half the CRSs are not installed correctly, the Dutch consumer guide underlined the need for proper manuals (*Consumentengids*, 1993b). Apparently, the designs were still not sufficiently self-explanatory, and written instructions therefore were still required. Additional CRS safety and comfort features were introduced after 2000. One example is Isofix, which makes it easier to install the CRS (see also the section on standardization). Maxi-Cosi started to market a

Figure 8.12 The safe fit belt adapter designated unsafe by Consumentenbond (Source: *Consumentengids*, 1993)

product called the FamilyFix (the base in Figure 8.15), which is connected to the car via Isofix connectors (Figure 8.13). Parents can simply snap in a Maxi-Cosi on top of the FamilyFix. The product uses electronics to indicate with a visual and auditory signal whether the CRS is connected correctly to the base. This ensures properly installed seats and therefore increases safety.

More and more manufacturers started adding so-called side wings (the side protection in Figure 8.15) to CRSs that helped protect children more effectively against injuries caused by the impact of a side collision. Legislation did not (yet) require these provisions, but consumer guides did assign a better score to products that had them. Helleke Hendriks, one of the researchers at Consumentenbond, claims that this was down to Consumentenbond's reviews. "Our demanding tests are thus market guiding, as legislation does not require these side wings" (*Consumentengids*, 2010b). Several brands stopped producing booster cushions without backrests, as these do not protect children sufficiently from injuries caused by side impacts. The extent to which this change can be attributed to the success of the consumer association(s) remains unclear.

Figure 8.13 The Maxi-Cosi Pebble above a Maxi-Cosi FamilyFix base with light and sound controls for correct installation and semi-universal Isofix (Source: Dorel, 2012)

8.3.11 Standardization and Safety Program Organizations

Euro NCAP[4] has carried out child occupant safety assessments since its inception to ensure that manufacturers take responsibility for children traveling in vehicles produced by them. In November 2003, Euro NCAP introduced a child occupant protection rating to make it easier for consumers to understand the outcome of these tests. In these assessments, Euro NCAP used dummies sized as 18-month- and three-year-old children in the frontal- and side-impact tests. Apart from studying the results of the impact tests, Euro NCAP assessed the clarity of instructions for seat installation in the vehicle. In 1990, the International Organization for Standardization (ISO) launched the Isofix standard in an attempt to provide a standard interface for fixing car seats into different makes of car. The system consists of a male connector on the

---

[4] The European New Car Assessment Programme (Euro NCAP) is a European car safety performance assessment program. Euro NCAP has created the five-star safety rating system to help consumers compare vehicles more easily on safety performance. Vehicle tests are designed and carried out by Euro NCAP, providing independent safety comparison of new vehicles.

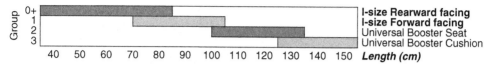

Figure 8.14 I-size classification based on length (Source: authors)

CRS and a female connector in the car seat (see also Figure 8.15). The US equivalent of this system is called Lower Anchors and Tethers for Children (LATCH). Obviously, to be of any use, this system needs to be adapted by manufacturers of cars and those of CRSs. Consequently, the proliferation of this feature in CRSs (the fitness in evolutionary language) is dependent on the extent to which both car and CRS manufacturers implement these connectors throughout their products. It took about a decade of discussions with the automotive industry before all involved agreed to the technical specifications. The current version of the standard was published in 1999. Some CRS manufacturers had started selling Isofix-compliant baby car seats in the EU from around 2000. The EU regulations required cars from 2009 to be fitted with Isofix anchorage points. As cars in EU countries until the 2004 expansion were, on average, 8.5 years old (ACEA, 2009), this meant, with the average age remaining constant, that it would take slightly less than a decade, or until 2018, before half the cars on the road were compulsorily equipped with Isofix. This sets the scene for the market adoption rate of Isofix in CRSs sold to consumers in the EU. And it shows that diffusion of new interface standards depends on changes in two types of products, each with very different life cycles.

The phasing in of LATCH in the United States was completed in 2002. Assuming that the average age and life expectancy of cars in the United States are similar to those in the EU, this means that 8.5 years later (at the beginning of 2011), LATCH would be compulsorily installed in the majority of cars on US roads. It could therefore be expected that LATCH would become the default installation method about seven years before Isofix reaches the same level in the EU. The European Association for the Co-ordination of Consumer Representation in Standardisation (ANEC), a European organization involved in standardization of consumer products, influenced legislation and standardization of CRSs. Since 2006, the organization (ANEC, 2006) has advocated an increase in the age up to which children are seated backward from the current 9 to 15 months or 16.5 kg, as this increases safety during frontal collisions. Furthermore, the ANEC promotes a stature-based system referred to as I-size to replace the current weight-based system (ANEC, 2011). CRS in this system refers to the minimal and maximum child length for the seat to fit (Figure 8.14). Further it requires rearward-facing transport until the child is 15 months of age and provides side-impact protection. The I-size regulation came into force in 2013 (ANEC, 2014) and over time will oust all old-style CRSs from the market (ANEC, 2012).

8.3.12 Consumer Associations

Consumer associations played a pivotal role in the advancement of CRSs by publishing comparative tests. Between 1970 and 2010, *Consumentengids* published a total of 18 comparative tests on CRSs. These articles reveal that, particularly in the 1970s and early 1980s, these products did not often perform very well as regards their primary functionality, namely to ensure safety during collisions for children traveling in cars. Consumer guides provide an independent and detailed overview of the quality and price of the products available in the market in the comparative tests. Pictures of articles tested, and relevant references to legislation, importers, and manufacturers are included. Products that perform best are designated "best choice." Producers often use these qualifications in their marketing, and retailers display copies of such articles at point of sale. Consumer associations therefore directly influence the purchasing behavior of consumers and, in that way, exert evolutionary pressure (selection of the fittest). Consumer associations also directly address legislators and manufacturers as described in an article by Consumentenbond, which mentions the use of video recordings of crash tests with CRSs. These videos have been shown to both legislators and manufacturers in order to convince them that there was a need to improve the standards with which the CRSs should comply (*Consumentengids*, 1993b). An example of the arguments used was that CRSs should not be tested with a lap belt, but with the retractable three-point belt instead. Those new requirements have subsequently been described in the ECE-44–03 legislation.

Consumer associations in various countries are united in different bodies such as ANEC, Consumers International (a federation of consumer groups), and International Consumer Research and Testing (ICRT) that focus on joint research and comparative testing. Consumer associations cooperate on product tests and share information used to compile the reviews published. Employees of various consumer associations participate in bodies like ANEC, for which they publish research into CRSs' safety with the objective of influencing legislation and standardization (ANEC, 2003). Along these routes the different international consumer associations cooperate and influence both legislation such as ECE-44 and standardization issues such as Isofix and I-size. Consumentenbond claims that this cooperation between various consumer associations in Europe has led to increasingly safe CRSs (*Consumentengids*, 1994).

8.3.13 Increasing Scale at Manufacturers Reduces Regional Design Differences

Similarly to cars and other consumer goods, regional differences can be found in people's preference for a specific technology, product architecture, or design language. In the United States, the larger car models like SUVs and trucks are widely sold. In Europe, where fuel has traditionally been taxed more heavily, the average car is smaller and more fuel efficient than in the United States. Similar differences can be observed for CRSs. In Scandinavia, rearward-facing CRSs are promoted for up to four years. Other parts in Europe will adapt to a new length-based standard (I-size) that increases current rearward-facing from 9 to 15 months or 16.5 kg.

Over the decades, a large number of companies have been involved in the development and production of CRSs. Historically they served different geographical markets. In recent years, mergers and acquisitions caused a consolidation of the CRS market. Currently, only a few large players remain. In Europe, the market is served by several large companies, plus a few smaller ones, and white label products from Asia. Dorel is a Canadian firm that acquired Maxi-Cosi, which primarily sells in Central and Western Europe, and Bebé-Comfort, which is traditionally strong around the Mediterranean. Britax Römer is an Anglo-German firm that, besides its own brand, also supplies CRSs to various automotive manufacturers that sell them under their own brand. Storchenmühle was originally a German manufacturer and is now owned by the globally operating Keiper Recaro Group that specializes in mobile seating. HTS (Hans Torgersen and Sønn AS), traditionally strong in Scandinavia, targets the European and Asian markets. These larger CRS manufacturers all have their own in-house development centers where they consolidate resources and know-how to develop new products. The CRS market, the international trade with ever more global companies, and the advent of the Information Age mean that know-what and know-how concerning CRSs will disseminate faster than it did in the early 1970s. These changes in the CRS ecosystem can be expected to drive design differences gradually to become smaller.

8.4 Perspectives on the Development of CRSs

The CRSs discussed in previous sections thus evolved into a product family that schematically can be pictured as shown in Figure 8.15. Variants of CRS designs through time consist of different executions of the subsystems that are configured according to prevailing views regarding the needs of the particular age, weight, or length group. Thus, over time, different design solutions evolved for different subsystems, each of which over time became more refined.

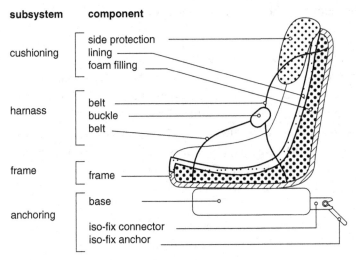

Figure 8.15. The system diagram of CRSs (Source: authors)

8.4.1 Mapping the Development of CRSs in a Product Evolution Diagram

The product evolution diagram as introduced in Chapter 4 is used in Figure 8.16 to map the development of CRSs over time juxtaposed with the ecosystem that played an important role in the evolution. As shown earlier, the CRSs did not originate at once, but evolved over a century from numerous designs at the hands of a "collective body of inventors," a varied group of people such as designers, salesmen, and test laboratory employees. As similarly remarked by Badke-Schaub (2007) on the subject of scientific discovery, CRSs have been shown to develop in incremental steps, based on past experience. The juxtaposed depiction of ecosystem above the product family tree in the product evolution diagram shows the influence over time of external events, such as the development of cars, safety belts, legislation, and the death of Dana Hutchinson, on the development of CRSs. Clearly these factors had a major impact on the evolution of CRSs.

Figure 8.16 shows a product family tree of CRSs that is rooted in earlier forms of baby cots and child seats. With the advent of the modern car, marked by the introduction of the Ford Model T, car ownership in the United States started to rise and provided a market for CRSs. In the early 1970s, the level of car ownership also started to rise in Europe to more than 200 vehicles per 1,000 people, a similar level as existed in the United States in the 1930s. Together with the diffusion of car safety technologies, this fed the awareness of and need for in-car safety for children. This set the scene for a rapidly increasing diversity in CRSs. Several designs proved unsafe, and, although they subsequently became extinct, they influenced legislation

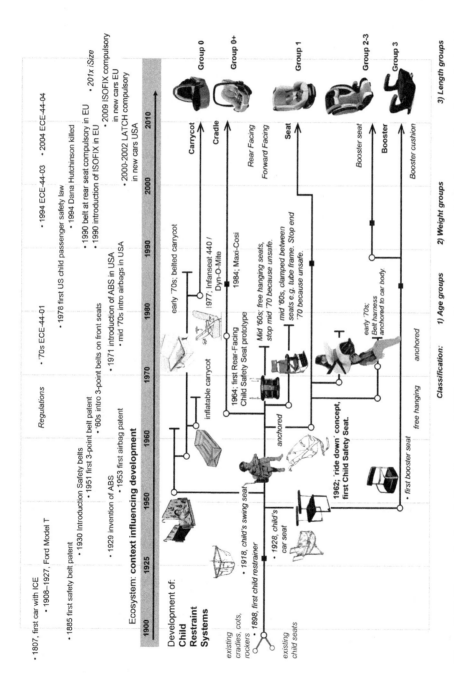

Figure 8.16 The product evolution diagram of CRSs. The approximate appearance of dominant designs is marked with squares (■) on branches. Strictly following the definition of dominant design (>50% of sales) would require information on market shares, which is not available. Instead, dominance is determined by reviewing the types tested in consumer guides (Source: authors)

for later generations of CRSs. The designs that provided better protection evolved into the dominant designs we know today.

The evolution of CRSs led to three different dominant designs that cater to different market segments (based on age, weight, or length). The first is the cradle type, in which babies and toddlers aged up to 1.5 years or weighing up to 12 kg lie rearward facing in a reclined position. The second is the seat type for small children aged up to seven or weighing up to 24 kg. Both these types have their own belt harnesses for children whose bone structure, muscles, and length are not yet mature enough to use the three-point belt for adults provided in the car. The third, the booster type for children aged up to 12 years or weighing up to 36 kg, does not have a belt system of its own and uses the three-point belt provided in the car. The evolution of the CRS product family into three types of dominant designs marks the segmentation phase as described in Chapter 5 of this book. The products literally evolved to meet the needs of three different market segments and, as can be concluded from this case study, the different product architectures evolved over time with certain designs surviving while others disappeared as they were designated as unsafe in consumer tests and/or banned by legislation that became stricter over time.

8.4.2 CRSs Developing Through the Product Phases

When the first CRS was introduced at the end of the nineteenth century, the product was new to the market. As noted before, the product was aimed at "restraining" the freedom of movement of children in cars. It did not yet provide safety because the concept of car safety did not yet exist. Variants of CRSs appeared on the market in the first six decades after introduction. As observed for other products (Eger, 2007a), the performance of CRSs was poor. In terms of product phases the CRS is in the performance phase. Figure 8.17 depicts the product family tree of CRSs juxtaposed with product phases.

In 1962, the Ameses introduced the first CRS aimed at providing safety (Figure 8.3). Two years later, Professor Aldman experimented with the first rear-facing CRS (Figure 8.4). These events marked the beginning of the optimization phase, characterized by new product development intended to improve the performance of products in terms of reliability, ergonomics, and safety. In the 1990s, the focus of CRS development and standards shifted to details. This characterizes the itemization phase. Reviews in consumer guides started focusing on aspects like ease of installation and cleaning. Isofix and LATCH were introduced to promote better installation of CRSs in cars. Since the end of the 1990s, almost all members of the target group (i.e., young parents using a car) became familiar with CRSs. Legislation also enforced its use. After

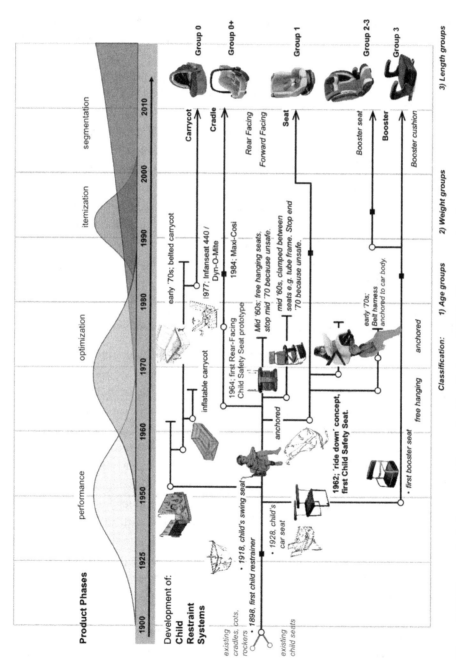

Figure 8.17 The product phases and the product family tree of CRSs (Source: authors)

2000, wide product ranges were being offered with increasingly complex features like snap-on bases (Figure 8.13) and CRSs that combine with strollers. Expressive styling became more common and CRS (and strollers) started following fashion trends. It transpired that the product phases for CRS were not sharply demarcated in time. Instead, a certain development marked the beginning of a phase while elements characterizing the previous phase were still available on the market. This is why the phases are mapped with a peak marking wherever, in terms of time, this phase best describes the evolution in the product family in time while the start and end of the phase overlap with other phases.

As far as CRSs are concerned, it transpired that not all product phases appeared simply in succession. The product family tree shows that the branching that eventually shapes the CRS product segments actually started with the introduction of the first booster seat around 1950 and led to the carrycot a few years later. Then safety-focused CRSs were introduced in 1962. For that reason, Figure 8.17 shows how initial segmentation coincided with the start of the optimization phase. For the product family of CRS, segmentation evolved over time, starting with the recognition of age groups, then weight groups, and currently length groups. Although the optimization and itemization phase were not yet finished, the elements that characterize the segmentation phase were already visible. Apparently, the segmentation phase overlaps with earlier phases.

8.4.3 Relation between Development of Product Family and Ecosystem

As noted in Chapter 4, the interaction between the development of product and ecosystem shapes the development of both. Other authors noticed similar systems and discussed the development of products in niches, which are influenced by developments in the wider ecosystem or socio-technical regimes and industrial landscapes (Geels, 2002; Joore, 2010). The role of legislation as an important element of these socio-technical regimes is discussed in connection with the development of forms of sustainable transport (Hoogema et al., 2002; Van den Hoed, 2004). Figure 8.18 depicts this mutual relation. The lower half shows a simplified CRS product family tree. The upper half summarizes the ecosystem that interacted with the CRS product family as it developed over time. The case of CRSs shows a strong and mutual influence (hence two-way arrows) between the evolving product family and consumers (including consumer associations and advocacy groups), standardization, and related legislative bodies. This has been described as a direct or primary influence in Figure 8.18. An indirect or secondary influence on the development of this product family can be observed from the wider environment of general (car safety) legislation, (car safety) technology development,

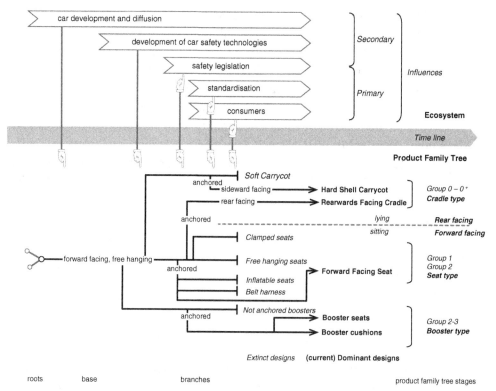

Figure 8.18 The relation between the product family tree and the ecosystem (Source: authors)

and general development and diffusion of the environment in which the products are used (cars).

8.5 Conclusion

The CRS case study shows an example of a new type of product that emerges from seats aimed to restrain child movement in cars and evolves into a product family providing child passengers safety catering to different segments. CRS segmentation evolved over time from age groups to weight groups and currently length groups and is related to the improving functionality. The first documented use of a child restraint system (CRS) in a car dates back to 1898. This first device was little more than a drawstring bag that would attach to the actual car seat intended as a system used to restrain children from moving through the car. The mass production of cars started with the Ford Model T in 1908. In the 1920s, the production of various CRSs started and patents for CRSs were filed. At that moment, the level of car ownership increased to more than 200 vehicles per 1,000 inhabitants in the United States, which formed a CRS market, and with it the diversity of CRS designs increased. Once car safety technology had diffused from the 1960s onward, the perception of required safety to be provided in cars changed. As a consequence, the then still latent needs for child passenger safety evolved into an awareness that child passengers did not receive the protection they needed. This created an environment in which CRS designs were developed that focused on providing safety to children traveling in cars. Slowly the perception of what functionality a CRS should provide changed among manufacturers, designers, salesmen, consumer organizations, legislators, and consumers. Then, in the 1960s, the level of car ownership increased in Western Europe as well to more than 100 vehicles per 1,000 inhabitants. This condition allowed the market for CRSs to grow in Europe as well.

The case study revealed that many different actors contributed in various ways to evolving CRS perception and designs. It was certainly not a process driven by designers alone. Besides that, international trade, consolidation among manufacturers, as well as coincidence, have been shown to influence CRS evolution. It has become apparent that the whole of influences from the context here defined as the ecosystem is part and parcel of the evolution of CRS products. The development history of CRS that covers more than a century has been mapped in a product evolution diagram using a product family tree, and an ecosystem. The architectures of CRSs sold in the Netherlands have been stable over the past two decades. That does not mean that evolution has halted. It was noted (*Consumentengids*, 2010b) that the room for improvement in side-impact protection, the relatively high levels of incorrectly installed CRSs, and the lack of support for booster-only cushions mean that further improvement of CRS designs is possible. A major review by the ANEC (2014) toward I-size, a stature-based system promoting rearward-facing CRSs until 15 months, further refines standardization for CRSs. These are examples of evolutionary forces that can be mapped in a product evolution diagram to provide direction for the design and development of new evolutionary versions of CRS (see also the next section). Based on this case study, it can be stated that CRSs have come a long way in terms of the safety they provide, their ease of use, and their comfort.

It can be asserted that the current CRSs perform well as regards their current basic function, namely to provide safety to child passengers in cars during driving in general, and in the event of a collision in particular. The performance of this basic function is expressed in qualitative terms like "bad, moderate, reasonable, and good." A single unit of performance allowing quantification of the performance or the price-performance is not available for CRSs.

8.6 Application of the Case Study in a Design by Noor Reigersman

Introduction

In the course "Evolutionary Product Development" at the University of Twente in the Netherlands, student Noor Reigersman designed a new CRS for BeSafe (Reigersman, 2014). Her findings with regard to the product evolution diagram (PED) and the product phases were added to the research described in the previous sections; this section describes the design of the new product.

Reigersman chose to make a redesign of the BeSafe iZi Combi X3. This CRS is brought to the market by the Scandinavian company BeSafe, a company that is one of the pioneers in rear-facing car seats for children up to four years. For this age group, rear-facing seats are safer than the still often used front-facing seats. At the time of Reigersman's research, the number of rear-facing seats was very small; however, it was foreseen that the competition would grow because of the expectation that in 2017 rear-facing seats for children up to 15 months of age would become mandatory (ANEC, 2012).

At the start of the design process the BeSafe iZi Combi X3 was compared with the two most important competitors: the Maxi-Cosi 2wayPearl and the Cybex Sirona (Figure 8.19). Figure 8.20 gives an overview of what BeSafe could do with regard to product development, based on the theory of evolutionary product development.

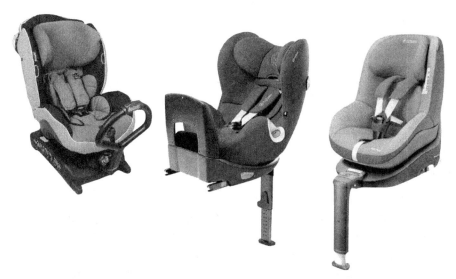

Figure 8.19 The three products that were compared left to right: BeSafe iZi Combi X3, Cybex Sirona, Maxi-Cosi 2wayPearl (Source: Noor Reigersman)

Product phase characteristic	Aspects	Short description of the present situation	Solution space for future products
Newness	Technology push Dominant design(s) Product is part of daily life	The product is well-known, the rear facing CRS may become a new dominant design because of changing regulations	No action intended
Functionality	Poor performance Reliability Safety	Functionality and reliability are good; however, regulations and car techniques change	Carefully follow new developments of cars and regulations
Ergonomics	Handling Comfort User interface	The ergonomics of the product can be improved	Pay attention to handling and user interface
Development	Assortment Emotional benefits Mass customization Individualization	The product does not offer much choice	There is room for segmentation aimed at extra features or lifestyles
Styling	Not very good Integration of form giving Expressive styling Emotional benefits Sober	The integration of form giving is good, but the styling is very neutral	Styling could be more expressive
Pricing	High Under pressure Low Customized	The prices are relatively high	Prices could be decreased; performance should be improved
Complexity	Number of parts Extra features/accessories	The number of parts is at its minimum	No action intended
Production	Assembly Manual Automated Outsourced	Production has a high level of automation Assembly is outsourced to low-wage countries	No action intended
Service	Not organized Organized Involves societal issues	The service is well organized	No action intended
Ethics	Sustainability Working conditions Energy saving Animal welfare Nontoxic materials Recyclability	The social behavior of the company is not a major concern for the users' purchasing behavior	No action intended

Figure 8.20 Solution space for BeSafe based on the product phases and the product phase characteristics (Source: authors)

Based on this overview of possible design directions, Reigersman selected the following – in her opinion most promising and in the short term most realistic – design directions: adding emotional benefits to justify the high price of the iZi Combi X3 in a market where the number of rear-facing seats will be growing, e.g., by designing a seat aimed at a specific lifestyle; or by developing a less expensive seat aimed at young parents, the biggest buyer group.

Figure 8.21 iZi Go Limited Edition (Source: BeSafe)

Safety is BeSafe's most important value. Its products have a rather "technical know-how look"; it seems like the design of the seats is not considered very important. However, a lot of attention is paid to user friendliness, child friendliness and – of course – safety. The redesign should meet the focus points mentioned earlier, without regarding these core values of BeSafe. One of the products looks more stylish and carefully designed: the iZi Go Limited Edition (Figure 8.21). It is striking that this product is used in many promotional activities. Therefore, Reigersman used this design as inspiration for the redesign. Mood boards were made, visualizing design and color trends, but also "Scandinavia" and "safety." Figure 8.22 shows some of the sketches with a short explanation.

Figure 8.23 shows parts of a study into combinations of colors and materials; in Figure 8.24 the final design is presented.

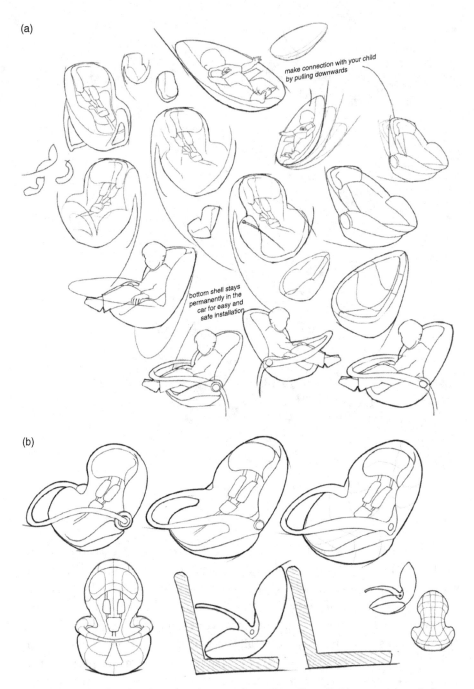

(a)

make connection with your child
by pulling downwards

bottom shell stays
permanently in the
car for easy and
safe installation

(b)

Figure 8.22 Design sketches aimed at creating a friendly, reliable, natural, and classy shape and looking for emotional benefits, such as the possibility to make a better connection with the child – being able to better reach the child – during a ride (Source: Noor Reigersman)

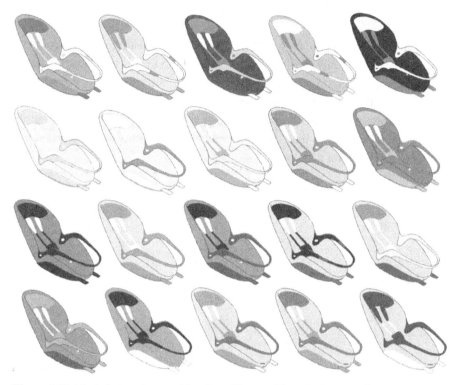

Figure 8.23 Study into color combinations (Source: Noor Reigersman)

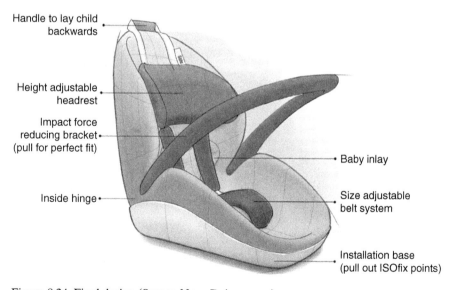

Figure 8.24 Final design (Source Noor Reigersman)

Conclusion

The example of the CRS showed that analyzing the history of this product, using the product family tree, its ecosystem, and the theory of product phases offered useful design directions. In the case described previously, the assignment given to the student required that the product had to be realized – made ready for production – within a period of one year. That limited the number of possible choices. Despite that, several opportunities were found and an interesting design direction was chosen.

9 Example Showing the Application of the Theory in the Work of Maarten Michel

9.1 Introduction

Nike Basketball Shoes

In the course "Evolutionary Product Development" at the University of Twente in the Netherlands, student Maarten Michel designed a new basketball shoe for Nike (Michel, 2014a, 2014b). The focus was on so-called signature shoes, which are developed in collaboration with famous NBA players. The NBA is North America's National Basketball Association and contains the world's top male professional basketball players. A basketball shoe consists of three components: the upper, the midsole, and the outsole (Figure 9.1). The upper encloses the shoe and provides stability. The midsole provides support for the foot and is essential for cushioning the forces that act on the foot. The midsole is connected to and protected by the outsole. The outsole also provides the necessary traction with the floor of the playing field.

Performance Product Phase

Basketball was invented in 1891 by James Naismith, who was searching for an indoor sport for his students during the winter season. The sport quickly gained popularity, and around 1900, there were enough basketball teams to start a competition. It became an Olympic sport in 1936. The first matches were played on standard soft leather sports shoes. However, many basketball players soon switched to tennis shoes, probably because they provided more grip and support. A. G. Spalding created a high-top variant of the (British) tennis shoe, which suited basketball players very well because of the ankle protection (Turner, 2013). The first shoe that was advertised as a basketball shoe was the Spalding "Expert" from 1904 (Figure 9.2). In 1907, the same company introduced a more flexible, canvas shoe with a rubber outsole. The main driver behind the development of the first basketball shoes was the development of the rubber industry

Figure 9.1 Basketball shoe: the upper, the midsole, and the outsole (Source: Maarten Michel)

Figure 9.2 Spalding "Expert" (1904) (Source: Converse/Nike)

(the T in the PEST acronym, the technology influence). With the invention of vulcanized rubber by Goodyear in 1860, it became possible to manufacture stable rubber soles. One of the companies to profit from this was Converse, which introduced its All-Stars in 1917. It became the best-selling product for the coming decades. Partly due to a protectionist law from 1933 (the P in PEST, the political influence), the hegemony of the All-Star would last until the 1960s. Because of this dominance of the All-Star, the performance phase lasted until the 1970s, when Nike entered the market.

Optimization Product Phase

The American import duty for foreign shoes based on 1933 legislation was lowered in 1966. This caused a turnaround in shoe design, as the German companies Adidas and Puma subsequently entered the market with innovative designs. They brought new, innovative models, such as the Adidas "Pro Model," which was introduced in 1968. It also offered Nike – then the distributor of Japanese running shoes – an opportunity to enter the market. Phil Knight, a former runner at Stanford University, was not very happy with the available running shoes that were produced in the United States. He found out that the shoes Adidas made were lighter and more comfortable than the American shoes; however, import taxes to protect the home market made the shoes very expensive. He discovered that Japanese shoes were of the same quality, but much cheaper. He went to Japan and made a deal with Onitsuka, a manufacturer of running shoes. Together with Bill Bowerman, he started Blue Ribbon Sports in 1964. In 1972, they introduced the first line of shoes of their own. The main models were the "Cortez" and the "Moon Shoe," both running shoes. They also introduced their own basketball shoes, the low-top "Bruin" and the high-top "Blazer" (Figures 9.3 and 9.4) and the Nike brand, with its famous swoosh logo. Unlike the American basketball shoe manufacturers, Nike was not rooted in the rubber industry and therefore used other materials as well. Like Adidas, Nike used padded leather and suede for the upper to improve support and comfort. The outsole consisted of a herringbone pattern that provided more grip and is still used today.

Itemization Product Phase

The 1980s proved a significant turning point for Nike. In 1979, NASA engineer Frank Rudy suggested a shoe with interconnected air pad cells (Plain, 2004). This was the start of the Nike Air technology. In 1982, Nike introduced the Nike Air Force 1, named after the presidential plane. It was the first basketball shoe that incorporated the Nike Air technology, developed since 1979 for running shoes. This technology gave Nike a great advantage, but it was not

Figure 9.3 Nike "Bruin" (1972) (Source: Nike)

Figure 9.4 Nike "Blazer" (1972) (Source: Nike)

the only innovation. The upper contained a window of mesh material, which provided more breathability than existing shoes. The third innovation was the outsole, which had a circular pattern to improve the turning movements of the player and a hollow "cup" that made bending the foot arch easier. This design became the standard for Nike until the 1990s.

In the early 1970s, Nike started to contract sports professionals to promote its brand. It started with tennis players Ilie Nastase (in 1973) and John McEnroe (in 1978). In 1984, Nike contracted its first basketball player: Michael Jordan.

In 1985, Nike introduced the Nike Air Jordan 1, the first so-called signature basketball shoe, a shoe created for or in close cooperation with a famous basketball player. During the 1980s, Nike became the biggest brand in basketball shoes. In 1980, it founded the Nike Sport Research Lab, where new materials and production methods were developed and tested.

Segmentation Product Phase

The innovations in basketball shoes really took off in the 1990s. The basketball shoe portfolio of Nike grew from 13 different shoes in 1990 to well over 50 different types around 2000. This was not only due to the rising popularity of basketball, but also to the growing number of people who started to wear the shoes in their leisure time or to work. Furthermore, the hip-hop culture was connected with basketball, and showing off with shoes (and clothing) became very important to its followers. This led to the design – and success – of very flashy, expressive, exciting basketball shoes. Nike started to focus on segments: high-end shoes for males, affordable shoes for consumers who could not afford the expensive (signature) shoes, and women's basketball shoes. There were also limited editions of existing shoes, for instance for the Olympics.

Besides introducing different styles to create a large range of products to choose from, Nike also started to design shoes for different types of players. An example was the Nike Huarache, introduced in 1992. It was aimed at big players who needed a stable shoe for their moves.

In 1998, Michael Jordan retired as a basketball player. In 2003, Nike signed up a proper successor: LeBron James. The success of this shoe line led to the contracting of other famous players. In 2006, the Nike Zoom Kobe I was introduced. The name giver – Kobe Bryant – had been contracted by Adidas in 1998. After the introduction of the Adidas KOBE TWO (in 2001), Bryant was contracted by Nike. Because of legal problems regarding his agreements with Adidas, his first "signature shoe" was introduced as the Huarache 2K4. In 2009, the third sequence of signature shoes started: the Nike KD1, named after Kevin Durant (See also Figure 9.13).

Individualization Product Phase

With the introduction of Nike iD in 1999, Nike entered the individualization phase. Nike iD is an online service that gives consumers the ability to perso-nalize their shoes (mass customization). Even though this is not real cocreation as the shoes are not custom-made, the enormous range of available shoes provides consumers with the possibility to mix and match their preferred style and technology. The platform is not used much; the broad portfolio that Nike offers seems to provide most consumers with enough choice. Although one could say that with Nike iD (Figure 9.5), the individualization product phase is entered, it does not cover a significant part of the market; it is more a sort of gimmick.

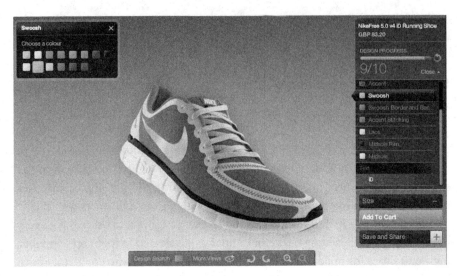

Figure 9.5 Nike iD website (Source: Nike)

For star players however, cocreation has become the norm. New signature shoes are designed in close collaboration with the athletes, such as LeBron James ("King James"), Kobe Bryant ("Black Mamba"), and Kevin Durant ("KD").

Awareness Product Phase

It has taken Nike some time to adapt to the awareness product phase. Since its founding, Nike was able to grow quickly because of its cheap production. Nike's shoes and, for instance, footballs were produced in low-wage countries, and Nike did not consider poor working conditions its responsibility. However, this changed after an article in *Life* in June 1996 about a 12-year-old boy called Tariq who was making footballs for Nike and earning 60 cents for nearly a full day's work. Shortly after this article, Nike began to take an active role in improving labor conditions. It also started reducing the use of toxic or harmful adhesives and materials. Since then, Nike has received several awards for its sustainability policy, including first place in the "Climate Counts" scorecard for sustainability seven years in a row up to and including 2013.

9.2 Conclusions of the Research

In the previous sections, the history of the Nike brand was analyzed. The first high-top shoe introduced by Nike in 1972 was called the Blazer. Until then, the basketball market had been dominated by Converse All-Stars shoes, which

Product phase characteristic	Aspects	Short description of the present situation	Solution space for future products
Newness	Technology push Dominant design(s) Product is part of daily life	The product is well known, there are two dominant designs (low and high shoes), research is aimed at improving the performance	Only minor improvements are possible; Nike has a major focus on innovation
Functionality	Poor performance Reliability Safety	Functionality and reliability are very good; most NBA players wear Nike or Air Jordan	No action intended
Ergonomics	Handling Comfort User interface	Good, different shoes for different physiques, designed to wear comfortably	No action intended
Development	Assortment Emotional benefits Mass customization Individualization	Much choice for the customer, mass customization (individualization) was realized with Nike iD	There is room for further segmentation, e.g., a signature shoe for a big player or a new women's signature shoe
Styling	Not very good Integration of form giving Expressive styling Emotional benefits Sober	Expressive, some shoes are a bit "over the top," ahead of competition	Not much room for improvement here, maybe design the next shoe for an existing line of shoes
Pricing	High Under pressure Low Customized	Good price in relation to the quality in all segments, but more expensive than the competition	A line of cheaper products is possible, but not recommended
Complexity	Number of parts Extra features/accessories	The number of parts is OK and is decreased with Flyknit and Hyperfuse[1]	No action intended
Production	Assembly Manual Automated Outsourced	Production is highly automated; newly introduced technologies are more efficient Assembly is outsourced (see ethics)	No action intended
Service	Not organized Organized Involves societal issues	Service organization is good	No action intended
Ethics	Sustainability Working conditions Energy saving Animal welfare Nontoxic materials Recyclability	Improved, but as a market leader this is always under a "magnifying glass"	Higher priority is recommended

Figure 9.6 Solution space for Nike based on the product phases and the product phase characteristics (Source: authors)

[1] Employing a new technology, the Nike Flyknit upper is precisely engineered to only use materials where they are needed, for a featherweight, form-fitting, and virtually seamless upper. It does not use the multiple materials and material cuts used in traditional sports footwear manufacture.

Hyperfuse creates a durable composite sole composed of three layers: one for stability, one for breathability, and one for durability. All three layers are fused together using heat and pressure. The unibody design results in lightweight, breathable footwear and minimizes seams that can wear on an athlete's foot. (Source: Nike, 2015).

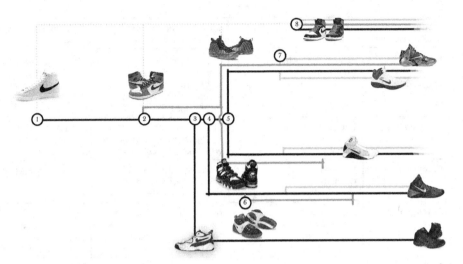

1: First basketball shoe: Nike Blazer, 1972
2: First signature shoe: Air Jordan I, 1985
3: Segmentation: cheaper basketball shoes
4: Segmentation: women's basketball shoes
5: Segmentation: shoes for different positions
6: First women's signature shoe: Air Swoopes Zoom, 1996
7: Nike iD, 1999
8: Throwbacks: reintroduction of earlier models

Figure 9.7 (Simplified) product family tree of the Nike basketball shoes (Source: Maarten Michel)

were quite simple, made from canvas and rubber. In the beginning, Nike was a small brand, but from the 1980s, its dominance of the market took off. The Nike Air Force 1 (1982) and the Nike Air Jordan 1 (1985) are the typical products that gave Nike its position as a top brand with the characteristic innovation and superstar appeal. The Nike Air Force 1, with its new features like Nike Air, and more recent developments such as Flyknit and Hyperfuse, illustrate Nike's being a front-runner in innovation. The other factor that gives Nike an edge over most competitors is the superstar appeal. In 1985, Nike signed up Michael Jordan, presumably the best basketball player ever. Nike recognized the potential of linking star players to its brand, and since then has contracted current players LeBron James, Kobe Bryant, and Kevin Durant. Nike has gone through all product phases and is now simultaneously in the three last phases: segmentation, individualization (Nike iD), and awareness.

A difficulty with designing basketball shoes for Nike is that they are already very successful, and all product phases have been reached. Consequently, there is not a lot of room for improving the functionality or increasing segmentation and individualization. To find out whether there are niches in the current portfolio, a closer look was taken at the product family tree and at the portfolio of the main competitor, Adidas. When we examine the product family tree (simplified for this purpose; see Figure 9.7), we can identify three viable options. An added challenge within this assignment was that the new design had to be launched onto the market within a year's time. This was part of the assignment to make sure that the students would aim for an evolutionary step in the product development, not for a revolutionary leap.

The research yielded the following three options.

1. Design the next shoe for an existing line of shoes. Currently, there are three players with signature shoes. They all release a new shoe every year. This is a realistic option, but – according to Michel (2014b) – not a real challenge.

2. Reintroduce a women's signature shoe. Since the Air Swoopes Zoom of 1996, there has not been a new introduction of such a shoe. However, women's basketball is relatively small, making the possible profitability also small, and the WNBA (Women's NBA) lacks a real superstar at the moment.

3. Design a signature shoe for a big player. Since the signature shoe for Kevin Garnett, there has not been a signature shoe for the center and power forward positions. Michel chose this strategy because he considered it the most interesting and viable option.

9.3 Design Considerations

Several young players in these positions (center forward and power forward) have star potential: Kevin Love, LaMarcus Aldridge, and Anthony Davis. Nike already has a contract with Anthony Davis for some limited editions of existing shoes. However, no signature shoe, cocreated with him, is available yet. Therefore, the selected strategy for this project became: "Design a signature Nike shoe for NBA star Anthony Davis."

Michel studied the characteristics of the selected player. First, he looked at the playing style.

> Anthony Davis' style of play is characterized by its versatility. . . . He changed from a guard to a power forward. This means he can both dribble and pass (guard), but is also able to rebound and is one of the best shot blockers in the NBA. He is very athletic with a great vertical jump ability, but is still very nimble on his feet. He therefore needs a shoe that is stable but light and bouncy enough to move quickly.
> (2014b, 18–20)

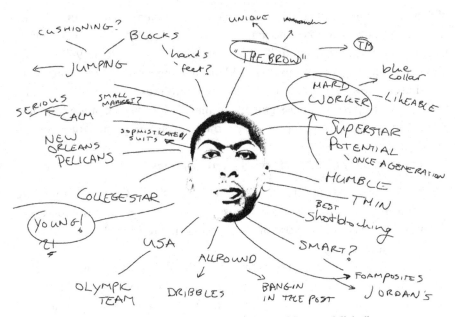

Figure 9.8 Characteristics of Anthony Davis (Source: Maarten Michel)

Second, Michel studied Davis's features. One feature – his unibrow – stands out and has brought him his nickname, The Brow. He has a so-called blue-collar attitude, working hard during the game, but with a sensible, calm presence both on and off the court (see also Figure 9.8).

Third, Michel researched the shoes that Anthony Davis prefers. The most important finding was that during matches, he prefers the 2013 Hyperposites, stating that he likes the ankle support they offer. Based on his research, Michel created a list of requirements. He designed a logo – which is customary with signature shoes – that is inspired by the eyebrows of Anthony Davis (see Figure 9.9). The logo also spells out the name Davis (Figure 9.10). About the design, Michel wrote:

> For the design of the shoe, I have taken all previous conclusions in consideration, and have tried to match all of those aspects into a coherent design that fits both Nike and Anthony Davis.   (2014b, 26) (see Figure 9.11)

Summary of the Chosen Design Strategy

In this section, the considerations to design a signature shoe for Anthony Davis are summarized.

1. In the portfolio of Nike there are signature shoes for guards and forwards, as well as regular shoes for all positions; however, there is no signature shoe for large players. At the moment this seems to be the only available niche.

Figure 9.9 The logo and its inspiration (Source: Maarten Michel)

Figure 9.10 The logo spells the name Davis (Source: Maarten Michel)

Figure 9.11 Sketches for the shoe design (Source: Maarten Michel)

2. The biggest competitor of Nike, Adidas, has an agreement with NBA star Dwight Howard, a large player, and one of the most popular players in the NBA. In the top 10 of best-selling signature shoes, this player takes the seventh place.

3. Large players seem to become more agile and athletic. If this is taken into account in the shoe design, it means that somewhat smaller players can use the shoe as well; this way, the target group can be expanded.

4. There are several young players on this position that have star potential: Kevin Love, LaMarcus Aldridge, and Anthony Davis. Many people expect Davis to be one of the next superstars in the NBA. An extra advantage is that he is quite young: 21 (at the moment of this design process).

5. Nike has already signed Davis to a contract for some limited editions of existing shoes. This has resulted in several throwbacks (reissues of earlier shoes) and a few modern shoes, but there is no signature shoe yet.

Elucidation of the Design

When looking at the exterior of Nike basketball shoes, a few things can be noticed. First of all, the shoes have different exteriors; there is no basic concept from which all shoes are derived. Every shoe is based on a unique concept, but there are similarities that turn the shoes into a product family: the shoes are relatively clean looking (especially when compared to the shoes of competitor Adidas), there is a very apparent distinction between the upper and the midsole, and the Nike swoosh is clearly visible in all shoes.

With regard to the upper of the shoe, the following possibilities exist: Flyknit and Hyperposite. Flyknit was introduced in 2014 with the Kobe 9 shoe. The lightweight wires make it a very light shoe, perfect for smaller players. The other technology – Hyperposite – uses an injection-molded shell. It makes a stable and comfortable shoe suited for larger, heavier players, mostly because of its stability and ankle support.

With regard to the midsoles, the following options can be considered: Nike Air, Air Max, and Zoom Air. Air Max is suited for heavy players, Zoom is for a little extra bounce, often in the forefoot, and Air is an intermediate version. Finally there is also the possibility to choose Luarlon, which is a very lightweight midsole in a Phylon (EVA^2) shell that adds a bouncy, reflective feel and evenly spread cushioning.

In competition, Anthony Davis mostly wears the 2013 Hyperposites, arguing that he likes the ankle support. Outside the court, he often wears its predecessor, the Foamposite. Based on his preference of shoes, Michel chose the following starting points for his design: a Hyperposite upper because of its

---

[2] EVA: ethylene-vinyl acetate, a copolymer of ethylene and vinyl acetate.

ankle support, a Lunarlon midsole for lightweight and responsive cushioning, and "throwback" features that refer to Davis's preference for retro shoes and that form a contrast with other, hypermodern signature shoes. The result is presented in Figure 9.12. In Figure 9.13, the three existing Nike basketball signature shoes are depicted next to the new design.

Figure 9.12 The final design of the Anthony Davis signature shoe (Source: Maarten Michel)

NBA Player	LeBron James	Kobe Bryant	Kevin Durant	Anthony Davis
Nickname	"king James"	"Black Mamba"	"KD"	"The Brow"
Shoe positions	Allround, guards, forwards	guards	Guards, forwards	(Power) Forwards
Characteristic	Powerfull, allround	Slick/Smooth, arrogant	Nimble, quickness, shooting	Shot blocking, allround athletic
Shoe style	Performance, allround	Luxurious, fashionable	Young men's Fashion, light weight	Allround, retro, performance
Upper	Hyperposite, Hyperfuse	Flyknit Flywire	Flywire	Hyperposite
Mid/outsole	Full length Zoom Air	Lunarlon	Air Max, Zoom Air	Lunarlon
Materials, graphics	New, lightweight materials	Luxurious materials Snake skin, leather	Graphics, pop-art	Foam/hyperposite, old school leather?
Colors	Red/white/black	Dark colors, gold, white	Bright, colorful	Gold, white, red, dark blue
Characteristic technology	Hyperposite	Flyknit	Ultra-thin Flywire	Lunarlon hyperposite?

Figure 9.13 Nike signature shoes including the new design created by Michel (Source: Maarten Michel)

In his report Michel wrote about his design:

Aside from the Hyperposite and Lunarlon, the design features that needed to be included were retro features from old shoes. What resulted was a shoe lace patch that in shape resembles the Jordan 3 shoe, and in material the Jordan 11, with the patent leather. The golden nose guard and side logo are made of course [from] leather, like the "elephant skin" on the Jordan 3 shoe. ... The small Nike logo and the complete upper are based on the 1997 Foamposite shoe. The overall shape follows the 2013 Hyperposite shoe that Davis wore this year. With its high ankle, it offers great support and stability. The outsole is a wink to the famous Waffle sole that Nike introduced in the 1970s.   (2014b, 28)

9.4 Conclusion

The case of the basketball shoe was added to this book to demonstrate that even in a seemingly saturated market, the method of evolutionary product development can be useful to find opportunities to introduce new products. To be able to find a niche, such as Michel did, it is inevitable to make a profound study of the product, the product history, and – in this example – also of the game. Michel also illustrated in his project that the product family tree can be created on different levels. In total, he created three PFTs: one for the upper, one for the midsole and sole, and one that was mainly aimed at the signature shoes (Figure 9.7). This design project also illustrates how a designer can revert to previous solutions from other products, something that is – as far as we know – not possible in biological evolution. Without this research and the knowledge of the technologies that Nike uses, it would not have been possible to create this kind of new design.

10 Abstracts of the Most Important Theories Used in This Book

This chapter presents an overview of theories developed to help designers, engineers, and managers with innovation policy, product development, and the design and styling of products. Evolutionary product development is not (yet) a research discipline. For the purpose of providing a theoretical background, we collected information from different disciplines, such as economics, sociology, marketing, management studies, organizational studies, (design) history, industrial design engineering, design methodology, and innovation studies. Another problem we encountered is that often the research that was found was developed in isolation within one discipline. And finally most innovation and technical change research has been done in high-tech business-to-business industries, or with producers of commodities. The closest the theoretical work gets to consumer products is when car manufacturers are the subject of research. There is hardly any research done on innovation and technical change in consumer products (Dosi and Nelson, 2013).

The theories that have been found are described in alphabetical order based on the name(s) of the (first) authors. Because history is important for the model of product phases, recent studies were considered in addition to some older ones. The conclusions drawn from the presented theories partially overlap. Some research directions, like the "numeric aesthetics" of Bense (1954), have been abandoned because they seemed to lead to a dead end. They have still been included in this chapter because they give an impression of ideas and research of the past and also because they make this chapter more complete.

10.1 Abernathy and Utterback (1975): "A Dynamic Model of Process and Product Innovation"

In the mid-1970s, Abernathy and Utterback (1975) proposed a model of innovation that is a synthesis of "two distinct but complementary models on innovation" (p. 639), one looking at the product and the other examining the process. For both product and process, three different stages of development are described.

The process model describes the relationship between production process characteristics and innovation. It recognizes that the production process develops over time toward improved output, becoming more capital-intensive and improving labor productivity through greater division of labor and specialization. The first or "uncoordinated" stage is characterized by the use of largely unstandardized and manual operations, relying upon general-purpose equipment. The process has not yet been optimized. The next stage, "segmental," is characterized by price competition, requiring improving the production process for efficiency. Parts of processes here become automated, which in effect only becomes feasible when sales volumes are increasing. In this stage, process innovation reaches its peak. Then, a "systemic" stage is entered, where the process becomes so highly developed and well integrated that any further improvement becomes very costly. The rate of innovation in the process decreases.

The product model describes the relation between competitive strategy and innovation. A product innovation is defined as a new technology or combination of technologies that are introduced commercially to meet a user or market need. The model is based on the idea that product innovations go through three stages that first target product performance, then emphasis product variety, and finally focus on standardization and cost.[1] The first stage of the product life cycle is characterized by "performance-maximizing," where rapid changes and large margins are expected. The innovation for by far the largest share is driven by new market needs and opportunities that translate into product requirements. The second stage is characterized by "sales maximizing," where increasing competition is based on product differentiation. It is noted that advanced technology is stimulating product as well as process innovation in this stage. It is in this stage that, according to Abernathy and Utterback, one "might expect a greater degree of competition based on product differentiation with some product designs beginning to dominate" (p. 644). This notion has become known as the first conception of the term "dominant design" in innovation literature. At the end of the product life cycle, the competition shifts to product price, leading to "cost minimizing" and standardizing. This is when production processes become more capital-intensive and may be relocated to areas with lower costs of labor.

The model described addresses three issues that have relevance for the management of technological innovation.

---

[1] Note here that these stages have strong parallels with the first three product phases (performance, optimization, itemization) defined by Eger (2007).

1. The locus of innovation or most likely the source of innovation shifts with the stage of development. In the first stage, critical input is not so much found in technology, but in insights in "needs." Then it shifts to "technology." Finally the needs are well defined and the stimulus of further innovation is found in "cost."

2. The stage of development influences what type of innovation is most likely to be successful. In the beginning of the life cycle, production process innovations are unlikely, as processes are still ill defined, uncertain, and unstructured. Vice versa, innovations in targeting needs seldom take place at the end of the life cycle.

3. The type of barriers to innovation change along with the stage of development. In the early stage of the life cycle, the main question is if a particular innovation is relevant. Will it work and meet a need, or not? At the end of the life cycle, the disruptive nature of the innovation defines the level of resistance that will be met.

Figure 10.1 is not the original version by Abernathy and Utterback. The figure has been slightly adapted for ease of interpretation in the context of this book. Between the curves, the word "stimuli" is added, and four times "stimulated" is removed to improve readability. The curves are provided with the same names, but between brackets the words "what" and "how" are added, designating what type of knowledge is involved. This distinction is added in order to link to Chapter 2 of this book that distinguishes between know-how and know-what. Although Abernathy and Utterback do not use the designations "know-how" and "know-what," they clearly describe them as "two distinct but complementary models on innovation" (p. 639).

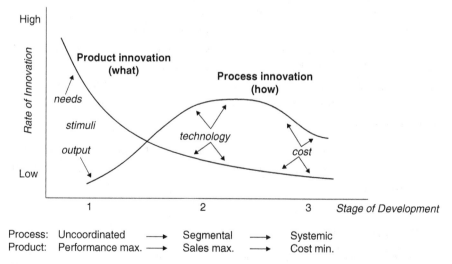

Figure 10.1 The technology life cycle (Free after Abernathy and Utterback, 1975)

The horizontal axis here includes stage numbers, and below it, in a matrix, the keywords per stage. In the original figure, no visual reference to the three stages has been added, and keywords for the second stage were not included.

10.2 Altshuller (1999): TRIZ, the Theory of Inventive Problem Solving

TRIZ[2] or the "Theory of Inventive Problem Solving" is a method for problem solving, analysis, and forecasting derived from a study of inventive patterns in patent literature, developed by Genrich Altshuller (1999) and associates. Altshuller, who was an inventor and science fiction writer, started developing TRIZ in 1946 while working as an "invention inspector" for the Soviet navy. Over three decades, a total of hundreds of thousands of patents have been analyzed for patterns of inventive solutions.

ARIZ,[3] which freely translates as "Algorithm of Inventive Problem Solving," was developed as an algorithmic approach based on the TRIZ theory. Because of its extensiveness, TRIZ is not an easy creative technique to teach or apply. For that reason, several modified versions are known such as SIT (Systematic Inventive Thinking) and USIT (Unified Structured Inventive Thinking).

While working with Soviet patents, Altshuller realized that a problem requires an inventive solution if there is an unresolved contradiction in the sense that improving one parameter negatively impacts another. He first based his theory on the concept of technical contradictions, the concept of ideality of a system, a contradiction matrix, and 40 principles of invention. After 1969, he added the concept of physical contradictions, SuField analysis (structural substance-field analysis), standard solutions, laws of technical system evolution, and many other practical and theoretical approaches. After the Cold War, TRIZ was brought to other countries. Based on TRIZ and ARIZ, various software tools have been developed (Wikipedia, 2015c).

This book discusses no other tools for creative problem solving. However, TRIZ is included in this abstracts section because an element of it, the "laws of technical system evolution," is associated with evolution in the technological domain. Altshuller positioned subdivided laws of technical system evolution in three categories (Wikipedia, 2015d):

- Statics – describing criteria of viability of newly created technical systems.
- Kinematics – defining how technical systems evolve regardless of conditions.

---

[2] TRIZ is a Russian acronym of *teoriya resheniya izobretatelskikh zadatch*, which is commonly translated as "Theory of Inventive Problem Solving."

[3] ARIZ is a Russian acronym of *algoritm resheniya izobretatelskikh zadatch*, which translates as "Algorithm of Inventive Problem Solving."

 – Dynamics – defining how technical systems evolve under special conditions.

These laws or patterns can be used to forecast the direction into which a technological system can develop, according to Altshuller. However, these laws have not evolved into general guidance rules in science, technology, or engineering studies. They remain an element of TRIZ, and as such an element of a creative technique. Therefore, TRIZ and its laws of technical systems evolution is better characterized as a tool for creative problem solving than the other theories listed in this section.

10.3 Anderson and Tushman (1990): "Technological Discontinuities and Dominant Designs: A Cyclical Model of Technological Change"

Anderson and Tushman (1990) propose an evolutionary model of technological change. Their model (Figure 10.2) recognizes that technology develops in cycles in which periods of fermentation and periods of incremental change alternate. The eras of fermentation are initiated by a technological discontinuity and followed by intense technological variation and selection, which culminates in one, sometimes a few, dominant design(s). Subsequently an era of incremental change starts, in which a dominant design is further elaborated until a new technological discontinuity punctuates the equilibrium. The model is called evolutionary as it recognizes that the process is driven by technological "variation," for which the rate is high in the eras of ferment when many alternative solutions or designs compete. Then "selection" of an industry standard or dominant design is accomplished at a certain moment by social, political, and/or organizational dynamics. The establishment of new industry standards heralds a period of incremental change in which further elaboration of the standard leads to "retention" of the dominant design.

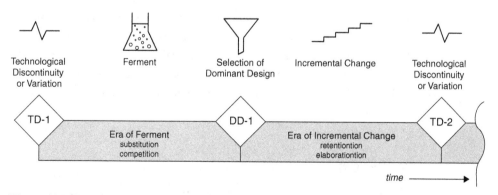

Figure 10.2 Technological discontinuities and dominant designs (Source: authors)

Discontinuities

The authors recognize two types of discontinuities. Process discontinuities are described as "fundamentally different ways of making a product that are reflected in order-of-magnitude improvements in the cost or quality of the product" (p. 607). An example of a process discontinuity discussed is the introduction of the float-glass process to produce flat-glass by leading the molten glass over a bath of a molten metal alloy. This provided about 400% improvement in square feet per hour output over the flat-glass processes used up to then. "Product discontinuities are fundamentally different product forms that command a decisive cost, performance, or quality advantage over prior product forms" (p. 607). Examples of a product discontinuity provided are diesel (vs. steam) locomotives and electronic (vs. mechanical) typing.

Technological discontinuities are characterized as either competence-enhancing or competence-destroying. The competence-enhancing discontinuities further build on the know-how embodied in the technologies they replace. The competence-destroying discontinuities, on the other hand, render existing competences required to master a technology obsolete. In other words, some lines of know-how further accumulate (evolve) while in other cases, new know-how structures are built, rendering the old versions obsolete and using them as fundaments. Competence-destroying discontinuities are typically followed by longer periods of ferment than observed for competence-enhancing cases. And, when a series of consecutive competence-enhancing discontinuities occur, they are characterized by eras of ferment that become shorter.

Anderson and Tushman remark that discontinuous technological advances do not always have the potential to once dominate the incumbent technological order. That is, discontinuous technological advances do not all lead to superiority, as was the case for the Wankel engine, which never challenged the dominance of the reciprocating or piston engine. However, once superiority of a new technology is established, supplanting happens rapidly.

The authors describe how technological competition processes can be forestalled for cases where firms fence off a technology by patents and licensing. The consequence is that various technological solutions keep competing. The opposite happens in regimes where a technological discontinuity becomes widely adopted by many competitors, which leads to the emergence of a dominant design.

Dominant Designs

Anderson and Tushman describe how dominant designs can emerge from market demand affected by technological possibilities and individual,

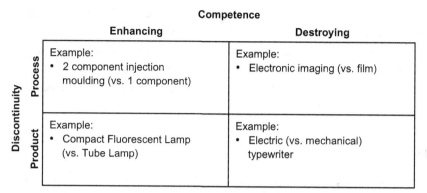

Figure 10.3 Examples of discontinuities and competences (Free after Anderson and Tushman, 1990).

Note: this figure is not included in the paper by Anderson and Tushman (Source: authors)

organizational, and governmental factors. Examples of such cases are found in the QWERTY typewriter and VHS videocassette recorder. Their packages of features were favored by the market. They did not necessarily have the best technical performance offered at that moment. There are also other ways for dominant designs to emerge. Market power of a dominant producer like IBM, which made a particular design standard in the early days of the personal computer, or a powerful user like the US Air Force, which mandated a standard for numerical control for programmable machine tools (now commonly referred to as computer numerical controlled or CNC), also provide a selection process that leads to dominant designs.

It is remarked that technical discontinuities themselves will not become the dominant design. The dominant design itself is shaped by actions of individuals, organizations, and networks of organizations, and emerges as the cumulative product of selection among technological variations produced in the era of ferment. Thus, the establishment of a dominant design marks the end of the period of ferment, which was initiated by the technological discontinuity. Since dominant designs are the product of selection not only by technical, but also by a set of social and political constraints, they will not be on the frontier of technological performance when emerging. By definition, a design becomes dominant when adopted by more than 50% of the market. The risk adverse, who adopt a design only once it becomes dominant, perceive state-of-the art designs that deliver superior technical performance as too unreliable and expensive. The introduction of the dominant design ends uncertain times as it reduces product-class confusion. It also promises dramatic cost reduction, as firms can design standardized and interchangeable parts plus optimize their processes for volume and efficiency.

Dominant designs that arise from competence-destroying discontinuities are likely to be initiated by new entrants in an industry as these benefit from attacking established structures with new know-what. On the other hand, incumbent firms commonly prefer to extend their established know-how. Hence they will typically initiate dominant designs arising from competence-enhancing discontinuities.

Reflection

The authors of this book remark that specifically for production processes, discontinuities are in general relatively simple to identify, as their cost or quality improvement can be measured well. Product discontinuities, on the other hand, can be more difficult to designate. According to Anderson and Tushman, product discontinuities command a decisive cost, performance, or quality advantage over prior product forms. With the introduction of the compact fluorescent lamp (CFL), which provided a much higher efficacy and lifetime, a decisive cost improvement was achieved over incandescent lamps (see also Chapter 7). However, it appears that lamp performance (start speed, ability to dim) and quality of the light produced by these lamps, in terms of human perception, did not improve, but declined. These aspects are more qualitative in nature than cost per unit of light. As the case study shows, CFL did not become a dominant design in terms of the product class general lighting solution (GLS), as it could not oust the incandescent lamp by its own merits in the eyes of consumers. Within the scope of the product family CFL, however, the transition from the CFL-G1 architecture, based on magnetic ballast, toward the CFL-G2 architecture, based on electronic ballast, was clear and decisive. The dominant design of a subsystem[4] of the CFL (the ballast) changed, allowing the lamp to become much smaller, lighter, and cheaper while it also improved its performance.

Even more difficult to interpret in quantitative terms is the advancement in child restraint systems (CRS) described in Chapter 8 of this book. The basic function of CRS is providing safety to children traveling in cars. However, no product review published in decades of consumer guides provides test information that indicates how much more safe one design is versus another. And price performance reviews provide relative rankings. Nevertheless, the test reviews published in the consumer guide provide a good overview of the evolution of CRS. Starting around 1970, there were no standards yet, and the products reviewed did often not offer any significant safety. Once in the 1990s,

---

[4]   Another publication (Tushman and Murmann, 1998) further explores the concept of dominant designs, its underlying causal mechanisms, and the levels of analysis used in literature. This publication argues that dominant designs apply most fundamentally to a product's subsystem.

common product architectures were established for different age or weight groups, the safety provided was generally good.

10.4 Arthur (2009): *The Nature of Technology, What It Is and How It Evolves*

This is one of the few books written to provide arguments for an evolutionary nature of "technology." According to Arthur, evolution in both biology and technology is a matter of accumulating changes. For both, the path of development defines what and how certain species or technologies develop. The history of development therefore is very relevant. In biology, adaptation and survival of the fittest lead to changes and new species. Adaptation occurs through slow mutations in the genetic information of species. In technology, adaptation for the major part takes place by recombining knowledge and techniques, or ways for solving problems. Arthur calls this process in technology therefore combinatorial evolution.

This *combinatorial evolution* points out that technology is about making new combinations of known routines, more than inventing completely new routines. Combinatorial evolution makes it possible to combine ideas from various technology domains to construct complex technologies in a rather short period compared to biological evolution. The turbine jet engine is used as an example to show this particular technology did not evolve by the accumulation of small, favorable changes over a long period of time; it was developed for a large part by recombining existing knowledge in a short period. This recombination of knowledge makes very rapid combinatorial evolution for technology possible. Change/adaptation in technology is foremost a routine, the work of inventors and development engineers. Combinatorial evolution is thus about creating novel things out of combinations of themselves.

In biology, evolution is slow paced, at least if observed from a human time scale. Every mutation needs to be "viable" to survive. Mutations then accumulate one by one over many generations as long as the species in which they propagate remains viable. Once a species dies off, its genome including the mutation disappears. Biological evolution is essentially about the accumulation of small changes over many generations. The changes appear via variation and selection. Recombination also appears (e.g., in bacteria swapping genes), but is less prevalent as in technology.[5] Arthur claims technological evolution is not so much characterized by the accumulation of small changes. It would not have provided a jet engine, as it is not an accumulation of small changes, but rather the recombination of ideas. Because technological development is an

---

[5] Note that in multi-celled life, gene swapping appears less prevalent. However, if one takes into account that the majority of biological diversity appears in single-celled life (Archaea and Bacteria), then the comparison looks different. See also Section 3.3.

accumulation process mainly driven by making novel combinations out of existing technologies, prior development is important (as a source of ideas), and innovation in technology is an evolutionary process.

In combinatorial evolution, ideas are recombined. Successful combinations lead to new ideas, technologies, products, etc. Arthur stays away from products. He specifically names *technologies* and gives it a rather wide scope as a *means to a purpose*. Technologies, according to Arthur, also encompass "nontechnical" systems, e.g., banking systems, contracts, and legal systems. Technology is described as recursive. It has a structure from large to small (e.g., systems > assemblies > parts or a fleet > an aircraft carrier > air crafts > jet turbine > fan blades).

Phenomena

The discovery of phenomena requires the accumulation of knowledge and techniques to reveal them. The discovery of a particular family of phenomena leads to the discovery of later ones. Technologies are programmed by a set of fixed phenomena in many different ways. For that reason, Arthur points at phenomena as the "genes of technology." He describes that knowledge cumulates over time. Technical universities, learned societies, national academies of science and engineering, published journals, and so on are a substrate from which technologies emerge. This pyramid of causality supports the microprocess of innovation as a logistic system supports an army in battle. This rough "readiness" in timing makes it rare for novel technologies to be the work of a single inventor. Technology begins a journey along a path of development. Once under way, different working versions of the technology emerge. Technologies tend to become more complex as they mature. This is referred to as structural deepening. Once component replacement or structural deepening do not add much more to the performance of a technology, it reaches maturity. Then a novel principle is needed for further development. Improvement speeds up if competition from other developers becomes heated, and slows down if competition is absent. Technology domains are described as coherent wholes, families. They are not invented; they emerge over decades, crystallizing around a set of phenomena or enabling technologies. The author refers to economics and that the era of equilibrium economics is over. However, Arthur does not substantially refer to evolutionary economics. The work of Nelson and Winter (1982) is mentioned in only two instances.

10.5 Basalla (1988): *The Evolution of Technology*

Since the 1980s, evolutionary theories have been applied more prominently to technological change. Basalla (1988) uses "the evolution of technology" as a metaphor to describe how the process of technological innovation produces novel artefacts, and how society applies selective pressure on available artefacts. As an historian, Basalla speaks of artefacts rather than products or technologies. Basalla argues that "necessity and utility alone cannot account for the variety and novelty of the artefacts fashioned by humankind" (p. 2), and suggests seeking other explanations. He proposes to apply the theory of organic evolution to the technological world, although cautioning of the "vast differences between the world of the made and the world of the born."

His theory of technological evolution is rooted in four broad concepts: diversity, continuity, novelty, and selection. "This diversity can be explained as the results of technological evolution because artefactual continuity exists; novelty is an integral part of the made world; and a selection process operates to choose novel artefacts for replication and addition to the stock of made things" (p. 25). His book is organized according to these four concepts and explores the evolution of many artefacts. Basalla states that "continuity implies that novel artefacts can only arise from antecedent artefacts – that new kinds of made things are never pure creations of theory, ingenuity, or fancy. If technology is to evolve, then novelty must appear in the midst of the continuous" (p. vii–viii).

Basalla describes the evolution of a range of different technologies. For example, the development of Edison's electric lighting system is described as an exhibit of continuity in change, because it builds on the idea of a network to distribute energy, like used for gas lamps and electric arc lamps. Both systems had their drawbacks. Gas lamps held a fire hazard. And the arc lamps could not be dimmed, nor individually switched on or off, and required power stations close to the point of use. Both solutions produced toxic fumes. The incandescent lamp was proposed as an answer, developed drawing from antecedent solutions. According to Basalla, this exemplifies the continuity in the evolution of artefacts that always builds on antecedent solutions.

10.6 Bense (1954): *Aesthetica, Metaphysische Beobachtungen am Schönen*

In the years shortly before and after World War II, a number of efforts was made to measure when an object (of art), a design, or a building is beautiful or ugly. In his book *Aesthetica*, Max Bense tried to find formulas for beauty in art, in technology, and in nature.

$$Ks = (W+[Cw.N']).M$$
$$Ts = (W+[Cw.N]).M$$
$$Ns = W+Cw$$

The abbreviations in these formulas have the following meaning.

Ks: beauty in art
Ts: beauty in technology
Ns: beauty in nature
W: reality
Cw: environment
N: necessity
N':   non-necessity (the opposite of necessity)
M: possibility

Bense did not manage to develop his formulas in any further detail. He only gives some reflections on them. In his book, he refers to the formula Birkhoff (1928) used for the aesthetic measure (M):

$$M = \frac{O}{C}$$

In this formula, O stands for the measure of order of the object and C for the complexity. According to Bense, this formula can be used only for objects or designs that are not too complex (*"möglichst einfache, nicht zusammengestelte ästhetische Objekte"* (Bense, 1954, 31–32)). The main problem with all the formulas described is that concepts on both sides of the equal sign cannot be filled in with numbers.

10.7 Berlyne (1971): *Aesthetics and Psychobiology*

Berlyne (1971) started his research to try and establish why people are interested in objects – such as works of art – that do not seem to have any biological benefit for them. According to Berlyne, people search (actively) for stimuli that trigger their senses in the right way. If the design is too easy or too complex to comprehend, it will be judged more negatively. The aesthetic appreciation of a pattern depends on the extent to which it can stimulate the senses. The graphic representation of this phenomenon has a reversed U-form. Patterns or designs with a level of interest that is too low do not stimulate the senses and are therefore not pleasing, although not unpleasant either. In the words of Berlyne, they are indifferent. If the level of interest intensifies, for instance because the pattern becomes more complex or because it contains unexpected irregularities, the level of interest grows and the senses are stimulated in a positive way. This continues until the pattern becomes too complicated and the observer starts to dislike it. In that case, the senses are stimulated in a negative way and the observer will find the pattern (or design) unpleasant (not beautiful, ugly). Three kinds of variables can stimulate the senses:

- Physiological aspects, such as size of the object, intensity, hue, and saturation of colors.
- Ecological aspects, such as learned or associative meaning of a picture or
  object.
- Comparative properties, such as newness, ambiguity, contradiction, and
  complexity.

Berlyne's research concentrated on the last category. He found a reversed U-
form that reflected the relationship between aesthetic appreciation and complexity (as shown in Figure 10.4), ambiguity, irregularity, and/or newness
(originality), where uniformity, order, and familiarity would lower the level
of interest and variation, complexity, and newness would enhance the level of
interest. Whether an increase in the level of interest is experienced as positive
depends on the level of enhancement, the situation, and the experience of the
beholder. Berlyne adds that the appreciation for complexity rises with both age
and the level of artistic training or education of the subjects. Over the years,
Berlyne's model has been quite widely disputed. Some researchers did not
agree with his reversed U-form, but instead advocated a linear, rising line (as
shown in Figure 10.5). It also seems as if Berlyne's model works best for simple,
artificially created designs. The model does not work so well as soon as the
designs, such as paintings, have an associative or learned meaning.

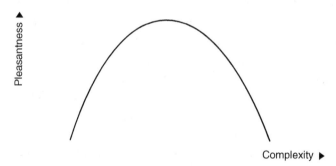

Figure 10.4 Pleasantness versus complexity (Source: authors)

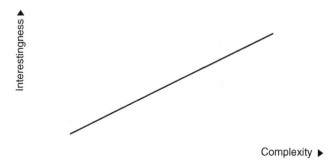

Figure 10.5 Interestingness versus complexity (Source: authors)

In later research, Berlyne made a distinction between "pleasantness" and "interestingness." According to these new insights, simple, easy-to-understand, redundant patterns are found pleasing, but a pattern is only considered interesting if it contains some disorientation that cannot be understood within seconds, but instead requires the observer to take a second look. Interestingness grows in a linear manner with complexity, whereas pleasantness gives a reversed U-form: not enough complexity is boring; too much complexity is annoying.

10.8 Bijker (1990): *The Social Construction of Technology*

As a sociologist studying technology, Bijker argues that technology does not determine human action, but that rather, human action shapes technology. To explain how this "shaping of technology" happens, Bijker distinguishes three "developmental configurations" in which a product can be: "social group," "technological frame," and "inclusion." A social group can best be compared to what an industrial design engineer would call a "stakeholder." A technological frame resembles "a body of knowledge." Inclusion finally can be compared to what in the (neoclassical) economy would be called "path dependence" and "technical lock-in." If there is no dominant social group, then, according to Bijker, there are many different products (or different solutions for a problem) aimed at these social groups. If there is only one important social group, then a dominant design will emerge. Sometimes there is only one dominant design. The bicycle is an example: There is one dominant design (with many variations; see Section 4.3). Sometimes there are a few dominant designs. Shaving has three dominant designs: wet shaving and electric shaving with either a rotating or a vibrating shaving principle (see Section 4.1). If there is one dominant group, there usually is a corresponding technological frame. Inclusion can prevent inventors (or innovators and designers) from finding new solutions because they cannot step out of their technological frame.

If there is no technological frame, then the number of solutions that are investigated is radical, in the sense that there are many solutions that are very different. All aspects of the product are subject to variation. On the other hand, if there is a technological frame, Bijker further distinguishes between actors with a high or a low inclusion. If the actor (designer, engineer) has a high inclusion, he is bound to generate rather conventional product improvements. Actors with a low inclusion will draw much less on standard problem-solving strategies and may also identify different problems than actors with a high inclusion.

10.9 Boselie (1982): *Over Visuele Schoonheidservaring*

Boselie researched what aspects of patterns lead to aesthetic appreciation. He distinguishes between aesthetic, hedonistic, and affective values that an object (or a piece of art or music) can have for the observer. According to Boselie, hedonistic value is more extensive than aesthetic value.

> We speak of a positive hedonistic value if the experience is pleasant, joyful. We speak of a negative hedonistic value if the experience is unpleasant, inconvenient.
>
> (1982, 2)

From earlier research, it can be concluded, according to Boselie, that stimuli are considered pleasant or unpleasant for various reasons. Subjects give qualifications such as: beautiful, funny, interesting, and exciting or, by contrast, ugly, boring, and farfetched. It was found that the stimulus that was considered the most beautiful was often not considered the most exciting. The qualifications mentioned previously describe the affective meaning of the stimuli. They are measured on what is called a semantic scale. That is a scale on which the subjects judge a stimulus on opposite qualifications, such as beautiful/ugly, small/big, or exiting/boring. Often the subjects can choose from a scale of five or seven steps.

In his research, Boselie uses two-dimensional patterns that consist of lines and dots. In short, his results can be summarized as follows: perceptual beauty is directly related to perceptual order. The perception of beauty is directly related to the experience of order perceived by the subject. If a pattern consists of a combination of different orders, the experience of beauty will grow if the perception of order is stronger and will diminish if the order is hard to perceive.

Even in his introduction Boselie remarks that, in empirical research into art, the statements of subjects are often considered typical for the subject, not for the work of art. He therefore concludes his thesis with a discussion of ecological validity. Because the situation in a laboratory differs from reality, one can question whether the results are still valid in the real world. If it is difficult to draw conclusions in daily life based on the experiments in a laboratory, one speaks of a low ecological validity. According to Boselie, many researchers and authors doubt the validity of experiments with regard to aesthetics. Arguments that these critics use include the following:

- The patterns offered to the subjects are of a kind that no one in his right mind would examine for longer than a fraction of a second (outside the experimental situation in which one "has to" look).
- The situations in which the subjects examine the patterns are very different from real-life situations. The subjects are asked to give an aesthetic judgment, but there is a substantial chance that the subjects instead try to show off their artistic expertise rather than to give their personal opinions.

In response to this, Boselie argues that some pieces of art – he mentions Kandinsky, Liberman, and Struycken – strongly resemble the patterns he used in his experiments.

He also states that the hypotheses that he considers to have "partially proved" – meaning that perceived beauty equals perceived order – are mainly valid for simple patterns. However, he does not exclude that in more complex patterns as well, such as in baroque, the patterns that have the highest perceived order – within the rules of the style – will be considered the most beautiful.

Boselie's research can also be regarded as an argument for large-scale variation. Although in his experiments he finds a majority of subjects who confirm his hypotheses, there is also always a substantial minority (of sometimes up to 40%) who do not agree and choose the other design. (In Boselie's experiments, the designs are compared "pair wise.") This is a minority that many marketers would find very interesting if it represented the possible market share.

10.10 Christensen (1997): *The Innovator's Dilemma*

Christensen states that, when trying to predict the future, specialists usually do not do much more than extrapolate the present:

> The only thing we may know for sure when we read experts' forecasts about how large emerging markets will become is that they are wrong. (1997, xxi)

He differentiates between two kinds of innovations, namely sustaining and disruptive innovations.

Sustaining and Disruptive Innovations

Why do well-organized and well-managed companies that seem to do what they should do, fail? They listen carefully to the wishes of their clients, they introduce new technologies as soon as possible, they strive for better products for a lower price, and they produce what their customers want.

In his book *The Innovator's Dilemma*, Christenen (1997) provides the following explanation as to why such companies fail. The fact that they listened to their clients, invested in the latest technologies, offer their clients better-performing products, that is, products that meet the needs of their clients better, based their developments on careful and thorough research of trends in the market, and invested in the markets that promised the best financial results, was the reason why they lost their market leadership.

In his study, he concludes that it sometimes makes sense not to listen to clients, but to invest in products that don't perform in line with the wishes of these clients and that have a lower profit margin. He also concludes that it is sometimes better to invest in small, not very interesting markets, rather than in big, much more promising markets.

Most of the time, innovations are sustaining. A sustaining innovation is an innovation that fulfills a desire held by existing clients. Often this means improving the performance of the product. Sustaining innovations hardly ever lead to the failure of an organization. A sustaining innovation leads to an improved product with an immediate, positive result for the company. The company's clients asked for the improvement and immediately buy it.

In the event of a disruptive innovation, there is, according to Christensen, no improvement of the product that the existing relations are interested in. On the contrary, the present clients will not want the innovation. Disruptive innovations have to find their own, new market. The problem for the present organization comes later, after the product has been developed in more detail, and sometimes only after several years, when the disruptive innovation has been improved in such a way that it has become interesting to their clients. In many cases, it is then too late. The new organization will have acquired such a strong position in the market that the existing organizations are unable to catch up.

A disruptive innovation is a competitive product that is cheaper than the existing products and that initially performs less well. The market for the product is small and therefore not interesting for the existing suppliers. Disruptive innovations usually fulfill most of the following criteria:

- The products are simpler in the sense that they perform less well and offer fewer possibilities.
- The products are cheaper.
- The profits are lower.
- The products are successful in small, uninteresting markets.
- The key clients of the present producers do not want the product (and usually have no use for it either).

10.11 Crilly, Moultrie, and Clarkson (2004): "Seeing Things: Consumer Response to the Visual Domain in Product Design"

This study discusses consumer responses to product visual form with an emphasis on the aesthetic, semantic, and symbolic aspects of the cognitive response to design. In this section, a selection is made of those aspects that are the most relevant for designers and that are related to evolutionary product development. Products are considered signs that users can interpret. A consumer can react to a product by cognition and an effect that may be followed by behavior.

Cognition

The first – cognition – can be described using the following categories: aesthetic impression, semantic interpretation, and symbolic association.

Aesthetic Impression

According to Coates (2003), the aesthetic impression is the result of two factors, namely information and concinnity. (Berlyne (1971) proposes pleasure and interest; see Section 10.7 of this volume.) He suggests that both stem from the objective qualities of a product and from the subjective experiences of the consumer. This leads to four components of aesthetic impression: objective information, subjective information, objective concinnity, and subjective concinnity.

- Objective information concerns the degree of contrast that a product presents against competing products, the environment in which it is used, and the (complexity of) its design.
- Subjective information is the novelty the consumer perceives in the product. A design that is completely new to one consumer may be quite familiar to a more experienced consumer.
- Objective concinnity is related to the order that can be perceived in the product (e.g., symmetry).
- Subjective concinnity refers to the extent to which the consumer understands the product. Aspects are the cultural background of the consumer and the degree of commonality with products known to him.

Coates suggests that these four factors are items on a weighing scale:

> If information outweighs concinnity, the product will be considered confusing, meaningless and ugly. Alternatively, if concinnity outweighs information, the product will be considered simple, dull and boring.   (Crilly et al., 2004, 558)

This principle seems related to the famous MAYA principle – Most Advanced Yet Acceptable – of Raymond Loewy. Loewy:

> The adult public's taste is not necessarily ready to accept the logical solutions to their requirements if the solution implies too vast a departure from what they have been conditioned into accepting as the norm.   (www.raymondloewy.com, 2011)

Semantic Interpretation

In their description of semantic interpretation, Crilly and colleagues use Monö's semantic functions (Monö, 1997): description, expression, exhortation, and identification.

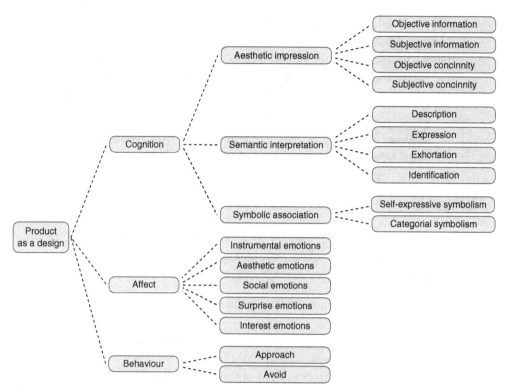

Figure 10.6 An overview of the aspects that involve consumer response to product visual form according to Crilly and colleagues (Source: authors)

- Description refers to the way a product is self-explanatory, the way its form explains its use (without the need of instructions).
- Expression has to do with the way that the properties of the product are perceived. The design can show the user that it needs to be handled with care or that it is very robust and can withstand some abuse.
- Exhortation refers to the interaction between the user and the product. For example, a sound may draw a user's attention to an action that has to be undertaken.
- Identification is about the origin and affiliation of a product: the brand, product type, specific model, etc.

Symbolic Association

Products – but also behavior, jewelry, or make-up – are used by consumers to express themselves, for example to show that they are unique and/or that they belong to a group: self-expressive symbolism and categorical symbolism. Consumers use self-expressive symbolism to try and express their individual qualities and differentiate themselves from other people around them. By contrast, they use categorical symbolism to try and express the fact that they belong to a certain group or social class.

According to Crilly and colleagues, the three cognitive responses to product design do not operate independently, but are highly interrelated:

> For example, assessment of what a product is (Semantic Interpretation), may influence judgements on the elegance of a design (Aesthetic Impression) and the social values it may connote (Symbolic Association).   (2004, 564)

Affect

Affect relates to the emotional responses that products may elicit. Desmet (2003) proposes five aspects: instrumental, aesthetic, social, surprise, and interest emotions.

- Instrumental emotions refers to the functioning of the product: is it pleasant to work with?
- Aesthetic emotions relate to the liking or disliking of a product based on its looks.
- Social emotions relate to what other people (may) think of the product.
- Surprise emotions relate to the novelty of the design in the eyes of the beholder.
- Interest emotions refer to the degree to which the consumer wants to possess and use the product.

Behavior

Behavior is about the way consumers respond to a product. This aspect is not given much attention in the paper by Crilly and colleagues. They distinguish between approach and avoid responses:

> Approach responses may be associated with further investigation of the product, product purchase and product use. Avoid responses may be associated with ignoring the product, failure to purchase and even hiding the product.   (2004, 554)

10.12 David (1985): "Clio and the Economics of QWERTY"

The QWERTY keyboard layout has become commonly associated with the concept of path dependence since Paul A. David (1985) published his seminal paper on this topic. QWERTY, as it is commonly known, is a keyboard layout standard named after the sequence of letters used on the top row. Clio refers to the muse of history in Greek mythology on which the name cliometrics is based. Cliometrics or economic history is a discipline that uses systematic application of econometric techniques and other mathematical methods to study social and economic history. For this paper, David used the economic historical account of the development of typewriter keyboards to describe the concept of path dependence, which has since become associated with QWERTY.

David uses his exposition of the developments that provided us QWERTY to describe how this particular layout became dominant over other possible layouts, like, for example, the Dvorak Simplified Keyboard (DSK). The DSK, patented in 1936, allegedly allows for faster typing. Nevertheless, QWERTY remained dominant, or locked-in, as phrased in the terminology of economic historians. According to David, the fifty-second man (. . .) to invent the type-writer named Christopher Latham Soles applied for a patent in 1867 for his primitive writing machine. This machine did not allow for hassle-free typing as it suffered from jamming type bars, of which, moreover, the results were not directly visible as the mechanism was visually hidden behind the paper carriage. The mechanical deficiencies of this early machine stood in the way of commercialization. Soles spent six years on trial-and-error experiments, rearranging the keyboard layout away from its initial alphabetical order. This eventually led to the QWERTY layout for which the manufacturing rights were acquired in 1873 by the company Remington and Sons, a famous gun maker. Remington's mechanics completed the evolution of this keyboard layout with many changes that fine-tuned the design. Among them was a change of the position for the R into the first row. This final layout allowed rapid pecking of letters that form the word TYPEWRITER by salesmen to impress customers.

The first typewriters, named No. 1 Remington, were marketed in an economic downturn and sold slowly. The model No. 2, marketed in 1878, witnessed better sales with the economic downturn ending. The annual typewriter production climbed to 1,200 units in 1881. At that time, it is said, the total available number of typewriters using the QWERTY layout could not yet have exceeded 5,000 and its layout was not yet deeply entrenched.

The typewriter boom started in the beginning of the 1880s with many competing keyboard layouts proliferating. In the late 1880s, the QWERTY-adapted "touch typing" was introduced, which allowed for easier operation, as was possible with the up to then used four-finger hunt-and-peck method. Touch typing, according to David, gave rise to three features causing QWERTY to become "locked-in." These were *technical interrelatedness, economies of scale,* and *quasi-irreversibility* of investment.

With the advent of the typewriter, these machines were taking their place in a large, complex system that involved typewriter operators or typists and organizations that provided training to prospective typists, as well as buyers and manufacturers.

Technical interrelatedness between "hardware," formed by keyboard layouts, and "software," represented by the typist's acquired skill using a particular keyboard layout, introduced the need for compatibility. Initial typewriter buyers were business firms who acquired the machine as an instrument for production. With only small numbers of those machines around, every decision to purchase a QWERTY keyboard typewriter instead of a competing design provided typists accustomed to QWERTY a better market position than those accustomed to other layouts. This increased the likelihood that new typists would prefer to learn QWERTY over other layouts. While QWERTY gained acceptance, economies of scale made its cost decrease relative to other systems, causing a self-reinforcing mechanism. In the battle of the keyboard layouts, the first economies of scale made the momentum tip toward QWERTY. Technical interrelatedness of the typewriter keyboard layout and related typing skills raised barriers between the available layouts. The typing skills acquired by typists formed a quasi-irreversible investment. In case of a conversion to a different system, the investment in acquiring the skill had to be written off. This produced a de facto standardization through the predominance of a single keyboard layout that remained locked-in, although from the mid-1890s, typewriter engineering advances removed the need for the QWERTY layout to prevent jamming.

The case David describes is intriguing because today, with electronic keyboards used for computers, or touch screens used on mobile devices, the days of the typewriter are so far gone by, that probably nobody entering university has experienced a mechanical typewriter anymore, let alone jamming mechanisms associated with the early days of the typewriter. Nevertheless, QWERTY still dominates.

Path dependence, as a phenomenon used *ex post* to explain how technologies are adopted and industries evolve, is commonly used. Nevertheless, David's reasoning is not without controversy. Liebowitz and Margolis (1990) are vocal critics, arguing there are three different types of path dependence. Only the third degree type would theoretically involve a lock-in, which, according to these authors, does not exist in real-world cases. To add to the controversy, Vergne (2013) states that empirical evidence for path dependence is so far absent. Vergne believes path dependence "is out there," but calls for better research to explore it aiming at coherent theories and predictable future trajectories. It appears that David initiated a path of thought that became dependent on the QWERTY case.

10.13 Dosi (1982): "Technological Paradigms and Technological Trajectories: A Suggested Interpretation of the Determinants and Directions of Technical Change"

Dosi introduced the term "technological paradigm " in analogy with the scientific paradigm as posed by Kuhn (1962).

Dosi defines "technological paradigm" as:

> A "model" and a "pattern" of solution of selected technological problems based on selected principles derived from natural sciences and on selected material technologies.

Subsequently, a technological trajectory is defined as:

> The pattern of "normal" problem solving activity (i.e., of "progress") on the ground of a technological paradigm.

The technological trajectory is the direction of advance within a technological paradigm. The technological paradigm strongly narrows the directions of technological change (solutions) pursued (investigated). It provides a framework that guides technological development. At the same time, such a framework also prevents investigation of alternative types of solutions. Thus, a technology paradigm has an exclusion effect, blinding technologists and engineers to other technological possibilities. According to Dosi, *paradigms are also an "outlook" that focuses the eye and the efforts of technologists and engineers in defined directions.*

Dosi describes two different states of technological development: "normal progress" and "extraordinary innovative effort" or breakthroughs. During "normal progress," technology develops along a path or trajectory that is framed or limited by the boundaries of the technological paradigm. This is also called "continuous technological change". Trajectories are disrupted by changes in the technological paradigm. When a technological paradigm changes, the problem-solving activity starts almost again from the beginning. This type of technological change is referred to as discontinuous. Often, the emergence of new technologies is characterized by new emerging firms.

Dosi describes two phases of technological change. First, in a "trial-and-error" phase, institutions produce and direct the accumulation of knowledge, experience, etc. A multiplicity of risk-taking actors tries different technical and commercial solutions. Then a second phase starts, the "oligopolistic maturity." In this phase, the production, exploitation, and commercial diffusion of innovations are commonly executed by a less diverse group of actors. Therefore, this phase is referred to as oligopolistic competition. Actors in this phase derive their oligopolistic power from the asymmetric capability to innovate successfully. Static entry barriers (such as economies of scale) protect the oligopolist from competition entering the market. This possibility for firms to enjoy oligopolistic positions is a strong economic incentive to innovate as it provides them market and technological leadership.

10.14 Foot (1996): *Boom, Bust,* & *Echo*

According to David Foot, two-thirds of everything that will happen in the near future (five to 10 years) can be predicted based on demographic shifts. If you want to know how people aged 40 will behave in five years, all you have to do is study the behavior of people aged 45 right now. If there are a lot of people aged 40, the behavior of people who are currently 45 will become a trend. Unfortunately, the results of Foot's research with regard to the behavior of people are spread throughout his book, and he does not use age categories. To make his theory useful for industrial design engineers, age categories have been created. The results of his research were collected and grouped according to these categories and are described next.[6]

Children, Zero to Nine Years

This group does not feature in Foot's research. Children of this age do not usually decide for themselves (although this may depend on their ability to nag). In general their parents decide (see Starters and Families).

Adolescents, 10–19 Years

Adolescents do not have much money, but they do have a lot of time. This means that they have enough time to look for the cheapest offers and that they are willing to read complicated instructions and assemble do-it-yourself products to save money. They live with their parents, attend concerts and sport events, go out a lot, and download lots of music, films, and games. They use public transport and think they are immortal.

Starters, 20–29 Years

Just like adolescents, starters do not have much money, but they do have a lot of time. They study and start living on their own, mostly in the center of a (big) city. They are not very critical about the quality of the products they buy. They look for bargains and spend time hunting them down. They buy in discount shops and assemble products themselves if that saves them money. Mostly they

---

[6] Note that the book was written in 1996 and that Foot is Canadian. Although some aspects were updated, not everything will be relevant in every country.

use public transport and they drink beer (a lot of cheap beer so that they can get drunk as cheaply as possible). They also behave as if they were immortal. Their favorite sports are football (soccer), tennis, and hockey. They use decorative cosmetics (fashionable, with expressive colors) and they are followers of the latest fashion. They are on the look-out for a potential partner. If they buy their first car, it is second-hand and an inexpensive one.

Families, 30–39 Years

Starter families with small children usually have a bit more to spend, but they also have a lot of expenses due to their houses, furnishings, cars, and children. (In the Netherlands, the average age of women when they gave birth for the first time was 29 in 1996 and 28 in 1992). Because they spend a lot of money, they often borrow (mortgage). They live in a suburb and want a house with a garden. They drink less, but more expensive alcohol in the form of special beers or wine. They buy a new car every two years to "keep up with the Joneses." As they approach 40, they start earning more money, but have less time to spend it. They become more critical of the quality of the products they buy. They select skincare products (instead of decorative cosmetics) and engage in fewer sports (or they switch sports to golf). Because they have children, the vehicle they own will be a minivan, space wagon, or SUV.

Career Oriented, 40–49 Years

The people who belong to this group have a lot of money to spend. Their career is midway and their participation in nightlife is declining. Their children start to go and live on their own, their mortgage has been nearly paid back, and many of the products they have are good enough and do not need replacing. They have busy lives, regard quality as important, and have no time (nor do they want to take the time) to look for bargains. They buy leading brands and want good advice. They do not have time to read the manual, so they want simple products. They like convenience and are willing to spend money on getting it. Instead of buying a head of lettuce, they buy prepacked, prewashed, ready-to-use "salad mix." They shop at supermarkets with a wide range of products. They do not mind that all this costs a bit more as long as it does not take much time. They buy a smaller, but more luxurious car. They pay almost no attention to fashion because they already dislocated their ankles by wearing platform shoes in their twenties. They buy clothes that they know from experience fit their style. They buy more lingerie, also "corrective" lingerie, because their body is not in as good shape as it used to be. About 80% need reading glasses. They are attracted to less contact-based sports, such as golf or walking. They go to musicals, ballet, and classic concerts, rather than to rock concerts and sports events. By the time they reach 45, they start having a midlife crisis about what they are going to do with the rest of their lives. They start their own company or set out on a new career. They are sometimes willing to make do with a lower salary.

Young Seniors, 50–59 Years

Young seniors have both time and money. Their children have left home and they want good quality and service. They have enough experience with products of poor quality to have become very critical and aware of good quality. They think they have everything they need as regards products. They therefore prefer to spend their money on holidays, going out for dinner, concerts, or the theatre. They prefer faraway, exclusive destinations. With regard to clothing, they know what fits and suits them and are willing to pay the asking price. They are keen to be given good financial advice about how to invest their money (private banking). They are aware of their mortality (often one or both of their parents have died) and are worried about and pay attention to their state of health. They use vitamins and preventive medicines. Men encounter prostate problems; women are in or are approaching menopause. They spend more money on games of chance such as casino games, the lottery, and bingo. They prefer quiet shops with dedicated and patient staff and have no desire to negotiate on prices. They prefer luxurious sedans and drive them for five years or more. They often get involved in voluntary work and spend more money than others on charity. They visit museums, start collecting things (or pick up where they left off with an old collection), start a hobby, or start to read (again) in their spare time.

Seniors, 60+

Seniors are – to a great extent – comparable to young seniors. Many of them are retired and because most of them have taken good care of themselves, they get a lot of money to spend and a lot of time to spend it.[7] They do not plan to save this money for their children. They are assertive and critical and want to enjoy the rest of their lives, as well as giving meaning (fulfillment) to it. However, they start to suffer more and more health problems and their need for medication slowly increases as their mobility slowly decreases.

---

[7] This may differ per country. In Europe, this is the case in many countries.

What Can Be Predicted and What Cannot?

Foot claims that the near future of two-thirds of "everything" can be predicted with the aid of demographic knowledge, at least if the behavior is related to age. According to Foot, that is almost always the case. However, some things cannot be predicted. A surprising example is the result of elections. One would expect an aging population to vote more conservatively. However, this is untrue. Indeed, there is no relationship between age and voting behavior. Therefore, a change in the age structure of the population has no predictive value. Another example is the introduction of new products (innovations) and their direct consequences, such as the computer (and the predicted paperless office that still has not become a reality), or the discovery that smoking causes cancer, which has led very slowly to a reduction in the number of smokers. After a number of years, when the influence of the new product has become clearer, the consequences will also have become more and more predictable.

Exclusive?

A critical note that has to be made with regard to Foot's model is that he seems to concentrate his research on people with both a higher education and a higher income. He states, for instance, that members of the "career-oriented" and "young seniors" groups have a lot of money to spend. However, considering the VALS-typology of Mitchell (1983, and Section 10.21 of this volume), it can be concluded that 60% of people are regarded as belonging to a low-income category. No significant change is to be expected in this situation between 1983 and 1996, although the situation improved considerably as regards Mentality (Motivaction International, 2017, and section 10.22 of this volume). Therefore it is questionable if Foot's theory is representative of the whole population or only of an elite group.

10.15 Forty (1986): *Objects of Desire*

In his book *Objects of Desire*, Adrian Forty provides an interesting vision of the sometimes lengthy existence of styles and the lack of generally applicable scientific theories in the world of (industrial) design. He concludes that most books about design primarily offer descriptions of the life and work of (well-known) designers.

> It seems odd that the biographies of individuals should be considered a satisfactory means of explaining an activity that is by nature social and not purely personal. . . . If political economy consisted only of the study of the economy in the light of the statements made by politicians, the subject would indeed do little to increase our understanding of the world. Clearly, it would be foolish to dismiss designers'

> statements altogether, but we should not expect them to reveal all there is to know
> about design.   (1986, 239)

In books about design and industrial design engineering, the created designs
are, in most cases, based on the careers, statements, ideas, and theories of
individual designers. No consideration is given to things such as the wants and
needs of consumers, the price of the product, the market segment that the
products were aimed at, or the way they were advertised. In this vision,
the existence of products is considered only the result of the creativity of the
designer. This way of looking at products is misleading and ignores the fact that
a lot more needs to be done to launch a successful product onto the market
than just design work.

> Although designers prepare designs, the responsibility for carrying them out rests
> with the entrepreneur; in the development of a manufactured article, it is normal
> for many preliminary designs to be prepared, from which one is chosen by the
> entrepreneur to be worked up for production.   (1986, 241)

In most cases, the entrepreneur will choose from several concepts created by
the designer. Although a designer may give his opinion on the concept that
should be chosen, it is rare for him to be the decision maker.

> Many designers will admit that when they put up their first proposals, the
> entrepreneur chose a different design from the one they themselves favoured,
> and that it was the entrepreneur's choice and not their own on which the
> development went ahead. It is the entrepreneur not the designer who decides
> which design most satisfactorily embodies the ideas necessary to the product's
> success, and which best fits the material conditions of production.   (1986 241)

However, because designers usually only talk and write about what they
themselves do, design is often considered a process that is completely controlled by them. According to Forty, this is even what is sometimes taught at
design schools. One consequence is that some students get a completely wrong
impression of what they can achieve. Another is that they may grow frustrated
in their later career.

> Students are liable to acquire grandiose illusions about the nature of their skills,
> with the result that they become frustrated in their subsequent careers. (1986, 241)

10.16 Geels (2002): "Technological Transitions as Evolutionary
Reconfiguration Processes: a Multi-level Perspective
and a Case Study"

Geels (2002) developed a model to describe how *technological transitions* come
about. Technological transitions (TT) are described as long-term and large-
scale technological developments that transform the way in which societal

functions are fulfilled. The model applies what is called a *multilevel perspective* (MLP) to connect developments and context at different levels and time scales with each other, to explain the interaction and dynamics that lead to TT. Two views on technological evolution are used to describe TT. The first view describes how a process of variation, selection, and retention challenges inertia in technological regimes. This reasoning is an extension of evolutionary economics (Nelson and Winter, 1982) that challenges equilibrium, assumed by neoclassical economic theory, and instead proposes a process of continuous change. The second view uses the Schumpeterian perspective of unfolding and reconfiguration that results in paths and trajectories of evolving technologies.

The model distinguishes three characteristic mechanisms: (1) *niche accumulation*, (2) *technology add-on and hybridization*, and (3) *riding along with the growth market*.

The first mechanism (niche accumulation) takes place in "incubation rooms" that allow radical novelties to grow in terms of specification and price performance. This stage of the process is referred to as the micro level or *technological niche*, and acts as a "nursery for change." Niches are important because they provide a protected environment for learning by doing, using, and interacting. As the use of particular radical novelties grows in the number of application domains and market niches, it cumulates. Some novelties become widely adopted and evolve into dominant designs. Others do not make it and become failed innovations. In Figure 10.7, this process is symbolized by the small arrows on the bottom left. As long as dominant designs are not yet established, development efforts (arrows) go in all kinds of directions leading to diversity. Then the arrows come together and slowly move upward and gain influence. Small arrows transforming into a first fat arrow represent the establishment of a dominant design.

The second mechanism (technology add-on and hybridization) links the novelty with established technologies and plays a crucial role in the breakthrough of radical innovations. The novelty first links with established technologies as an "add-on" to solve particular bottlenecks. The paper illustrates the model with a case study, describing the transition from sailing ships to steamships in which "steam engines were first used as auxiliary add-ons to sailing ships, used at times of little winds" (p. 1265). Once the novelty further matures and grows in connectedness with the established technology, it starts forming hybrid solutions.

The third mechanism described marks how novelties break out from niches. Once technology matures well past its radical stage, it "rides along with the market growth." Growing in importance and influence, what once started as a novelty now becomes potent enough to start influencing on the regime level. As an example, the development of steamships is described. Toward the end of the 1840s, steamships became so advanced

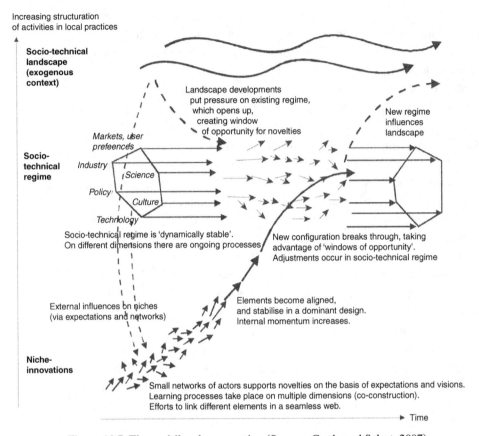

Figure 10.7 The multilevel perspective (Source: Geels and Schot, 2007)

they could be used for large-scale transport of passengers. The market for this was developed by landscape developments such as the Irish potato famine, European political revolutions and the Californian gold rush. Together, the conditions were created for a wave of mass immigration from Europe to North America. The immigration waves then fueled further development of steamships.

The model Geels developed applies what is called a dynamic, multi-level perspective to describe how technological transitions evolve through dynamics in and interactions between different levels: the micro level or niche, the meso level or socio-technical regime, and the macro level or landscape. The three levels can be understood as a nested hierarchy in which niches are embedded in regimes, which in turn are embedded in landscapes. Developments in niches occur on a relatively short time scale. The socio-technical regimes account for the stability of technological development in trajectories. The landscape consists of slow-changing, external, heterogeneous factors and provides gradients for the trajectories.

Examples of landscape elements are economic developments, wars, emigration, demographic shifts, and environmental problems (e.g., global warming).

Technological transitions do not occur because there is a sudden shift from one regime to another. Rather, a stepwise process of reconfiguration allows new regimes to grow out of old ones. A cascade of dynamics triggers changes in elements across all levels. Novelties grow from niches, and only become breakthrough innovations in interaction with processes on the level of regimes and socio-technical landscapes. The alignment of these developments determines if regime shifts occur. Technological transitions occur as the outcome of developments at different levels; they are not the cause. The model recognizes that technological transitions are multidimensional in nature, with technology being only one aspect of change next to user practices, regulation, industrial networks, infrastructure, and symbolic meaning or culture.

Reflection

Geels describes how technological transitions emerge and transform the way in which societal functions are fulfilled. The object of the model is the technological transition, which manifests itself as a systems change. This involves not only changing technologies or products, but above all changing socio-technical regimes and landscapes. This perspective is wider than the questions addressed in this book that specifically investigate how new (types of) products come about. Not every new (type of) product that emerges is also accompanied by a technological transition. However, every TT is accompanied by many new types of products. The case used illustrates how a new type of product, the steamship, emerged and eventually replaced the sailing ship. However, the case is not so much about the product steamship, as well as the dynamics of the process that brings about change in the way societies use particular technologies. The paper pays particular attention to the interaction of developments and contexts between different levels and explains that novelties only turn into breakthrough innovations (i.e., escape the niche) because of interaction with regimes and landscapes. This perspective contributes to the understanding of how new types of products emerge.

The compact fluorescent lamp, described in Chapter 7 of this book, is used as a case study of an emerging new type of product. However, it can also be portrayed as an example in the technological transition to energy-efficient societies. The trigger to develop the CFL came from socio-technical landscape developments: the first oil crisis and the awareness that there are "limits to growth." The breakthrough for the CFL was fostered by a landscape development more than two decades later, the awareness that limiting global warming required us to reduce the use of fossil fuels. This made political regimes prioritize massive adoption of energy-saving strategies in which the forced adoption of the already available CFL was a relatively easy step. The CFL did not oust the incandescent lamps because of consumer preference. It was politics that did the trick.

Geels's MLP model is used to describe how technological transitions emerge. As such, it is the theoretical framework for transition management, a type of policy used to orchestrate societal change, and in particular to address environmental and sustainability issues.

10.17 Hekkert (1995): *Artful Judgements*

In his research into aesthetic preference for visual patterns, Hekkert distinguishes four influential factors.

1. Physiological properties: physiological properties are the objective and quantifiable properties of pieces of art or designs, such as measures (length, width, stroke width), arcs, planes, colors (hue, brightness, saturation), textures.
2. Organization: the organization of the features, the way the elements are organized to create harmony, unity, balance, homogeneity, or, on the other hand, complexity, absurdity, variety, and heterogeneity.
3. Meaning: the qualities that give meaning to an object, such as semantic meaning, reference to an archetype, associative meaning, etc.
4. Denotation: the meaning of a work of art is denotative if the work refers to an (historic) event.

Hekkert excludes emotional meaning (emotional benefits) from his study. In the introduction to his research, he distinguishes objective and subjective theories. Objective theories suppose that aesthetic judgments are not dependent on the background, level of education, or experience of the observer of the work of art. On the other hand, subjective theories suppose that the observer's background does have some influence. According to the first group, there should be some kind of "objective aesthetic truth." According to the subjective theories, there will be a joint aesthetic meaning only if the background, education, and experience of the observers is comparable, if they belong to the same social group, or if they judge under comparable circumstances. He quotes Hume as an example of an "extreme" subjective theory. According to Hume, beauty is not a quality of an object or a work of art, but exists only in the mind of the observer. Every observer has a different aesthetic judgment. It is most likely that Hekkert is referring here to the statement: "Beauty is in the eye of the beholder." Opinions differ regarding the real source of this statement: "The first appearance of this phrase seems to have been in *Molly Bawn*, 1878, a novel about a frivolous, flirtatious Irish girl. The novel was written by Margaret Wolfe Hungerford (Hamilton) (1855–1897)" (Yahoo Answers, 2011; The Phrase Finder, 2011).

Hekkert describes three groups of theories about aesthetic reviews that partly overlap. The first group – the theory of Berlyne is an example – examines the stimulation of the senses and may have a kind of common conclusion, namely that not enough stimulation of the senses is boring, too much stimulation results in rejection, with aesthetic appreciation lying somewhere in between. The second group looks at the familiarity with the "rules" of the observer. The phenomena that play a role appear to be similar to those of the first group. Excessive proximity to the archetype (being seen too often) is not very exciting, and an excessive difference from the archetype is not recognized (does not belong to the archetype) and is therefore not appreciated. Appreciation is based on a differentiation with the archetype that is not excessive, but still sufficiently surprising. The third group of theories adds that the observer's degree of expertise plays an important role in the observations.

10.18 Jordan (2000): *Designing Pleasurable Products, an Introduction to the New Human Factors*

According to Jordan, features such as the usability of a product start as – what in marketing terminology is referred to as – satisfiers. Later, however, they come to be expected, and this transforms them into dissatisfiers. He identifies three hierarchical levels of human factors.

– Level 1: functionality
– Level 2: usability
– Level 3: pleasure

Each level is a satisfier until most of the products have reached a certain quality. From that moment on, the lack of enough functionality or usability causes them to become dissatisfiers.

Four Pleasures

At the third level – pleasure – Jordan distinguishes four different types. The first is physio-pleasure, which refers to touch (think of a pen or an electric shaver), taste, or smell (the first thing some people do when they have bought a new book is open it and smell it). Then comes what he calls socio-pleasure. This concerns pleasure derived from relationships with other people and is accompanied by questions such as, "Does the product suit me?" or "What does the product say about me?" The next pleasure is psycho-pleasure, which refers to the emotions felt by experiencing the product. The product is, for instance, "fun to use." Finally, he refers to ideo-pleasure (ideological pleasure), which refers to the value a product has for its owner.

Although the Four Pleasure model gives some insight into the emotional aspects of products, it is very difficult to separate them. For instance, Jordan states that a product made of a biodegradable material embodies the value of environmental responsibility and is therefore an example of ideo-pleasure. However, this characteristic can also offer the owner psycho-pleasure (the product is emotionally satisfying because of this material), or socio-pleasure (people will see me as responsible and environmentally friendly because of this product).

10.19 Krishnan and Ulrich (2001): "Product Development Decisions: A Review of the Literature"

The paper by Krishnan and Ulrich provides an overview of the literature relating to research into product development. The research focuses on research within firms, which means that it, for example, excludes market developments or governmental rules and regulations. It includes the organizational process (within the firm): e.g., the structure and organization of the design team, operations management (e.g., supplier and material selection, production sequence, and project management), marketing (product positioning and pricing, collecting and meeting customer needs), and engineering design (product performance, size, configuration, and dimensions).

In their research, product development is divided into four categories, namely concept development, product design, supply-chain design, and production ramp-up and launch. In their concluding remarks, they state:

> "We noted that there is essentially no academic research on industrial design, the activity largely concerned with the form and style of products. Yet aesthetic design may be one of the most important factors in explaining consumer preference in some product markets, including automobiles, small appliances, and furniture"
>   (2001, 14).

10.20 Maslow (1976): *Motivation and Personality*

American clinical psychologist Abraham Maslow distinguishes between five levels of human needs, which he describes as follows:

1. Physiological needs: food, water, sleep, homeostasis, sex, and air to breathe: to live

2. Safety needs: safety, protection, need for structure, order, laws, and borders; security of employment; freedom from fear, tension, and chaos; health, property
3. Love and belonging: belonging to a group or family, someone to love, a partner or children
4. Esteem: a stable, firmly founded, usually high self-esteem; self-respect; respect of others; achievement, competence, confidence vis-à-vis the world, independence, and freedom; desire for reputation or prestige, standing, fame, and glory, dominance, acknowledgment, attention, importance, dignity, or appreciation
5. Self-actualization

According to Maslow, self-actualization leads to a different way of life and a different opinion about life. Self-actualized people are capable of understanding the heart of matters. They accept their environment, the people who surround them and themselves as they are, without feelings of guilt. They can recognize untruthful behavior. They can see things in perspective. They have no fear of the unknown. They are more interested in the problems of their surroundings and of the world, instead of worrying continuously about their "own little problems." They form their own opinions and do not allow others to tell them what they should believe or think. They do not depend on adoration, status, income, popularity, and prestige. They do not need expensive artefacts to show to the outside world. They feel responsible and emphasize with other (human) beings and nature. They transcend the egocentric way of life that is typical for Maslow's fourth level of needs. The fact that they have gone beyond this level probably explains why they are capable of seeing it. Self-actualizing people are far from perfect and can be weary, stubborn, or annoying. They are often vain, proud, arrogant, and impatient. They are capable of – unexpected – ruthlessness (they not only form their own opinions themselves (as mentioned earlier), but sometimes put their ideas into practice without much empathy for others).

According to the theory of Maslow, higher needs can be satisfied only if the needs at a lower level are more or less satisfied.

– A satisfied need does not motivate. If a need is satisfied to a certain extent, the motivation to satisfy it slowly disappears.
– Lower levels of need must be satisfied before motivation to a higher level is possible.
– When lower levels are satisfied, there is an automatic motivation toward the next higher level.

10.21 Mitchell (1983): *The Nine American Lifestyles: Who We Are and Where We're Going*

In 1978, Arnold Mitchell introduced his VALS typology (value and lifestyle). He distinguished groups of consumers based on behavior, activities, interests, and values. He describes four main categories and nine subcategories.

1. "Need-Driven," which can be subdivided into "Survivors" (5%) and "Sustainers" (10%). According to Mitchell, this group mainly consists of elderly people with low incomes who often live in big cities.
2. "Outer-Directed," a group whose motivation is greatly influenced by their peers. This group can be subdivided into "Emulators" (45%), "Pursuers" (10%), and "Achievers" (22%). The biggest subgroup is the "Emulators." They have an income that is below average; they are conventional and nostalgic (in the past everything used to be better). The "Pursuers" have an average income, are younger, and are very ambitious. The "Achievers" have a higher income, are well educated, somewhat older (middle-aged), ambitious, and like to show their success to the outside world.
3. "Inner-Directed," a group who is self-motivated, divided into "I-am-me" (2%), "Experiential" (2%), and "Societally Conscious" (2%). These are relatively small groups. Members of the "I-am-me" group are young, have a high education, and are individualistic. Many of them are students on low incomes for themselves, but who come from rich families. The "Experiential" group is in some ways comparable to this group, but includes more women. Its members are also young, earn a good income, and are looking for "experiences." The "Societally Conscious" are socially aware and care about the environment. They often have a high income and are well educated, but despite that they live sober lives.
4. "Combined Outer- and Inner-Directed," or "Integrated" (2%). The members of this group have high incomes (either because they have good jobs or live from "old money"), are well educated, self-assured, tolerant, and interested in art and culture.

A disadvantage of this model used to be that it was rather static, while in reality, new groups form and the original groups change both in behavior and numbers of people. At present, the model is kept up to date by SBI (Strategic Business Insights) in California.

10.22 Motivaction International (2017): *Mentality*

The "Mentality" model is comparable to the VALS typology (Mitchell, 1983), but was introduced more recently, in 1995. It was introduced under the name "Socioconsult." This model is based on both opinion polls and one-to-one

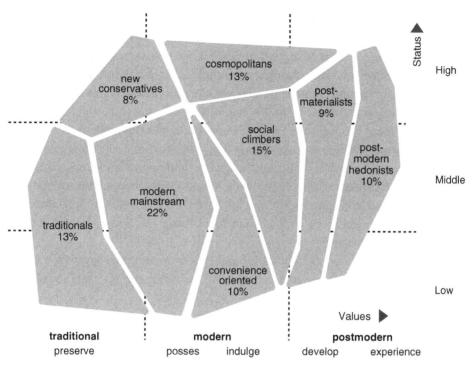

Figure 10.8 Motivaction International: The "Mentality" model (Source: authors, permission granted by Motivaction International)

interviews. Apart from acquiring demographical information, emphasis is placed on the interviewees' standards and values. This type of longitudinal information gathering can be used to measure changes within and between market segments. However, these changes are small and very gradual, being 1% or 2% per annum at the most. The following segments have been distinguished within Motivaction (see Figure 10.8 for an overview of the 2017 results):

- Traditionals (13%): moralistic, law-abiding, and status quo–oriented citizens who hang on to traditions and material possessions.
  Key words: the family as the cornerstone of society; quiet and harmonious lifestyle; solidarity with minorities and concern about the environment; acceptation of authority and rules; risk avoidance; sober and thrifty; geared toward passive entertainment; family as the central point; traditional division of roles; more women than men; few young people; fewer highly educated people.
- Modern mainstream (22%): conformist, status-conscious citizens who look for a balance between traditional versus modern values such as consumption and enjoyment.

Key words: the family as the cornerstone of society; acquisition of status and respect; a desire for authority and rules, but also for recognition and appreciation; work and performance; conformism and risk avoidance; materialistic and status conscious; technology minded; traditional division of roles; equal percentage of men and women; relatively low education.

- Convenience oriented (10%): impulsive and passive consumers whose main focus is on a stress-free, pleasant, and comfortable lifestyle.
  Key words: be free and live an easy life; pleasure oriented; not interested in society and politics; desire for recognition and appreciation; no certitudes or responsibilities; impulsive; living in and for the here and now; materialistic and consumption oriented; geared toward outward appearances; individualistic; more women than men; fewer old people, more people with low education.

- New conservatives (8%): the liberal-conservative upper layer of society who are keen to promote technological development but resist social and cultural innovation.
  Key words: hanging onto traditional norms and values; protection of social status; interest in politics and history; work and performance; sober; risk avoidance; insistence on good manners; central role of family relationships; more men than women; more elderly; more people with high education; more people with high incomes.

- Social climbers (15%): career-oriented individualists with a strong fascination with social status, new technologies, risk, and stress.
  Key words: build a career; free of tradition and obligations; open to innovation and change; international orientation; materialistic and status conscious; technology minded; impulsive and adventurous; orientated around kindred spirits; more men than women; relatively high percentage of younger people.

- Post-materialists (9%): idealists, social critics with a wish for self-development who denounce social injustice and stand up for the environment.
  Key words: solidarity and social engagement; awareness of immaterial values; tolerant; international orientation; people who search for a balance between work and private life; play a constructive role in society; not consumption and amusement oriented; partners have their own friends; more women than men; somewhat higher age bracket; more people with high educational levels.

- Post-modern hedonists (10%): the pioneers of the experience culture, in which experiment and the breaching of moral and social conventions have become targets in themselves.
  Key words: freedom; little societal and political engagement; equal opportunities; impulsive; adventurous; no commitments; oriented toward

experience; individualistic; friends more important than family; equal percentages of men and women; more young people; more people with high education.

– Cosmopolitans (13%): open and critical citizens of the world who integrate postmodern values, such as the development of their own talents and experience, into modern values such as social success, materialism, and hedonism.

Key words: self-development; international orientation; social and political awareness; ambition; materialistic and technology minded; impulsive and adventurous; status-conscious; well-mannered; networker; oriented toward peers and kindred spirits; equal percentages of men and women; more young people; more people with high incomes.

10.23 Pine and Gilmore (1999): *The Experience Economy*

In their book *The Experience Economy*, Pine and Gilmore distinguish between the following four phases for products and services:

– Commodity
– Good
– Service
– Experience

According to them, "commodities" are taken from raw and basic materials. They are very similar, and that makes price the main means of competition. As examples they refer to coffee beans, crude oil, and cereals. If a company burns, grinds, and packages coffee beans, it makes what Pine and Gilmore call a "good." Although the company can demand a better price than if it sold only burned coffee beans, the level of competition means its price cannot be set very high. "Services" are aimed at individuals. Service products use goods to create services for their clients. A hairdresser uses – among other things – scissors, combs, and a hairdryer to cut and style his clients' hair. A gardener needs a complete set of tools and machines to construct and maintain someone's garden. According to Pine and Gilmore, people are more interested in services than in goods and are therefore willing to pay more for them. They call the fourth level "experience." Companies that offer an experience use their products and services to commit the customer. Pine and Gilmore explain this as follows:

> While commodities are fungible, goods tangible, and services intangible, experiences are memorable.   (1999, 11–12)

It is the memory that makes an experience stand out while, in general, commodities, goods, and services are soon forgotten.

10.24 Prahalad and Ramaswamy (2004): *The Future of Competition: Co-creating Value with Customers*

A development that attracted a great deal of interest around the turn of the century is cocreation. Cocreation is defined as the active and direct involvement of users in the development of new products. The advantage for companies is that it gives them a better insight into the wishes and ideas of users. The advantage for consumers is that it gives them products better attuned to their individual wishes.

Prahalad and Ramaswamy (2004) suggest that the interest in cocreation is based primarily on the availability of information. Thanks to smartphones and the Internet, consumers have access to large amounts of information about companies, products, techniques, trends, etc. and can share this information very quickly. Therefore, it is no longer possible to operate anonymously. The new communication tools mean consumers can and will communicate with companies. Consumers' power and influence will increase. Three forms of cocreation can be distinguished, namely in production, in final design, and in concept development.

Cocreation in the Production Phase

In the production phase, consumers hardly have any influence on the end result and, most of the time, they are involved only in assembling the product. The advantages for the users are an often substantial cost reduction and the pride of authorship: "I made it myself." Examples are Ikea and many DIY products.

Cocreation in the Final Design

In this case, the consumer can choose from a (very) large number of possibilities and combinations. This is what is often called "mass customization." The consumer defines the final design – often via the Internet – with the aid of a toolkit. The main advantage for the user is that he owns a unique product. A disadvantage is that it sometimes takes a lot of time to learn to work with the sometimes complicated toolkit.

Cocreation in the Concept Phase

Cocreation in the concept phase of product design is often related to market research. The most important differences are that the participating consumers are the future users of the product and that they stay involved during the whole design process. In traditional market research, they are only asked for their opinion, and it is unsure whether any of this is used in the end result. There are different ways to organize cocreation in the concept phase. Companies sometimes organize "cocreation workshops." However, the participants in these workshops are often not the future users of the product. If that is the case, the workshops are not much more than a new form of market research. Sometimes consumers themselves take the initiative. One reason may be that they are not satisfied with existing products. They can, for instance, form an Internet community to develop a better product. According to Shah (2000), these communities are often formed by sports practitioners such as windsurfers, snowboarders, or skateboarders. Another well-known example of a product developed by a community is the computer operating system Linux.[8]

10.25 Rogers ([1962] 1995): *Diffusion of Innovations*

In his book entitled *Diffusion of Innovations*, first published in 1962 Rogers describes how new products are generally introduced and adopted by users described as different types. At the time of publication of the fourth edition (1995), more than 4,000 studies had been carried out. Based on this large number of studies, Rogers concludes that the acceptance of product introductions generally follows a well-defined pattern. The most important variation within this pattern is the amount of time it takes between the introduction and the moment of complete acceptance. This can vary from between a few years to a few centuries. According to Rogers's definition, a product is accepted if at least 90% of the potential users own the product. The market penetration of a product is about 50% if it is owned by what he calls the "innovators," the "early adopters," and the "early majority." He adds that "status" is one of the important motivations of these three groups.

> Status motivations for adoption seem to be more important for innovators, early adopters, and early majority, and less important for the late majority and laggards.
> (1995, 214)

According to Rogers, the first buyers of new products are the "innovators." They are followed by the "early adopters" and the "early majority." If these three groups own the product, the market penetration will be about 50% (see also Figure 10.9 for a visual representation of the distribution). The "early majority" is followed by what he calls the "late majority." This is followed – if at all – by the "laggards." Rogers provides descriptions of the most important lifestyle characteristics and values of each of the adoption categories. After each category, he indicates the percentage of people who suit his description.

---

[8] See also *Democratizing Innovation* (Hippel, 2005), which extensively discusses the contribution of users to innovation. The cases of kite surfing and Linux are discussed there.

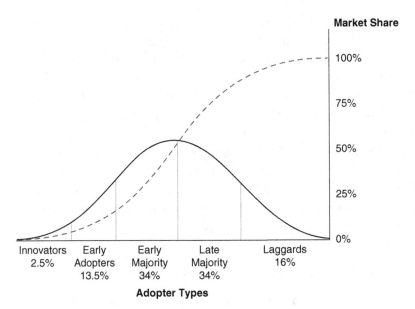

Figure 10.9 The diffusion of innovations and types of adopter associated with different adoption levels according to Rogers (1995) (Source: authors)

Innovators (Venturesome) (2.5%)

Innovators are very interested in new ideas, new techniques, and new products. They have "cosmopolite social relationships" and plenty of contacts with other innovators, who sometimes live a long way away from them. They are capable of understanding (technologically) complicated products, and have enough money to spend on them. They are able to live with the uncertainty that a new product can sometimes fail and do not mind if it does not function perfectly all the time. They look for new, cutting-edge, sometimes even dangerous experiences. (They have a "desire for the rash, the daring and the risky.") They can easily handle disappointments. However, they are not highly respected in their immediate social circles. They are often regarded as rather eccentric.

Early Adopters (Respected) (13.5%)

Early adopters are much better integrated into their local communities than innovators. They have a lot of prestige and authority, but are less internationally oriented. Their opinion is highly valued. They are "the individuals to check with."

Early Majority (Deliberate) (34%)

People who belong to the early majority have plenty of social contacts, but are seldom opinion makers ("not the first by which the new is tried, nor the last to lay the old aside").

Late Majority (Skeptical) (34%)

The late majority will implement an innovation or buy a product only after it has been generally accepted and functions reliably. They often make decisions based on economic or technological needs (the old system is no longer supported) or under pressure of their surroundings. They are skeptical toward innovations and careful in their decisions.

Laggards (Traditional) (16%)

Laggards have a small social network or are sometimes quite isolated. Their point of reference is the past: we have been doing things like this all the time; why would we suddenly want to change that? They often communicate only with people who share their opinion, do not trust innovations, need a long time to come to a conclusion, and often lack the means to afford an innovation that may prove a failure.

10.26 Veblen (1899): *The Theory of the Leisure Class*

One of the first researchers to describe groups based on demographic criteria was American sociologist Thorstein Veblen. In 1899, Veblen (1899, 1994) explained the behavior of the upper classes ('leisure class') as signs that they use to show their wealth. According to Veblen, members of the leisure class do not work with their hands, meaning that well-cared-for hands with clean, unbroken nails are important to them. If they perform any physical activity, it has to be "unproductive" and "consumptive," such as sports (golf, tennis). They own country houses or estates. Therefore, their meadows are used to keep nonproductive animals such as deer or to raise horses instead of cows or sheep. They wear clothes that make working with their hands difficult or impossible: clean, white shirts, lacquered shoes, and folded trousers. Their wives wear tight skirts and high-heeled shoes. Their activities are obviously useless since they learn "dead" languages (Greek, Latin) or study music or art history. A lot of attention and time is devoted to good manners and correct spelling and pronunciation of the language. They become connoisseurs of antiques and wine because these are useless (not life-essential) products that only members of their class can afford to consume. A number of these signs are later copied by other, lower classes. A description such as "white-collar profession" speaks for itself.

10.27 Woodring (1987): *Retailing New Product or Design*

During the "Design Congress '87" in Amsterdam, Cooper Woodring presented an interesting theory on the hierarchy of products based on the history of retail in the United States. Before 1900 – according to Woodring – products were sold in small shops spread all over cities and neighborhoods. After 1900, department stores were built so that different, small shops could combine their activities under one roof. In around 1930, bakers, butchers, greengrocers, and delicatessens started offering their products in one shop, and this is how super-markets came about. They became a huge success, due partly to the increase in the number of cars, which greatly enhanced people's mobility. In around 1950, discount stores were started that offered low-priced brand products because of their volumes and the principle of self-service.

"Wants" and "Needs"

Woodring distinguishes four product categories that all need their own selling strategy and their own kind of shop. He starts with a division into "wants" and "needs". Needs are products that we use on a daily basis. Wants are products that make life more pleasant. Many products start as wants and become needs some time later. An example of such a product is the refrigerator, once a product for rich people, now a commodity in every Western household.

Wants can be subdivided into lifestyle products and specialist products. Needs can be divided into service products and (fast moving) consumer products.

"Lifestyle Products"

Lifestyle products are new, desirable, fashionable, and exciting. They offer satisfaction and status. Examples are jewelry, clothing, furniture, and art. They can be bought in shopping malls that house lots of shops within close reach of each other. International examples are: Maxfield (Los Angeles), KaDeWe (Berlin), GUM (Moscow), or Siam Paragon (Bangkok). Alternatively, you can find them in warehouses. The people who want to buy them are not in any hurry to do so. They might even decide not to buy there and then, but to try and do so at another time and place. It is good for all parties, both buyers and sellers, if there is a wide range as regards choice and price in a small area.

"Specialty Products"

Specialty products promise the user good performance and are often techno-logically high quality (high technology). Examples are products for sports, cameras, computers, audiovisual products, some glasses and lenses, smart-phones, and hobby products. They often need well-educated sellers who have (technological) knowledge. The potential buyers research the products using brochures, websites, and articles in magazines and by exchanging information with peers. These products can be found in specialty shops and warehouses.

"Service Products"

Service products start their economic life cycle as lifestyle products, then become specialty products and end up as service products. Sometimes they are freestanding products that change into fitments. Examples are heating, ventilation, air conditioning, bath, shower, domestic appliances (vacuum cleaners, irons, coffee machines), or tools (drilling machines). Because they often do not have (or no longer have) unique selling points, no differentiating features of design, consumers often do not have a brand preference. Therefore, these products are often sold via discounters. Some products are bought with a service contract.

"Fast-Moving Consumer Goods"

"Fast-moving consumer goods (FMCG) are needed on a daily basis. Examples are food, beverages, cleaning products, medicines, fuels, and newspapers or magazines. They are bought routinely and frequently. Usually they are not very expensive (per unit). Often people buy well-known brands that are heavily advertised. In almost all cases, the products are bought in the nearest available shop. Often that is a supermarket or (for example in the United States and France) a hypermarket or convenience store.

A product can be presented in all four of the aforementioned categories and can be sold via all the market channels discussed here, to both consumers and professional users. Woodring describes the camera as an example (please note that this example was given in 1987). A "coloured, yellow disc-camera with funky product graphics and a suiting wrist bag" is a lifestyle product and will be sold in a shopping mall or department store. A Nikon with a 35 mm lens is a specialty product and will be sold in a specialty shop. A security camera for a bank is a service product and will be sold with a service contract. A preloaded panorama camera is a consumer product and will be sold in a supermarket near the cashier.

Woodring's Hierarchy

In 1920, the volume of products that was sold was related to price: the lower the price, the higher the volume (see Figure 10.10). In around 1950, this changed. People had more money to spend and did not always want to buy the cheapest product. The volume was then somewhere in the middle. There had to be a cheap, expensive, and medium-priced version of each product. The latter

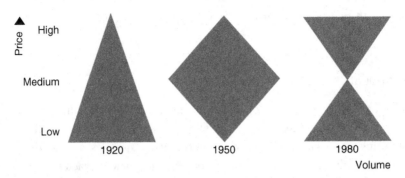

Figure 10.10 The number of products sold (horizontal) versus their price (vertical) in three periods (horizontal) (Source: authors)

category contained the greatest volume of products sold. Adding a high-priced new product raised the attractiveness of the product "in the middle."

This strategy became very unprofitable for a number of companies around 1980 because of the "enhancement sacrificial purchase syndrome" which can be summed up as follows.

> I buy my clothes in a discount shop, flew tourist class to a conference in Amsterdam, stopped my subscription to pay-tv and decided not to buy the essential new furniture so that I can buy a Hasselblad camera with Carl Zeiss lenses for $10,000.

According to Woodring, this is a clear example of the "enhancement sacrificial purchase syndrome" that formed the basis for a change in people's purchasing behavior around 1980. It was also a consequence of the worldwide recession at the time. The outcome was that the volume of purchases was no longer associated with the medium-priced category, but in the extremes. The diamond shape changed into an hourglass shape. It is not difficult to understand what this meant for manufacturers still using the diamond-shaped model: they consequently took the wrong products out of the market and introduced new products with the wrong pricing.

11 Conclusion: Evolution in Products

11.1 Introduction

This book addresses the question how new (types of) products emerge and typically develop over time. Next, it provides designers a low-risk new product development strategy. Building on practical design experience and the work of many other authors, an evolutionary perspective on products was taken. The way in which products evolve in the world of made is very different from the way in which biological species evolve. Beyond the realm of biology, the evolutionary perspective has most notably been applied to economics and defined a school of thought referred to as evolutionary economics (Nelson and Winter, 1982). Further, the evolution of technology (Basalla, 1988, and Section 10.5 of this volume) is a widely used conception.

Describing *how products come about and develop through time*, this study deliberately takes a product-centric perspective. To that end, experience with product development in practice was evaluated, and relevant schools of thought were reviewed, patterns and mechanisms of innovation were listed, and some new definitions were introduced.

The authors were educated as industrial design engineers and had many years of theoretical and practical experience with product development before they started their research and wrote this book. The professional experience as well as the personal interest and fascination of both authors has been the basis of this writing. The purpose of this book is to provide a method for new product development that takes recurring patterns in the evolution of products as its point of departure, aiming to reduce the risk of product failure, as well as to provide starting points for new product development. To that end, the product phases have been defined and used in a course named "Evolutionary Product Development." Using the product phases requires understanding how the product in focus came about, and how it developed thus far. For that purpose, an analytical tool named the

Product Evolution Diagram is proposed. The authors have used students as a first audience for their figments, although an earlier version of the product phases was used in the design practice of the Dutch design company Van Dijk/Eger/Associates, nowadays known as WeLL Design. We are convinced that this book offers interesting reading to a wider audience as it provides a conceptual framework and terminology that can be used to describe the process of product innovation and design without leaving it to magic. It describes how new types of products emerge in the world of made. Subsequently, it appears that new types of products evolve into a family of advanced versions.

Most commonly, innovation in products is described from a technology-centric perspective. Related literature suggests innovation as a series of disjointed processes in which every next product should be disruptive and radical to be any good. The premise of this book is the idea that an evolutionary approach provides a better explanation for the origin of products and their subsequent further development. In support of this evolutionary perspective, a theory of product evolution is proposed using the product evolution diagram to plot how new types of products emerge and evolve gradually. As a tool for designers, the Product Phase Model is proposed that provides clues for designing the next version of a product.

11.2 Product Phase Model: General Conclusions and Discussion

The phenomena that appear during the phases of the life of a product have been described. Regularities that were found have been analyzed and delineated. This has led to the Product Phases Theory that labels how products evolve through six product phases.

Placing the six product phases in a chronological order makes it possible to make predictions about new or future products. This is done by positioning a product, based on its product phase characteristics, in one of the product phases. When developing a future product, a designer can add to the product phase characteristics of (one of) the next product phase(s), thus creating added value for the intended user. In this way, the product phases can help a designer to create the next generation of a product.

For each separate product phase characteristic, a short description has to be made of the present situation. Based on the present situation and the product phase characteristics of the next product phase (or product phases), intended actions can be formulated. From these possible actions a choice has to be made. If making such a choice causes problems, selection methods such as those described in Eger and colleagues (2013) can be used. Examples of the short descriptions can be found in Chapters 8 and 9.

Discussion

Some remarks can be made regarding the theory of product phases. The first phases can be defined with more accuracy than the latter. It appears that the "career" of a product varies considerably, displaying more variation as time progresses. Perhaps there is an analogy between the career of a human being and that of a product. External factors, which are analyzed with the aid of the PED, can disturb the course of the product phases. It also appears that it is hard to draw a fine line between two different, successive product phases, as features from different product phases can exist at the same time. Despite these limitations, the theory of product phases has proven to be a useful thinking aid in order to make the large variation in "product careers" well-structured and unambiguous.

Education

With regards to design education, the theory has proven to be a useful tool to teach students to incorporate the history of a product into their design process when developing a new product and to develop a next logical step instead of trying to make a wild guess or undirected "innovative jump." This is important as most of the products that are developed are very rarely "completely new" (and sometimes "not new at all"), since they are commonly the successors of existing products that have minimal differences from their predecessors. Work on what in this book is defined as "new types of products" makes up only a very small part of the work of product developers. In successful cases, these new types of products give rise to a new product family. The majority of work for designers is developing next versions in such product families. Hence, it makes sense to include in the education of future designers and product developers a design strategy that in particular aims to understand how products typically come about and develop into families of advanced versions. This will support finding directions for the next evolutionary version of a product and reduces the risk that this expensive and labor-intensive process of new product development is delivered in vain.

As discussed in previous literature (Abernathy and Utterback, 1975; Anderson and Tushman, 1990; Tushman and Murmann, 1998), dominant designs are the hallmark of a successful product design. However, an important caveat is placed at how these highly successful designs are established.

> "Dominant designs emerge as [the] outcome of institutional dynamics constrained by economic and technical conditions. Dominant designs can only be known in retrospect and they evolve over time"   (Tushman and Murmann, 1998, 231).

Consequently, designers cannot be taught tricks to produce dominant designs. However, they can be taught the processes that shape product families and assisted in identifying the solution space of a next product, possibly entering a next product phase.

From the nearly 300 student cases so far, it can be concluded that students always succeed in finding one or more design directions, but also that the talent and motivation of the individual designer are important factors that influence the final result. The first students participated in this course in 2005. It was interesting to notice that, since then, some products have appeared on the market that closely resembled the design of the students. So far, no systematic research has been carried out to find out how often this was the case. Complicating factors to carry out this kind of research are the already mentioned different talents of the design students, the problem of judging how much the product that was brought to the market resembles the design of the student, and if it was a success. Still it would be interesting to carry out a further study on this subject.

Design Practice

In his design practice, a designer can use the product phases as a design methodology in order to guide the new product development. He can also use them as a tool in the decision process. Designers seldom decide whether a product will be manufactured and introduced into the market, since this decision is usually made by the entrepreneur or manager who is in charge of the project (Forty, 1986, and Section 10.15 of this volume). However, in most cases, the designer has to convince his client. When doing so, he can make use of the product phases to explain why and on what grounds certain decisions were made. Finally, a designer who has his own agency can use the product phases as an acquisition tool. If he studies the history of the products of his prospects, he can give them (even in the first meeting) a vision of the main lines of his future product assortment.

In general it can be concluded that the product phases theory offers a useful tool in the first steps of a new product development project: the preliminary phase (Figure 11.1), where existing, competing products are studied with regard to their functionality, ergonomics, safety, and marketing; and in the phase where ideas are generated for the preliminary design (design phase, Figure 11.1). On the other hand, the theory does always offer several options, never only one, and these options are not very detailed, leaving a lot of room for the designer to choose and detail the chosen concept.

Styling

According to the product phases theory, a new product starts in the performance phase and then goes through the next phases to finally come into the last

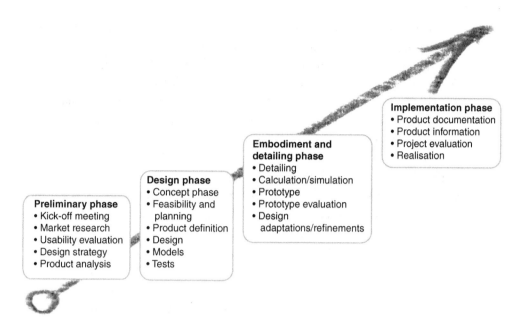

Figure 11.1 Road map for industrial design engineering (Source: authors)

three phases: segmentation, individualization, and awareness. The higher the product phase reached, the more important styling becomes. Up to the phase of itemization, the styling should be rather neutral, not too expressive. However, in the phase of segmentation, the styling will become more expressive. On one hand, the designer needs to make the product attractive for the chosen target groups; on the other hand, he needs to distinguish the product from the often rich offerings in this phase. In the awareness phase, the behavior of the producer or the brand will become more important. The price/performance ratio between products becomes so equal that the image of the brand may start to play a role in the buying decisions. What is the social behavior of the company? What does it do to improve the environment? Etcetera. This may lead to a much less expressive, more sober styling of the products.

11.3 The Product Evolution Diagram

The product evolution diagram provides a conceptual framework to analyze how new (types of) products emerge and subsequently develop into a family of more advanced versions. Other authors from backgrounds as diverse as economics, sociology, and innovation studies have described how technology typically develops. Based on these insights, an analytical framework is proposed, called the product evolution diagram, abbreviated as PED. The PED integrates ideas from different schools of thought and is as such an example of "appreciative theory" (Nelson and Winter, 1982). Further, some new definitions have been introduced that support the interpretation of developments in, and characteristics of the evolution of products.

The PED consists of two parts. The first maps the development of a product in a tree-like diagram. Similar to the family tree used to map lines of descent, the product family tree (PFT) maps when in time new products are introduced and how they relate to earlier versions, i.e., build onto antecedent products or technologies. The PFT recognizes different stages in the evolution of products. The roots link a new product family to antecedent products or technologies. The first product in a family is designated as a node between the roots and the base. Then the product further evolves, and types that deviate from a particular product line are marked as new branches. When the product matures, variants of the product of which the architecture is tuned to specific segments of the market mark the segmentation phase. Dominant designs in particular branches are marked with a square to signal where in time these designs appear.

The second element in the PED diagram maps the whole of influences from the context that influenced the development history of the product in focus. This element is also referred to as the ecosystem. Together, these two juxtaposed elements – each of which in isolation is already known – present an effective means to capture elements that picture the process of evolution in products.

Two cases of evolving products are studied. Using the PED diagram to map these cases makes clear the ecosystem is part and parcel of the evolution of products. It appears evolution in products is not a self-contained phenomenon. Rather, it is the result of complex interactions between a product (/product family/products class) and a context made up of many different factors. Thus the PED provides a tool to plot the complex process of product evolution schematically instead of mapping lineage unambiguously.

Discussion

This book describes cases of evolution in products; the patterns in their development are very similar to those described in the rich body of literature covering different schools of thought to which is referred. Because these patterns seem to be characteristic for the development of products, it is here assumed that products in general develop in a similar fashion. This is confirmed by the research carried out on 170 products by 294 students. (See also Eger, 2013, and Ehlhardt, 2016.)

One can argue about whether it makes sense to compare the origin of new (types of) products with the origin of species. It is clear there are major differences between evolution in the world of made and the world of born. After all, products do not breed and there is no undisputed carrier of hereditary information that is the basis of evolution in products. Because of this heredity issue, it has been argued that the product family tree cannot be constructed unambiguously. And, as described before, this is also not what is intended. The product evolution diagram is plotting the development history of a product family and the context that influenced it. The purpose of this diagram is to provide a comprehensive perspective on the question of the origin of products.

In Chapter 2, the evolution in telephones and telephone network systems was used to elucidate how changes in a product, visible to consumers, are driven by changes in an underlying, large technological system that is less visible. In Section 6.2, the case of the mobile phone was used to illustrate the product phases. However, the evolution of software and related products like the personal computer and smartphone were not specifically analyzed, although they are characteristic of the new types of products that mark the Age of Information and Telecommunication.

The evolution of products is described as an accumulation of knowledge distinguished as know-what (product to make) and know-how (to make the product). New types of products form knowledge structures on which the product family further evolves. Obviously, how people share information is instrumental to the accumulation of knowledge. And advances in sharing information from the emergence of language, writing, and printing to the Internet are likely causes of acceleration in the evolution of products. However, providing an explanation for the acceleration in the evolution of products is beyond the scope of this book. The same applies to the question into the unit of hereditary information for products.

Education

The PED proved a useful tool to students of industrial design engineering who had to analyze the evolution of a specific product in the first course before they were asked to provide a design for an evolutionary next version of the product in a second course. Between 2005 and 2010, it appeared that students who analyzed the evolution of a product commonly mapped pictures of product variants from different times along a timeline. Often, this mapping included an indication when in time characteristics of the product phases could be recognized. Between 2011 and 2014, students were asked to map the evolution of a product family in a PED. In lectures, the PED was explained, as well as some innovation patterns, as described in the literature, were elucidated. The work students delivered from here onward provided mappings with greater detail than found between 2005 and 2010. In general, students were well able to provide a PED, illustrating the evolution of a particular product. However, recognizing and interpreting relevant technological developments and changes in product architecture appeared to be more difficult. Not all students understood as well how developments took place and could indicate how the cause-and-effect relation between evolving product and ecosystem shaped the evolutionary path.

It was observed that students often added certain elements to the PED, like particular innovations that were instrumental in the evolution of the product. An example of this is shown for the evolution of the bicycle, in Figure 6.25. The bottom of this figure shows subsystems like spokes and the roller chain that were crucial elements required before the Rover Safety bike could be conceptualized and introduced in 1885. Shortly after, in 1888, the Dunlop inflatable tire became available, that allowed it to become the high-speed anti-vibration device that made it so successful. All in all, it can be said that the PED provides a useful tool for drawing out how a product family evolved in interaction with the ecosystem. Taking into account that students before had no reference in how to analyze the history of a product, the conceptual framework offered proved very useful.

Student, Product, Year, and Number of Times Researched

The researchers would like to thank the following students who participated in their courses. The research presented in this book is partly based on the studies carried out by 294 students who took part in the master course "Evolutionary Product Development." Over a period of 11 years (2005–2015), they investigated 170 products. Some were analyzed only once, some several times, with a maximum of seven. In the table presented here, the students' names are presented, followed by the product they researched, the year they participated in the course, and the number of times the product was examined. Most theses remained unpublished; however, the authors disposed of hard copies of all of the reports and digital copies of a selection of them.

Abbink, Bert	kitchen timer	2008	1
Addink, Carmen	electric toothbrush	2011	7
Adolfsen, Kyra	hairdryer	2010	2
Al-shorachi, Albert	digital camera	2011	1
Andriessen, Rosanne	baby carrier	2015	1
Anninga, Eelco	espresso machine	2014	5
Appelhof, Hans	game computer	2009	1
Arragon, Charlotte van	dyno torch	2008	1
Baaijens, Ruud	sanding machine	2012	2
Bakker, Anneke	bathroom scales	2009	5
Bakker, Jikke	lady shaver	2007	1
Bakker, Robbert	bicycle	2013	4
Balk, Remco	navigation system	2013	2
Barelds, Petra	ironing board	2010	2
Beens, André	jig saw	2010	4
Beer, Manon de	slr camera	2011	4
Berga, Geeske	soccer shoe	2009	1
Berge, Hans van den	iron	2007	2
Bergsma, Job	toaster	2014	4
Beurs, Dennis de	drawing tablet	2009	1

(continued)

Biemans, Bianca	facial tanner	2008	1
Bijkerk, Jennifer	electric toothbrush	2011	7
Bijvank, Jessika	slr camera	2013	4
Blankendaal, Hans	thermostat	2013	3
Blokker, Lara	mobile phone	2013	4
Blom, Martine	wristwatch	2010	3
Boer, Wouter de	loudspeakers	2008	4
Bogt, Oscar ter	steam iron	2011	2
Boiten, Hugo	backpack	2005	3
Bolding, Stefan	bicycle pump	2011	4
Boon, Liza	kitchen machine	2013	2
Bootsveld, Jorien	coffee machine	2013	3
Bos, Marianne	telephone	2008	1
Bosch, Jeroen van den	twilight lamp	2007	2
Bosma, Hedde	toy guitar	2009	1
Braakhuis, Peter	handheld vacuum cleaner	2011	4
Brandenburg, Stephan	game controller	2007	3
Brilman, Bas	running shoes	2015	1
Brinkman, Wouter	backpack	2008	3
Bruijn, Arnout de	juicer	2010	2
Brummelman, Annelies	wristwatch	2009	3
Buijs, Amke	loudspeakers	2013	4
Capota, Kevin	ironing board	2006	2
Claessen, Martijn	thermos flask	2008	1
Claus, Julian	clinical thermometer	2015	2
Commandeur, Ard	lawn mower	2012	3
Damhuis, Miranda	sanding machine	2008	2
Davina, Oliver	garden lighting	2009	1
Dijk, Christel van	child bicycle seat	2007	2
Dijkstra, Jurriën	coffee machine	2012	3
Dijkstra, Karin	hockey sticks	2008	1
Dijkstra, Minke	universal remote control	2013	1
Dijkstra, Wouter	electric shaver	2006	5
Domburg, Stephan	disposable camera	2008	1
Donker, Jacques	slr camera	2011	4
Dooren, Thijs van	toy car	2008	1
Doorn, Maike van	ballpoint pen	2009	1
Doppenberg, Alfred	mini audio system	2011	1
Draijer, Benne	angle grinder	2007	2
Dreissen, Cyriel	snowboard	2015	2
Eekelen, Victor van	moped	2005	1
Egberts, Frank	jig saw	2012	4
Eilering, Sanne	remote control	2011	3
Einmahl, Erik	garden hose nozzle	2010	1
Eising, Tessa	deep fryer	2012	1
Elders, Ruud	toaster	2006	4
Endert, Christiaan	suitcase	2012	2
Endert, Margreet	water cooker	2008	2
Erkel, Hendri	mixer	2009	2

(continued)

Everlo, Marloes	kitchen scales	2008	4
Evertzen, Renée	mattress	2014	1
Ewijk, Luuk van	kick scooter	2015	1
Fouw, Eddo de	food processor	2006	4
Frehe, Sebastiaan	microphone	2007	2
Friso, Thomas	car navigation system	2009	2
Galen, Ronald van	food processor	2011	4
Garde, Julia	espresso machine	2007	5
Geraedts, Vincent	clock	2006	2
Gerrits, Abel	video game console	2014	1
Geurds, Nina	child's bicycle	2012	2
Giesberts, Bob	smoke detector	2011	1
Goedheer, Sietse	wet shaving	2007	3
Gommeren, Martijn	kitchen scales	2012	4
Gorp, Lieke van	fountain pen	2008	1
Graat, Bob	baby monitor	2012	1
Grint, Annemiek van de	glasses	2008	2
Grob, Mark	game controller	2010	3
Groen, Bart	electric shaver	2010	5
Groenendaal, Niek	kitchen machine	2012	2
Groot, Felke de	electric drill	2007	2
Grunsven, Kai van	football	2015	1
Gude, Johan	radio	2007	1
Haagsman, Hjalmar	monopoly	2009	1
Haan, Robert-Jan den	bicycle pump	2012	4
Haar, Wouter van der	remote control	2015	3
Haisma, Arjen	wall socket	2006	1
Hartman, Tycho	socket	2009	1
Haverslag, Christiaan	cordless drill	2007	4
Heemst, Rick van der	writing desk	2010	1
Heezen, Jennifer	fan	2009	2
Heijs, Yannick	kitchen blender	2013	2
Helmich, Werner	computer mouse	2007	4
Henckel, Claudia	sewing machine	2014	3
Hengst, Thomas den	navigation system	2013	2
Henning, Michiel	multi tool	2010	1
Herder, Renske	bootee	2009	1
Heteren, Martijn van	coffee machine	2012	3
Heuvel, Linda van den	sewing machine	2009	3
Hidding, Jet	bicycle	2012	4
Hilgerink, Tom	toaster	2011	4
Hofsink, Ashley	mp3 player	2013	2
Hoogendoorn, Niels	windsurf board	2008	1
Hoogsteder, Kay	car radio	2015	1
Hop, Erik	electric shaver	2007	5
Hout, Niek van den	handheld vacuum cleaner	2015	4
Hout, Ruben van den	electric toothbrush	2015	7
Houwers, Thomas	speaker box	2012	1
Huijing, Sanne-Marye	keyboard	2009	2

(continued)

Hurk, Anne van den	hair clipper	2010	1
Jansma, Sybren	steamer	2009	1
Janssen, Fenna	binocular	2011	5
Janssen, Lydia	Nespresso machine	2010	1
Jokker, Jorn	hairdryer	2008	2
Joling, Kevin	headphones	2015	7
Jonkman, Marin	portable PlayStation	2010	1
Karsten, Rianne	sewing machine	2012	3
Kemp, Laurens	lawn mower	2011	3
Kerkhoffs, Etienne	remote control	2010	3
Kessel, Pleuni van	mobile phone	2013	4
Kilic, Yusuf	wet shaving	2010	3
Kneefel, Josja	tennis racket	2008	1
Knook, Eilien	kitchen scales	2013	4
Kodde, Annet	handheld vacuum cleaner	2013	4
Koelman, Marcel	computer mouse	2009	4
Koenderink, Mark	mobile phone	2010	4
Kolkman, Lonneke	racing bicycle	2014	1
Konink, Rik de	headphones	2010	7
Kopke, Melina	ice skate	2015	2
Korber, Matthias	loudspeakers	2011	4
Korfage, Bas	food processor	2011	4
Korteling, Niels	gas mask	2010	1
Kraaijvanger, Marten	clock radio	2009	1
Kranen, Martijn	cd player	2008	1
Kruiper, Ruben	laptop	2013	2
Kuiper, Kyan	hair dryer	2013	1
Land, Jan	espresso machine	2008	5
Landman, Renske	glasses	2007	2
Lemmens, Pim	snowboard	2014	2
Lenferink, Rob	pc	2008	1
Leusink, Erna	electric toothbrush	2014	7
Licht, Lasse	iPhone	2009	1
Lohmeijer, Jannes	car navigation system	2014	2
Maanen, Frank van	circular saw	2013	2
Maatman, Bjorn	wireless router	2009	1
Maljaars, Jacob	head torch	2009	1
Manen, Jorn van	espresso machine	2013	5
Mansour, Sara	camera	2009	2
Markerink, Willem-Sander	bathroom scales	2011	5
Martens, Maarten	paper cutter	2010	1
Martina, Dennis	cordless drill	2013	4
Meekhof, Linda	headphones	2014	7
Meer, Manon van der	wristwatch	2015	3
Meijers, Franke	vacuum cleaner	2014	4
Meinders, Nienke	alarm clock	2008	2
Mengerink, Tim	binocular	2007	5
Michel, Maarten	basketball shoes	2014	2
Molen, Pieta van der	steam iron	2012	2

(continued)

Molenaar, Marijn	inhaler	2010	1
Mooren, Remco	external hard disk drive	2010	1
Mulhof, Huub	Walkman	2007	1
Muller, Imo	vacuum cleaner	2006	4
Nieuwboer, Sander	iPod docking station	2010	1
Nifterik, Jan van	electric shaver	2013	5
Nijkamp, Maaike	wet shaving	2008	3
Offringa, Marleen	ice skate	2014	2
Olivier, Falco	bathroom scales	2007	5
Oosterhuis, Susan	clinical thermometer	2009	2
Ortiz Ambriz, Elisa	bicycle pump	2010	4
Oteman, Paul	cordless drill	2010	4
Otten, Gijs	food processor	2014	4
Oudehand, Leon	vibrator	2009	1
Pagter, Niels de	microphone	2010	2
Peeters, Nienke	kettle	2008	1
Pelgrum, Rinus	toothbrush	2005	1
Pepping, Matthijs	fan	2007	2
Peters, Harm	bread maker	2009	1
Peters, Jan Willem	iron	2009	2
Plant, Mark	heart rate monitor	2010	1
Poolen, Daniel	sneaker	2010	1
Praamstra, Klaas Michiel	perforator	2006	1
Prinsen, Wilco	electric guitar	2008	1
Pris, Boris	jig saw	2014	4
Pruyssenaere, Robin de	handheld vacuum cleaner	2007	4
Ramaker, Freddy	home cinema	2014	1
Rasser, Haske	electric toothbrush	2013	7
Rassers, Pierre-Yves	lawn mower	2013	3
Raven, Annemieke	tent	2005	1
Regeling, Kyle	headphones	2013	7
Reigersman, Noor	child restraint system	2014	1
Reijners, Ellen	electric toothbrush	2012	7
Reilink, Derk	slr camera	2009	4
Renkens, Anke	stapler	2010	2
Renswouw, Kim van	kitchen blender	2008	2
Reuvers, Remco	electric drill	2014	2
Rinsema, Hugo	calculator	2007	1
Roodink, Wesley	beer packaging	2015	1
Rouwenhorst, Maartje	child bicycle seat	2015	2
Rozema, Mart	desktop printer	2014	2
Schäffer, Laura	headphones	2012	7
Schelfhout, Roeland	mobile phone	2008	4
Schijvens, Renske	cooker	2005	1
Schol, Henri	washing machine	2012	1
Scholder, Frank	mixer tap	2009	1
Schoonderbeek, Anouk	bicycle	2015	4
Schotman, Rick	desk lamp	2010	1
Schouwenburg, Richard van	headphones	2011	7

(continued)

Schreurs, Marleen	bathroom scales	2014	5
Schrijver, Sander	walkie-talkie	2008	1
Schuddeboom, Lisette	laptop	2013	2
Schuring, Bart	stapler	2009	2
Sesink, Anke	electric hand mixer	2014	1
Settelaar, Evan	electric toothbrush	2008	7
Siahaya, Pim	juicer	2007	2
Siepel, Anika	child's bicycle	2013	2
Slob, Han	computer keyboard	2014	1
Sloot, Sander	electric coffee grinder	2008	1
Slot, Jasper	computer mouse	2014	4
Smilde, Bas	webcam	2008	1
Smit, Jeroen	Living Colors	2013	1
Smulders, Laura	suitcase	2013	2
Snippert, Bas	electric shaver	2012	5
Snippert, Jeroen	computer monitor	2014	1
Sönmez, Gökhan	game controller	2015	3
Spikkert, Emmy	horse saddle	2014	1
Sprenkeling, Ellen	contact grill	2010	1
Stam, Liesbeth	backpack	2012	3
Steen, Dirk van der	ski	2007	1
Swart, Lotte	electric fan	2015	1
Taatgen, Rik	electric deep fryer	2013	1
Theunissen, Rik	percolator	2011	1
Thung, Michael	bicycle computer	2008	2
Tibbe, Annemarie	bathroom scales	2012	5
Tijssen, Jan	keyboard	2006	2
Titsing, Tineke	circular saw	2012	2
Tol, Liza van	alarm clock	2015	2
Tromp, Casper	binocular	2010	5
Vaessen, Tim	mp3 player	2007	2
Valerio, Chiara	waterproof clothes	2012	1
Veen, Zeno van	jig saw	2008	4
Vekerdy, Balint	fan heater	2008	1
Velde, Erwin ten	camera	2010	2
Veldhuizen, Gilbert van	bicycle computer	2015	2
Verduijn, Leendert	lighter	2010	1
Versteegh, Christiaan	basketball shoes	2011	2
Vette, Frederiek de	binocular	2012	5
Veugelers, Puck	toaster	2014	4
Vis, Carlijn	twilight lamp	2010	2
Visbeek, Mark	record player	2008	1
Visschedijk, Manou	desktop printer	2015	2
Visscher, Pim	water cooker	2014	2
Vissers, Judith	piano	2015	1
Voorde, Gijs ten	barbecue	2014	1
Voorde, Pien ten	compact camera	2011	2
Voorthuizen, Judith van	clock	2009	2
Vos, Olivier	sandwich maker	2008	1

(continued)

Vries, Clareyne de	artificial cardiac pacemaker	2015	1
Vries, Gijs de	espresso machine	2013	5
Vries, Marleen de	pressure cooker	2012	2
Vries, Wessel de	binocular	2013	5
Vriesen, Maarten	pressure cooker	2013	2
Vriezenga, Stan	mixer	2007	2
Vrolijk, Jasper	vacuum cleaner	2010	4
Waard, Paul de	television	2014	3
Wal, Koen van der	bicycle	2005	4
Weeda, Herman	television	2008	3
Weerd, Henk de	bicycle pump	2014	4
Wensink, Ruud	paintball gun	2009	1
Werf, Sam van der	compact camera	2014	2
Wesselink, Alex	thermostat	2015	3
Westdijk, Mike	digital picture frame	2008	1
Wieringa, Rianne	pram	2015	1
Wiersma, Jordi	headphones	2009	7
Wiggers, Ellis	loudspeakers	2015	4
Wit, Marlien de	kitchen scales	2014	4
Witteveen, Gerrit	thermostat	2013	3
Wolf, Fernand de	cordless drill	2012	4
Worm, Bernd	angle grinder	2009	2
Wullems, Mathijs	receiver	2007	1
Xu, Ning	game darts for kids	2010	1
Young, David	vacuum cleaner	2014	4
Zandt, Joep van de	computer mouse	2015	4
Zanten, Julian van	television	2013	3
Zwart, Martijn	frying pan	2009	1
Zweers, Wout	TIG welding torch	2008	1

References

Abernathy, W. J. and Utterback, J. M. (1975). A dynamic model of process and product innovation. *Omega*, 3, 6, 639–656.

ACEA. (2009). Average car age in the EU. www.acea.be/images/uploads/files/20090529_average_car_age.pdf, accessed: November 17, 2010.

Agar, J. (2003) *Constant Touch: A Global History of the Mobile Phone*. Cambridge: Icon Books.

Ajzen, I. and Fishbein, M. (1980). *Understanding Attitudes and Predicting Social Behavior*. Englewood Cliffs, NJ: Prentice-Hall.

Altshuller, G. S. (1999). *The Innovation Algorithm: TRIZ, Systematic Innovation, and Technical Creativity*. Worcester, MA: Technical Innovation Center.

Ames, J. H. and Ames, F. J. (1964). *Improvements in or Relating to Children's Safety Seats for Use in Vehicles and Crafts*. The Patent Office.

Ammelrooy, P. van. (2005). Bellen is slechts bijzaak op de nieuwe gsm. *De Volkskrant, Bijlage Economie*. November 4.

Anderson, P. and Tushman, M. L. (1990). Technological discontinuities and dominant designs: a cyclical model of technological change. *Administrative Science Quarterly*, **35**, 4, 604–633.

Andriani, P. and Cattani, G. (2016). Exaptation as source of creativity, innovation, and diversity: introduction to the Special Section. *Industrial and Corporate Change*, **25**, 1, 115–131.

Andrianto, I. (2013). Top 10 smartphone market share in Q1 2013. www.smartphonezero.com/top-10-smartphone-market-share-in-q1-2013/, accessed: January 30, 2015.

ANEC. (2003). Vroman, R. (Consumentenbond), Gloyns, P. (VSC), Roberts, J. (VSC), Testing of rear seat strength in cars February 2003. www.anec.org/attachments/tr005-03(pictures).pdf, accessed: November 14, 2010.

ANEC. (2006). ANEC position on UNECE Regulation 44: requirements for child restraint systems. www.anec.org/attachments/ANEC-TRAF-2006-G-040.pdf, accessed: November 14, 2010.

ANEC. (2011). I-size: better protection of children's lives. www.anec.org/attachments/ANEC-PR-2011-PRL-026.pdf, accessed: November 25, 2010.

ANEC. (2012). One-pager on a new regulation on child-restraint systems (the "I-size Regulation"). www.anec.eu/attachments/ANEC-TRAF-2012-G-034.pdf, accessed: April 5, 2013.

ANEC (2014). Enhanced child restraint systems (R129). www.anec.eu/attachments/ANEC-TRAF-2014-G-039.pdf, accessed: January 4, 2015.

Anon. (1997). Mobile phones. *Design Engineering.* London, January, 11.

Anon. (2001). Digitaal Museum van de Volkshuisvesting. www.iisg.nl/volkshuisvesting/index.html, accessed: June 2, 2008.

Anon. (2004). Mobile 2003. www.motorola.com/MotoInfo, accessed: January 20, 2004.

Anon. (2005a). Retrobrick – the home of vintage and rare mobile phones. www.retrobrick.com/moto8000.html, accessed: January 20, 2005.

Anon. (2005b). The history of Nokia 1865–2002. www.nokia.com/nokiahistory/toimialat/print_tietoliikenne.html, accessed: January 20, 2005.

Anon. (2013a). The folding cyclist. www.foldingcyclist.com, accessed: March 19, 2013.

Anon. (2013b). Toestellen. www.retroscoop.com/toestellen.php?artikel=195, accessed: August 19, 2013.

Arthur, W. B. (2009). *The Nature of Technology: What It Is and How It Evolves.* New York: The Free Press.

Aunger, R. (2000). *Darwinizing Culture: The Status of Memetics as a Science.* Oxford: Oxford University Press.

Aunger, R. (2002). *The Electric Meme: A New Theory of How We Think.* New York: Simon & Schuster.

Badke-Schaub, P. (2007). Creativity and innovation in industrial design: wishful thinking? *Journal of Design Research,* **5**, 3, 353–367.

Bagozzi, R. P., Davis, F. D., and Warshaw, P. R. (1992). Development and test of a theory of technological learning and usage. *Human Relations,* **45**, 7, 660–686.

Bakker, R. P. (2013). *The history of the bicycle.* Unpublished master thesis. Enschede: University of Twente, Enschede, the Netherlands.

Basalla, G. (1988). *The Evolution of Technology.* Cambridge: Cambridge University Press.

Baudet, H. (1986). *Een vertrouwde wereld; 100 jaar innovatie in Nederland.* Amsterdam: Bert Bakker.

Bell, A. G. (1876). Patent No. 174.465. United States of America.

Bense, M. (1954). *Aesthetica, Metaphysische Beobachtungen am Schönen.* Stuttgart: Deutsche Verlags-Anstalt.

Benyus, J. M. (1997). *Biomimicry.* New York: William Morrow.

Berlyne, D. E. (1971). *Aesthetics and Psychobiology.* New York: Appleton-Century-Crofts.

Bijker, W. E. (1990). *The Social Construction of Technology.* Enschede: University of Twente.

Bijker, W. E. (1997). *Of Bicycles, Bakelites and Bulbs: Toward a Theory of Sociotechnical Change.* Cambridge, MA: MIT Press.

Bijker, W. E., Hughes, T. P., and Pinch, T. J. (1987). *The Social Construction of Technological Systems: New Directions in the Sociology and History of Technology.* Cambridge, MA: MIT Press.

Birkhoff, G. D. (1928). *Quelques éléments mathématiques de l'art.* Atti del Congresso Internazionale dei Matematci di Bologna, Bologna (Italy).

Blackmore, S. (1999). *The Meme Machine.* Oxford: Oxford University Press.

Boselie, F. A. J. M. (1982). *Over Visuele Schoonheidservaring.* Nijmegen: Katholieke Universiteit Nijmegen.

Bouckaert, R., Lemey, P., Dunn, M., Greenhill, S. J., Alekseyenko, A. V., Drummond, A. J., Gray, R. D., Suchard, M. A., and Atkinson, Q. D. (2012).

Mapping the origins and expansion of the Indo-European language family. *Science*, **337**, 6097, 957–960.

Bouwknegt, A. (1982). Compact fluorescent lamps. *Journal of the Illuminating Engineering Society*, **11**, 4, 204–2012.

Brittain, J. E. (2004). William D. Coolidge and ductile tungsten. *IEEE Industry Applications Magazine*, **10**, 5, 9–10.

Brodie, R. (1996). *Virus of the Mind: The New Science of the Meme*. Seattle, WA: Hay House, Inc.

Bryson, B. (2003). *A Short History of Nearly Everything*. London: Transworld Publishers.

Butler, S. (1863). Darwin among the machines. *The Press*, June 13, 1863, New Zealand: Christchurch.

Butler, S. (1872). *Erewhon*. London: Trübner & Co.

Bytheway, C. W. (1965). Basic function determination technique. *Proceedings of the FIFTH National Conference*, **2**, 21–23.

Candi, M., Gemser, G., and Ende, J. van den. (2010). *Effectiviteit van Design*. Rotterdam: RSM, Erasmus University.

Cao, H. (2009). RFID in product lifecycle management: a case in the automotive industry. *International Journal of Computer Manufacturing*, **22**, 7, 616–637.

Cao, H. and Folan, P. (2011). Product life cycle: the evolution of a paradigm and literature review from 1950–2009. *Production Planning & Control*, **23**, 8, 641–662.

Carlson, W. B. (2000). Invention and evolution: the case of Edison's sketches of the telephone. *Technological Innovation as an Evolutionary Process*. Ed. Ziman, J. (pp. 137–158). Cambridge: Cambridge University Press.

Casson, H. N. (1910). The birth of the telephone: its invention not an accident but the working out of a scientific theory. *The World's Work: A History of Our Time*, **XIX**, 12669–12683.

CBS (2015). *Factsheet Nederland Fietsland*. www.cbs.nl/NR/ rdonlyres/4CCAB732-FD1B-441F-B0C9-9CDF1A4A443F/0/2015factsheetnederlandf ietsland.pdf, accessed: August 30, 2015.

Chapman, R. J. (2006). *Simple Tools and Techniques for Enterprise Risk Management*. Hoboken, NJ: John Wiley & Sons.

Christensen, C. M. (1997). *The Innovator's Dilemma*. Boston, MA: Harvard Business School Press.

Coates, D. (2003). *Watches Tell More Than Time: Product Design, Information and the Quest for Elegance*. London: McGraw-Hill.

Colella, J. (2010). *Safe Ride News*, thirty "dynamic" years of FMVSS 213. www.safe ridenews.com/SRNDNN/CPSTsProfessionals/HistoryofChildPassengerSafety/ ThirtyDynamicYearsofFMVSS213/tabid/249/Default.aspx, accessed: November 7, 2010.

Collan, M. and Tetard, F. (2007). Lazy user theory of solution selection. *Proceedings of the CELDA 2007 Conference*, **227**, 273–278.

Consumentengids. (1970). Autozitjes en autogordels, voor kleine kinderen. *Consumentengids*, **18**, 5, 148–153.

Consumentengids. (1974). Kinderzitjes en -gordels in de auto. *Consumentengids*, **22**, 5, 242–245.

Consumentengids. (1977). Het kind in de auto. Reiswieggordels, zitjes en gordels. *Consumentengids*, **25**, 4, 140–147.

Consumentengids. (1983). Zitjes en kussens veilig en prettigst voor uw kind. Kinderbeveiliging in de auto. *Consumentengids*, **31**, 8, 358–361.

Consumentengids. (1984). Besparen op verlichting: TL-buis en bespaarlamp. *Consumentengids*, **32**, 2, 60–64.

Consumentengids. (1984). Kinderzitje schiet soms doel voorbij. *Consumentengids*, **32**, 6, 268–270.

Consumentengids. (1987). Nu ook een goed zitje voor de allerjongsten. *Consumentengids*, **35**, 6, 304–306.

Consumentengids. (1988). Meeste spaarlampen voordelig; op een paar legt u geld toe. *Consumentengids*, **36**, 4, 188–192.

Consumentengids. (1989). Helft spaarlampen blijft branden. *Consumentengids*, **37**, 7, 441–444.

Consumentengids. (1990a). Marathontest onthult de spaarzaamste lampen. *Consumentengids*, **38**, 1, 17–19.

Consumentengids. (1990b). Kind in autozitje niet altijd goed beschermd. *Consumentengids*, **38**, 6, 344–347.

Consumentengids. (1993a). Profijt van spaarlampen overtreft de gebreken. *Consumentengids*, **41**, 8, 552–556.

Consumentengids. (1993b). Veel kinderzithes passen slecht in moderne auto. *Veel kinderzitjes passen slecht in moderne auto*. *Consumentengids*, **41**, 10, 566–569.

Consumentengids. (1994). Kinderzitjes in auto veiliger. *Consumentengids*, **42**, 6, 373.

Consumentengids. (1995). Spaarzaam licht en toch gezellig? *Consumentengids*, **43**, 6, 450–457.

Consumentengids. (1996). Voordeliger uit met een spaarlamp. *Consumentengids*, **44**, 2, 80–83.

Consumentengids. (1999). Spaarlamp spekt spaarvarken. *Consumentengids*, **47**, 9, 44–48.

Consumentengids. (2001). 50 Mobieltjes! *Consumentengids*, **49**, 5, 46–49.

Consumentengids. (2004). Verlicht uw energierekening. *Consumentengids*, **52**, 1, 38–41.

Consumentengids. (2008). Spaarlampen: meer licht voor minder geld. *Consumentengids*, **56**, 2, 59–61.

Consumentengids. (2009). Spaarlampen doorgelicht. *Consumentengids*, **57**, 5, 38–41.

Consumentengids. (2010a). Laat led peertje nog even liggen. *Consumentengids*, **58**, 2, 27–29.

Consumentengids. (2010b). Test autokinderzitje. Maxi-Cosi domineert. *Consumentengids*, **58**, 6, 68–71.

Consumentengids. (2010c). Opvolger van de gloeilamp gezocht. *Consumentengids*, **58**, 7, 28–31.

Consumentengids. (2011). Goede spaarlamp voor €4,-. *Consumentengids*, **59**, 10, 18–21.

Consumentengids. (2012). De gloeilamp is bijna uitgegloeid. *Consumentengids*, **60**, 5, 16–19.

Consumentengids. (2013a). Ledlamp uit de kinderschoenen. *Consumentengids*, **61**, 3, 10–13.

Consumentengids. (2013b). Prijsdoorbraak eindelijk een feit. *Consumentengids*, **61**, 10, 38–41.

Consumer Reports. (1972). Crash tests of car safety restraints for children. *Consumer Reports*, **36**, 8, 484–489.

Cooper, A. (1999). *The Inmates Are Running the Asylum: [Why High-Tech Products Drive Us Crazy and How to Restore the Sanity]*. **261**, Indianapolis, IN: Sams Publishing.

Crilly, N., Moultrie, J., and Clarkson, J. (2004). Seeing things: consumer response to the visual domain in product design. *Design Studies*, **25**, 547–577.

Darwin, C. (1837). First Notebook on Transmutation of Species.

Darwin, C. (1845). *Journal of Researches into the Natural History and Geology of the Countries Visited during the Voyage of H.M.S. Beagle Round the World, Under the Command of Capt. Fitz Roy, R.N. 2d edition. 1*. United Kingdom: J. Murray.

Darwin, C. (2008). *The Origin of Species*. United Kingdom: Crw Publishing Limited. Originally published 1859.

David, P. A. (1985). Clio and the economics of QWERTY. *The American Economic Review*, **75**, 2, Papers and Proceedings of the Ninety-Seventh Annual Meeting of the American Economic Association, 332–337.

David, P. A. and Bunn, J. A. (1988). The economics of gateway technologies and network evolution: lessons from electricity supply history. *Information Economics and Policy*, **3**, 2, 165–202.

Davis, F. D. (1989). Perceived usefulness, perceived ease of use, and user acceptance of information technology. *MIS Quarterly*, **13**, 3, 319–340.

Davis, S. C., Diegel, S. W., and Boundy, R. G. (2003). *Transportation Energy Data Book: Edition 23* (No. ORNL 6970). Washington, DC: US Department of Energy.

Dawkins, R. (1976). *The Selfish Gene*. New York: Oxford University Press.

Dawkins, R. (1986). *The Blind Watchmaker*. New York: W.W. Norton & Company, Inc.

Dennett, D. C. (1996). *Darwin's Dangerous Idea: Evolution and the Meanings of Life*. New York: Simon and Schuster.

Desmet, P. (2003). A multilayered model of product emotions. *The Design Journal*, **6**, 2, 4–13.

Desmet, P. and Hekkert, P. (2007). Framework of product experience. *International Journal of Design*, **1**, 1, 56–66.

Dhalla, N. K. and Yuspeh, S. (1976). Forget the product life cycle concept! *Harvard Business Review*, **54**, 1, 102–112.

Diamond, J. (2005). *Collapse: How Societies Choose to Fail or Succeed*. New York: Viking Press.

Didde, R. (2004). Nieuw leven voor elk mobieltje. *De Volkskrant, Bijlage Economie*. February 19.

Dijkstra, W. (2005). *De ontwikkeling van het scheerapparaat*. Unpublished master thesis. Enschede: University of Twente.

DOE. (2011a). DOE announces Philips as first winner of the L Prize Competition. www.lightingprize.org/philips-winner.stm, accessed: February 15, 2015.

DOE. (2011b). Solid-state lighting research and development: multi-year program plan. US Department of Energy: http://apps1.eere.energy.gov/buildings/publications/pdfs/ssl/ssl_mypp 192011_web.pdf, accessed: September 18, 2011.

Dorel. (2005). *Around the World with Maxi-Cosi*. Helmond: Dorel Netherlands.

Dorel. (2012). FamilyFix, Base for Pebble and Pearl car seats. www.maxi-cosi.com/car-seats/familyfix.aspx, accessed October 14, 2012.

Dosi, G. (1982). Technological paradigm and technological trajectories: a suggested interpretation of the determinants and directions of technical change. *Research Policy*, **11**, 149–162.

Dosi, G. and Nelson, R. R. (2013). The evolution of technologies: an assessment of the state-of-the-art. *Eurasian Business Review*, **3**, 1, 3–46.

Drucker, P. F. (1985). The discipline of innovation. *Harvard Business Review*, **63**, 3, 67–72.

Economist, The, VI (May 13, 1848), 536; as cited in Tarn (1973).

Edmonds, B. (2005). The revealed poverty of the gene-meme analogy – why memetics per se has failed to produce substantive results. *Journal of Memetics – Evolutionary Models of Information Transmission*, **9**.

Eger, A. O. (1987). Who actually designs? *Holland in Vorm, Dutch Design 1945–1987*. Ed. Staal, G. (pp. 69–75). The Hague: Stichting Holland in Vorm.

Eger, A. O. (1993). Productniveaus bepalend voor vormgeving, promotie en presentatie (parts 1 and 2). *Nieuws Tribune*, **47**, 32–35 and **48**, 27–32.

Eger, A. O. (1996). *Succesvolle Productontwikkeling*. Deventer: Kluwer Bedrijfswetenschappen.

Eger, A. O. (2007a). *Evolutionaire productontwikkeling: productfasen beschrijven de meest waarschijnlijke levensloop van een product*. The Hague: Lemma Publishers.

Eger, A. O. (2007b). *Evolutionary Product Development: How "Product Phases" Can Map the Status Quo and Future of a Product*. The Hague: Lemma Publishers.

Eger, A. O. (2009). Evolutionary product development in working-class housing. *Comparative Methodologies: Bringing the World into Culture*. Liber Amicorum Richard Foqué (pp. 298–317). Antwerp: University Press Antwerp (UPA Editions).

Eger, A. O. (2013). *An Introduction to Evolutionary Product Development*. The Hague: Eleven International Publishing.

Eger, A. O., Bonnema, G. M., Lutters, E., and Voort, M. C. van der. (2010). *Productontweren*. 4th printing. The Hague: Lemma Publishers.

Eger, A. O., Bonnema, G. M., Lutters, E., and Voort, M. C. van der (2013). *Product Design*. The Hague: Eleven International Publishing.

Eger, A. O. and Drukker, J. W. (2010). Phases of product development: a qualitative complement to the product life cycle. *Design Issues*, **26**, 2, 47–58.

Eger, A. O. and Drukker, J. W. (2012). Evolutionary product development as a design tool. *Journal of Design Research*, **10**, 3, 141–154.

Eger, A. O. and Wendrich, R. E. (2011). Knowledge exchange between master and PhD students with regard to evolutionary product development. *Proceedings of the 13th International Conference on Engineering and Product Design Education*. City University (London). September 8–9, 2011. London: The Design Society.

Ehlhardt, H. (2012). Child restraint systems: an analysis of their development from an evolutionary perspective. *Journal of Design Research*, **10**, 4, 324–343.

Ehlhardt, H. (2013). Product evolution diagram: a systematic approach used in evolutionary product development. *Proceedings of the 15th International Conference on Engineering and Product Design Education*. Dublin, Ireland. September 5–6, 2013. London: The Design Society.

Ehlhardt, H. (2016). *Product evolution: how new (types of) products come about & develop over time into families of advanced versions*. PhD thesis. Enschede: University of Twente.

Ehrnberg, E. (1995). On the definition and measurement of technological discontinuities. *Technovation*, **15**, 7, 437–452.

Eisenhardt, K. M. (1989). Building theories from case study research. *The Academy of Management Review*, **14**, 4, 532–550.

Elkington, J. and Hailes, J. (1992). *Holidays That Don't Cost the Earth*. London: Victor Gollancz.

Encyclopædia Britannica. (2013). Peter Cooper Hewitt. www.britannica.com/EBchecked/topic/264522/Peter-Cooper-Hewitt?anchor=ref196631, accessed: May 19, 2014.

Fischer, C. S. (1994). *America Calling: A Social History of the Telephone to 1940*. Oakland: University of California Press.

Foot, D. K. (1996). *Boom, Bust & Echo*. Toronto, Canada: Macfarlane Walter & Ross.

Forty, A. (1986). *Objects of Desire*. New York: Thames and Hudson.

Freeman, C. and Louçã, F. (2001). *As Time Goes By: From the Industrial Revolution to the Information Revolution*. Oxford: Oxford University Press.

Friedel, R. and Israel, P. (1985). *Edison's Electric Light: Biography of an Invention*. New Brunswick, NJ: Rutgers University Press.

Garcia, R. (2010). Types of innovation. *Encyclopedia of Technology & Innovation Management*. Ed. Narayanan, V. K. and O'Connor, G. C. (pp. 89–95). Chichester, UK: John Wiley & Sons.

Gaulin, S. J. C. and McBurney, D. H. (2004). *Evolutionary Psychology*. 2nd edn. Upper Saddle River, NJ: Prentice Hall.

Geels, F. W. (2002). Technological transitions as evolutionary reconfiguration processes: a multi-level perspective and a case-study. *Research Policy*, **31**, 8–9, 1257–1274.

Geels, F. W. and Schot, J. (2007). Typology of sociotechnical transition pathways. *Research Policy*, **36**, 3, 399–417.

General Electric (GE). (2011). Three bulbs in one: GE's hybrid halogen-CFL with incandescent shape arrives in April (Press release). www.genewscenter.com/content/Detail.aspx?ReleaseID=12188&NewsAreaID=2, accessed: May 24, 2012.

Golder, P. N. and Tellis, G. J. (2004). Growing, growing, gone: Cascades, diffusion, and turning points in the product life cycle. *Marketing Science*, **23**, 2, 207–218.

Gould, S. J. and Vrba, E. S. (1982). Exaptation – a missing term in the science of form. *Paleobiology*, **8**, 1, 4–15.

Gray, R. D. and Atkinson, Q. D. (2003). Language-tree divergence times support the Anatolian theory of Indo-European origin. *Nature*, **426**, 6965, 435–439.

Grove, N. (1997). *National Geographic Atlas of World History*. Washington, DC: National Geographic Society.

Gyr, U. (2010). The history of tourism: structures on the path to modernity. *Europäische Geschichte Online (EGO)*. Institute of European History (IEG), Mainz 2010–12–03. www.ieg-ego.eu/gyru-2010-en URN: urn:nbn:de:0159–20100921246, accessed: November 27, 2014.

Haan, B. de and Vliet, G. van der. (2005). *Doordouwers en verhalenbouwers*. Enschede: SIR.

Haitz, R., Kish, F., Tsao, J., and Nelson, J. (1999). The case for a national research program on semiconductor lighting. *Annual Forum of the Optoelectronics Industry Development Association*. Washington, DC: Sanida National Laboratories.

Haitz, R. and Tsao, J. Y. (2011). Solid-state lighting: "The case" 10 years after and future prospects. *Physica Status Solidi A 208*, 1, 17–29.

Hansard, CXV (new series, April 1851), 1260–1; as cited in Tarn (1973).

Hekkert, P. P. M. (1995). *Artful Judgements*. Delft: TU Delft.

Hertog, F. den and Sluijs, E. van. (1995). *Onderzoek in organisaties*. Assen, The Netherlands: Van Gorcum.

Hippel, E. von. (1986). Lead users: a source of novel product concepts. *Management Science*, **32**, 7, 791–805.

Hippel, E. von. (2005). *Democratizing Innovation*. Cambridge, MA: MIT Press.

Hoed, R. van den. (2004). *Driving Fuel Cell Vehicles. How Established Industries React to Radical Technologies*. Delft: Design for Sustainability Program, Delft University of Technology.

Hoogema, R., Kemp, R., Schot, J., and Truffer N. (2002). Experimenting for sustainable transport. *The Approach of Strategic Niche Management*. London: Spon Press, Taylor & Francis Group.

Huxley, J. (1942). *Evolution. The Modern Synthesis*. London.

Hybs, I. and Gero, J. S. (1992). An evolutionary process model of design. *Design Studies*, **13**, 3, 273–290.

Iwafune, Y. (2000). *Technology Progress Dynamics of Compact Fluorescent Lamps*. Austria: International Institute for Applied Systems Analysis.

Jacobs, J. J., Hoorn, F. M. M. van, Ooy, C. M. van, Rolf, R., Muller, W., Kruit, J., and Mourik, F. van. (1987). *De telefoon blijft: archetypische verkenningen rond een massaprodukt*. Delft: Delftse Universitaire Pers.

Joore, P. (2010). *New to Improve. The Mutual Influence between New Products and Societal Change Processes*. Delft: VSSD.

Jordan, P. W. (2000). *Designing Pleasurable Products, an Introduction to the New Human Factors*. London: Taylor & Francis.

Karjaluoto, H. (2005). Factors affecting consumer choice of mobile phones: two studies from Finland. *Journal of Euromarketing*. 14, 3, 59–82.

Kay, N. M. (2013). Rerun the tape of history and QWERTY always wins. *Research Policy*, **42**, 6, 1175–1185.

Kelley, T. and Littman, J. (2005). *The Ten Faces of Innovation: IDEO's Strategies for Defeating the Devil's Advocate and Driving Creativity Throughout Your Organisation*. New York: Random House LLC.

Kessel, P. van. (2013). *Evolutionary product development: the evolution of the mobile phone*. Unpublished master thesis. Enschede: University of Twente.

Kondratiev, N. (2004). *The World Economy and its Conjunctures During and After the War*. Moscow: International Kondratieff Foundation. Originally published 1922.

Krishnan, V. and Ulrich, K. T. (2001). Product development decisions: a review of the literature. *Management Science*, **47**, 1–21.

Kroeber, A. L. (1948). *Anthropology*, rev. edn. New York: Harcourt Brace.

Kuhn, T. S. (1962). *The Structure of Scientific Revolutions*. Chicago: University of Chicago Press.

Lacohée, H., Wakeford, N., and Pearson, I. (2003). A social history of the mobile telephone with a view of its future. *BT Technology Journal*, **21**, 3, 203–211.

Langrish, J. Z. (2004). Darwinian design: the memetic evolution of design ideas. *Design Issues*, **20**, 4, 4–19.

Latour, B. (1993). *Aramis, or, The Love of Technology*. Cambridge, MA: Harvard University Press.

Lefèvre, N., T'Serclaes, P. de, and Waide, P. (2006). *Barriers to Technology Diffusion: The Case of Compact Fluorescent Lamps*. Paris: International Energy Agency, OECD.

Lessing, H. E. (1997). The Evidence against "Leonardo's Bicycle." *Eighth International Cycling History Conference*, Glasgow, 1997.

Levitt, T. (1965). Exploit the product life cycle. *Harvard Business Review*, **43**, 6, 81–94.

Liebowitz, S. J. and Margolis, S. E. (1990). The fable of the keys. *Journal of Law and Economics*, **33**, 1–25.

Loewy, R. (2011). Raymond Loewy, the father of industrial design. (www.raymon dloewy.com), accessed: August 30, 2011.

Losev, O. V. (1927). *Telegrafiya i Telefoniya bez Provodov*, **44**, 485–494.

Marylyn Carrigan, A. A. (2001). The myth of the ethical consumer – do ethics matter in purchase behaviour? *Journal of Consumer Marketing*, **18**, 7, 560–578.

Maslow, A. H. (1976). *Motivatie en Persoonlijkheid*. Rotterdam: Lemniscaat. Translation, original edition: *Motivation and Personality*, 1954.

McDonald Dunbar, R. I. and Knight, C. D. (1999). *The Evolution of Culture: An Interdisciplinary View*. Edinburgh: Edinburgh University Press.

McGarry, D. D. (1955). *The Metalogicon of John of Salisbury: A Twelfth-Century Defense of the Verbal and Logical Arts of the Trivium*. University of California Press.

McPherron, S. P., et al. (2010). Evidence for stone-tool-assisted consumption of animal tissues before 3.39 million years ago at Dikika, Ethiopia. *Nature*, **466**, 857–860.

Meadows, D. H., Meadows, D. L., Randers, J., and Behrens, W. W. (1972). *The Limits to Growth*. New York: Universe Books. 102.

Menanteau, P. and Lefebvre, H. (2000). Competing technologies and the diffusion of innovations: the emergence of energy-efficient lamps in the residential sector. *Research Policy*, **29**, 3, 375–389.

Mentalfloss (2013). A brief history of 7 baby basics. http://mentalfloss.com/article/ 49280/brief-history-7-baby-basics, accessed: June 14, 2015.

Meyer, R. de and Smets, M. (1982). De recente stedenbouwkundige geschiedschrijving in België omtrent negentiende en begin twintigste eeuw. *Belgisch Tijdschrift voor Nieuwste Geschiedenis*, **XIII**, 2–3.

Miaskiewicz, T. and Kozar, K. A. (2011). Personas and user-centered design: how can personas benefit product design processes? *Design Studies*, **32**, 5, 417–430.

Michel, M. (2014a). *Evolutionary product development: research Nike basketball shoes*. Unpublished master thesis. Enschede: University of Twente. (Source: http://news .nike.com/, accessed March 3, 2015).

Michel, M. (2014b). *Evolutionary product development: design basketball shoe*. Unpublished master thesis. Enschede: University of Twente.

Millward, S. (2014). 15 new Asian smartphone makers hoping to crush Samsung and Apple. www.techinasia.com/2013-list-new-asian-homegrown-smartphone-brands/, accessed: January 30, 2015.

Mitchell, A. (1983). *The Nine American Lifestyles: Who We Are and Where We're Going*. New York: Macmillan Publishing Co.

Mokyr, J. (1996). Evolution and technological change: a new metaphor for economic history. *Technological Change*. Ed. Fox, R. (pp. 63–83). London: Harwood Publishers.

Mokyr, J. (1998). Induced technical innovation and medical history: an evolutionary approach. *Journal of Evolutionary Economics*, **8**, 119–137.

Mokyr, J. (1999). Invention and rebellion: why do innovations occur at all? An evolutionary approach. *Minorities and Economic Growth*. Ed. Brezis, E. and Temin P. (pp. 179–203). Amsterdam: Elsevier Publishers.

Mokyr, J. (2000a). Innovation and selection in evolutionary models of technology: some definitional issues. *Technological Innovation as an Evolutionary Process*. Ed. Ziman, J. (pp. 52–95). Cambridge: Cambridge University Press.

Mokyr, J. (2000b). Knowledge, technology, and economic growth during the Industrial Revolution. *Productivity, Technology and Economic Growth*. Ed. Van Ark, B., Kuipers, S., and Kuper, G. (pp. 253–292). The Hague: Kluwer/Springer.

Monö, R. (1997). *Design for Product Understanding*. Stockholm, Sweden: Liber.

Motivaction International. (2017). Mentality. www.motivaction.nl/specialismen/mentality-tm, accessed: March 2017.

Murmann, J. P. and Frenken, K. (2006). Toward a systematic framework for research on dominant designs, technological innovations, and industrial change. *Research Policy*, **35**, 7, 925–952.

Nelson, R. R. and Winter, S. G. (1982). *An Evolutionary Theory of Economic Change*. Cambridge, MA: Belknap Press of Harvard University Press.

Nierop, O. A. van, Blankendaal, A. C. M., and Overbeeke, C. J. (1997). The evolution of the bicycle: a dynamic systems approach. *Journal of Design History*, **10**, 3, 253–267.

Nifterik, J. van. (2013). *The evolutionary development of the electric shaver*. Unpublished master thesis. Enschede: University of Twente.

Norman, D. (1988). *The Psychology of Everyday Things*. New York: Basic Books.

Norman, D. (1992). *Turn Signals Are the Facial Expressions of Automobiles*. Reading, MA: Basic Books.

NXP (2009). A journey for next-generation lighting solutions.www.arrownac.com/offers/nxp-semiconductors/nxpparts/journey_for_next_generation_lighting_solutions_19200909.pdf.accessed: October 23, 2011.

O2 (2012).Making calls has become fifth most frequent use for a smartphone for newly-networked generation of users. http://news.o2.co.uk/?press-release=making-calls-has-become-fifth-most-frequent-use-for-a-smartphone-for-newly-networked-generation-of-users, accessed: August 31, 2015.

Oost, E. van. (2003). Materialized gender: how shavers configure the users' femininity and masculinity. *How Users Matter*. Ed. Oudshoorn, N. and Pinch, T. (pp. 193–208). Cambridge, MA: The MIT Press.

Ormerod, P. A. (1994). *The Death of Economics*. London: Faber and Faber.

Ormerod, P. A. (1998). *Butterfly Economics: A New General Theory of Social and Economic Behavior*. London: Faber and Faber.

Ormerod, P. A. (2005). *Why Most Things Fall: Evolution, Extinction and Economics*. London: Faber and Faber.

OSRAM.(2008).www.osram.com/media/resource/HIRES/333322/watts-new-11%962008.pdf?search_result=%2fosram_com%2fsearch%2fadvanced_search.jsp%3faction%3ddosearch%26inp_searchterm_1%3dduled%26website_name%3dosram_com, accessed: March 23, 2014.

PA Consulting Group (2009). Exploring the future to meet environmental targets. www.paconsulting.com/our-experience/arn-exploring-the-future-to-meet-environmental-targets/, accessed: February 2, 2016.

Pagel, M. (2012). *Wired for Culture: Origins of the Human Social Mind*. New York: WW Norton & Company.

Pauw, G. de (ed.). (2006). *De Productie van Sociale Woningen*, Art. 23, 22. Brussels: BBRoW.

Perez, C. (2002). *Technological Revolutions and Financial Capital: The Dynamics of Bubbles and Golden Ages*. Cheltenham, UK: Edward Elgar.

Petroski, H. (1992). *The Evolution of Useful Things*. New York: A. Knopf.

Phaal, R., Farrukh, C. J., and Probert, D. R. (2004). Technology road mapping – a planning framework for evolution and revolution. *Technological Forecasting and Social Change*, **71**, 1, 5–26.

Philips. (2012). Introducing Philips hue: the world's smartest LED bulb, marking a new era in home lighting. www.newscenter.philips.com/main/standard/news/press/ 192012/20121029-introducing-philips-hue.wpd#.UoXx9JSxN1A, accessed: November 15, 2013.

Phrase Finder, The. (2011). Beauty is in the eye of the beholder. (www.phrases.org.uk/meanings/59100.html), accessed: July 19, 2011.

Pinch, T. J. and Bijker, W. E. (1984). The social construction of facts and artefacts: or how the sociology of science and the sociology of technology might benefit each other. *Social Studies of Science*, **14**, 3, 399–441.

Pine, B. J. and Gilmore, J. H. (1999). *The Experience Economy*. Boston, MA: Harvard Business School Press.

Plain, C. (2004). *Apollo's Small Steps Are Giant Leap for Technology*. NASA's John F. Kennedy Space Center, www.nasa.gov/missions/science/ f_apollo_11_spinoff.html, accessed March 3, 2015.

Prahalad, C. K. and Ramaswamy, V. (2004). *The Future of Competition: Co-creating Value with Customers*. Boston, MA: Harvard Business School Press.

Pruitt, J. and Adlin, T. (2010). *The Persona Lifecycle: Keeping People in Mind Throughout Product Sesign*. San Francisco, CA: Morgan Kaufmann.

Pruitt, J. and Grudin, J. (2003). Personas: practice and theory. *Proceedings of the 2003 Conference on Designing for User Experiences*. 1–15, ACM.

Rae, J. (2014). *What Is the Real Value of Design?*. Alexandria, VA: The Design Management Institute (DMI) and Motiv Strategies.

Ramakers, R. (1984). Van sigaar naar pijp en verder. *Vorm & industrie in Nederland 1: huishoudelijke artikelen*. Rotterdam: Uitgeverij 010.

Reigersman, N. (2014). *Evolutionary product development: design of a child car seat for BeSafe*. Unpublished master thesis. Enschede: University of Twente.

Renfrew, C. (1987). *Archaeology and Language: The Puzzle of Indo-European Origins*. Cambridge: Cambridge University Press.

Robert, P. and Weil, P. (2016). *Typewriter: A Celebration of the Ultimate Writing Machine*. New York: Sterling.

Rogers, E. M. (1995). *Diffusion of Innovations*. 4{{sup}}th edition. New York: The Free Press. Originally published 1962.

Rosenberg, N. (1996). Uncertainty and technological change. *The Mosaic of Economic Growth*. Ed. Landau, R., Taylor, T., and Wright, G. 334–356. Stanford, CA: Stanford University Press.

Rosenbloom, J. L. (2010). Technology evolution. *Encyclopedia of Technology & Innovation Management*. Ed. Narayanan, V. K. and O'Connor, G. C. (pp. 9–18). Chichester, UK: John Wiley & Sons.

Roozenburg, N. F. and Eekels, J. (1995). *Product Design: Fundamentals and Methods* (Vol. 2). Chichester, UK: Wiley.

Roy, R. (1994). The evolution of ecodesign. *Technovation*, **14**, 6, 363–380.

Sandahl, L. J., Gilbride, T. L., Ledbetter, M. R., Steward, H. E., and Calwell, C. (2006). *Compact Fluorescent Lighting in America: Lessons Learned on the Way to Market*. Pacific Northwest National Laboratory. Prepared for the US Dept. of Energy.

Sandhu, S., Ozanne, L. K., Smallman, C., and Cullen, R. (2010). Consumer driven corporate environmentalism: fact or fiction? *Business Strategy and the Environment*, **19**, 6, 356–366.

Save (2015). Function analysis systems technique – the basics. www.value-eng.org/pdf_docs/monographs/FAbasics.pdf, accessed: September 13, 2015.

Schäffer, L. S. (2014). *The awareness phase in theory and practice: a study of the position of awareness products in the theory of evolutionary product development.* Unpublished master thesis. Enschede: University of Twente.

Schmidt, P., et al. (2013). Heat treatment in the South African Middle Stone Age: temperature induced transformations of silcrete and their technological implications. *Journal of Archaeological Science*, **40**, 9, 3519–3531.

Schumpeter, J. A. (1939). *Business Cycles (2 vols.).* New York: McGraw-Hill.

Schumpeter, J. (1942). *Capitalism, Socialism and Democracy.* New York: Routledge.

Semaw, S., et al. (1997). 2.5-million-year-old stone tools from Gona, Ethiopia. *Nature*, **385**, 333–336.

Shah, S. (2000). *Source and patterns of innovation in a consumers products field: innovations in sporting equipment.* MIT Working Paper no. 4105.

Sleeswijk Visser, F. (2009). *Bringing the Everyday Life of People into Design.* Delft: Delft University of Technology.

Smith, W. (2008). The history of the car seat. www.articlesbase.com/education-articles/the-history-of-the-car-seat-593547.html, accessed: October 31, 2010.

Southworth, F. C. (1964). Family-tree diagrams. *Language*, **40**, 4, 557–565.

Spencer, H. (1864). *The Principles of Biology.* London: Williams and Norgate.

Srivastava, L. (2005). Mobile phones and the evolution of social behavior. *Behaviour & Information Technology*, **24**, 2, 111–129.

Staal, P. E. (2003). *Automobilisme in Nederland. Een geschiedenis van gebruik, misbruik en nut. Zutphen.* The Netherlands: Walburg Pers.

Steadman, P. (1979 and 2008, rev. edn.). *The Evolution of Designs: Biological Analogy in Architecture and the Applied Arts.* Cambridge, UK: Cambridge University Press.

Switch Lighting. (2011). The first 100 watt-equivalent LED bulb shines at 2011 LIGHTFAIR. http://switchlightbulbs.com/lib/pdf/PressRelease-051711.pdf, accessed: March 4, 2012.

Tarn, J. N. (1973). *Five Per Cent Philanthropy: An Account of Housing in Urban Areas between 1840 and 1914.* Cambridge: Cambridge University Press.

Tempelman, E., Pauw, I. C. D., Grinten, B. V. D., Mul, E. J., and Grevers, K. (2015). Biomimicry and cradle to cradle in product design: an analysis of current design practice. *Journal of Design Research*, **13**, 4, 326–344.

Thøgersen, J., Jørgensen, A. K., and Sandager,S. (2012). Consumer decision making regarding a "green" everyday product. *Psychology & Marketing*, **29**, 4, 187–197.

Triggs, R. (2014). State of the smartphone industry – Q3 2014. www.androidauthority.com/smartphone-industry-q3-2014-567890/, accessed: January 30, 2015.

Turner, T. (2013). The sports shoe: a social and cultural history. *PhD thesis.* London: Birbeck, University of London.

Tushman, M. L. and Murmann, J. P. (1998, August).Dominant designs, technology cycles, and organisation outcomes. *Academy of Management Proceedings*, **1998**, 1, A1–A33. Academy of Management.

Valverde, S. and Solé, R. (2015).Punctuated equilibrium in the large scale evolution of programming languages. *Journal of the Royal Society Interface*, **12**, 107.

Veblen, T. (1994). *The Theory of the Leisure Class*. New York:Penguin Books. Originally published 1899.

Venkatesh, V., Morris, M. G., Davis, G. B., and Davis, F. D. (2003). User acceptance of information technology: toward a unified view. *MIS Quarterly*, **27**, 3, 425–478.

Verbeek, P. P. C. C. (2000). *De daadkracht der dingen: over techniek, filosofie en vormgeving*. Boom.

Vergne, J. P. (2013). QWERTY is dead, long live path dependence. *Research Policy*, 42, (6–7), 1191–1194.

Volvo. (2014). Dudes to dads. Baby sense. Volvo genuine child safety. www.volvo cars.com/za/Documents/MY%2014%20Brochures/ChildSafety.pdf, accessed: January 2, 2015.

Waide, P. (2010). Phase out of incandescent lamps, implications for international supply and demand for regulatory compliant lamps. International Energy Agency. www.iea.org/papers/2010/phase_out.pdf, accessed: September 16, 2011.

Wal, K. van der. (2005). *Productfasen Fiets; Onderzoek & Ontwerp*. Unpublished master thesis. Enschede: University of Twente.

Wikipedia. (2011). Edison screw.www.en.wikipedia.org/wiki/Edison_screw, accessed: March 4, 2012.

Wikipedia. (2014). Phase-out of incandescent light bulbs. www.en.wikipedia.org/wiki/ Phase-out_of_incandescent_light_bulbs,accessed: May 25, 2014.

Wikipedia. (2015a). Invention of the telephone. http://en.wikipedia.org/wiki/ Invention_of_the_telephone, accessed March 20, 2015.

Wikipedia. (2015b). Dual-tone multi-frequency signaling. http://en.wikipedia.org/wiki/ Dual-tone_multi-frequency_signaling, accessed March 27, 2015.

Wikipedia. (2015c). TRIZ. http://en.wikipedia.org/wiki/TRIZ#ARIZ_- _algorithm_of_inventive_problems_solving, accessed: May 10, 2015.

Wikipedia. (2015d). Laws of technical systems evolution. http://en.wikipedia.org/wiki/ Laws_of_technical_systems_evolution, accessed: May 10, 2015.

Wikipedia. (2015e). Incandescent light bulbs come in a range of shapes and sizes. http://en.wikipedia.org/wiki/Incandescent_light_bulb, accessed: September 6, 2015.

Wikipedia. (2016a). Phylogenetic tree of life. https://commons.wikimedia.org/wiki/ File: Phylogenetic_Tree_of_Life.png#, accessed: January 11, 2016.

Wikipedia. (2016b). Ecosystem. https://en.wikipedia.org/wiki/Ecosystem, accessed: January 11, 2016.

Witte, E., Berg, V. van den, and Meijering, J. Eigen belang prevaleert steeds sterker bij keuze voor duurzaamheid, Burger-consument paradox uitvergroot door crisis. From Dossier Duurzaam: www.dossierduurzaam.nl/Cms_Data/Contents/ DossierDuurzaamDB/Folders/Files/Resultaten/~contents/99W2EFFQPE22U9EN/ ResultatenbDossierbDuurzaamb2012.pdf, accessed: on September 20, 2012.

Witte, E., Berg, V. van den, Meijering, J., and Bruggenwirth, B. (2013). Consument steeds kritischer over duurzame communicatie: Vijf lessen uit vijf jaar Dossier Duurzaam. *Dossier Duurzaam*.

Woodring, C. (1987). Retailing new product or design. *Design Congress '87 Amsterdam*, Utrecht: Tekstotaal.

Yahoo Answers. (2011). Beauty is in the eye of the beholder. (http://answers.yahoo.com/question/index?qid= 1920071004192052AACqS2G). accessed: July 19, 2011.

Yang, X. (2001). *Economics: New Classical versus Neoclassical Frameworks*. Malden, MA: Blackwell Publishers.

Yang, X., Moore, P., and Chong, S. K. (2009). Intelligent products: from lifecycle data acquisition to enabling product-related services. *Computers in Industry*, **60**, 3, 184–194.

Ziman, J. (ed.) (2000). *Technological Innovation as an Evolutionary Process*. Cambridge: Cambridge University Press.

Index

Printed in the United States
by Baker & Taylor Publisher Services